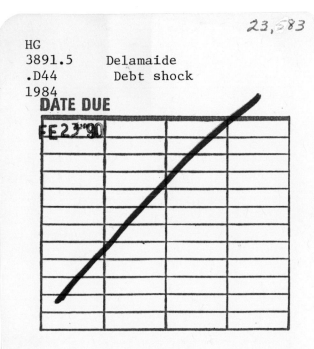

DEBT SHOCK

The Full Story of the World Credit Crisis

Debt Shock

*The Full Story of the World
Credit Crisis*

DARRELL DELAMAIDE

DOUBLEDAY & COMPANY, INC.,
Garden City, New York
1984

Library of Congress Cataloging in Publication Data
Delamaide, Darrell, 1949–
Debt shock

Bibliography: p. 257
Includes index.
1. Debts, External.   2. Debts, External—Developing countries.   I. Title.
HG3891.5.D44   1984   336.3'435'091724
ISBN 0-385-18899-4
Library of Congress Catalog Card Number 83–45009

To Veronika Hass

Acknowledgments

My first acknowledgment has to go to my agent, June Hall, who got the ball rolling. I am grateful to George Weidenfeld of Weidenfeld's and Phil Pochoda of Doubleday for their enthusiasm and support for the project. I also want to thank Gilbert Kaplan, editor and publisher of *Institutional Investor,* for granting me the time off to write the book.

I am, of course, indebted to the many bankers and officials who talked to me: Jacques de Larosière, Henry Wallich, Karl Otto Pöhl, Wilfried Guth, Rimmer de Vries, Johannes Witteveen and many others. I am especially grateful for the insights of three young, thoughtful European bankers: Christoph von Metzler, Helie de Pourtales and Hervé de Carmoy.

I benefited from the advice and help of several colleagues, notably Veronika Hass, Peter Koenig, David Marsh, and Jane Baird.

Writing a book works hardships on many people. I am grateful for the support and interest from many friends and family members whom I neglected.

CONTENTS

THE MEXICAN WEEKEND
PROLOGUE

The U.S. Treasury looms imposingly across the street from the White House. Its imperial Greco-Roman façade dwarfs the colonial-style mansion. Inside, wide hallways with marble floors, generous staircases with sweeping banisters hark back to the pre-air-conditioning torpor of a Southern city.

That city was sweltering in August 1982. On Thursday evening August 12, Treasury Secretary Donald T. Regan took a call from Jesús Silva Herzog, the Mexican finance secretary. "Chucho," as his friends call him, was telephoning from the Hacienda, Mexico's finance ministry. There were "a number of problems" that he wanted to discuss with Regan the next day. Silva Herzog and his aides boarded the private jet of Mexico's central bank and flew to Washington.

Friday the thirteenth the Mexicans met with Regan at the Treasury. Then they traversed the few blocks to 19th Street to meet with Jacques de Larosière, the French civil servant who heads the International Monetary Fund. The delegation went on to Constitution Avenue to lunch with Paul Volcker, the chairman of the Federal Reserve Board.

Silva Herzog had a simple message. Mexico was broke. The country had loan payments of $10 billion due to banks in the next

1

few months. Something had to be done, quickly. The Mexican Weekend had begun.

After lunch the Mexicans returned to Treasury. Regan was closeted with President Reagan prior to a weekend meeting at Camp David with congressmen to discuss tax issues. It fell to R. Timothy McNamar, a laid-back Californian who played Mr. Inside to Regan's Mr. Outside, to do something.

Tom Dawson, the Treasury man responsible for developing countries, was signed out for a weekend in New Hampshire. He actually was at home in Washington, but the switchboard operator at Treasury did not try to reach him because she just *knew* he was in New Hampshire. Charles Siegman, a top international finance official at the Fed, really was away in the Berkshires.

But Fed chairman Paul Volcker was there, roaming the Treasury halls in a trail of cigar smoke. The atmosphere was tense. A U.S. negotiator balked at the suggestion of paying cash for increased oil deliveries. The oil would be too expensive that way. "I don't give a damn what you pay for oil," Volcker said forcefully. "If you *don't* do it, the whole thing is going to come crashing down—and it'll be your fault."

The meeting adjourned until Saturday. Silva Herzog summoned the head of Pemex, Mexico's national oil company, to talk over the oil deal. John Gavin, the U.S. ambassador to Mexico, interrupted his vacation in the British Isles to fly to Washington. A bevy of lawyers from the Department of Energy joined the crowd.

Saturday morning, McNamar got a call from Agriculture Secretary John Block, who was unaware of the Mexican visit. He was calling to see if McNamar wanted to go jogging along Washington's C&O Canal, as they had done on previous weekends. McNamar was in no mood to jog, but he added, "Say, as long as I have you on the line . . ." McNamar proposed to Block that the Commodity Credit Corporation put up $1 billion in additional guarantees for credits to finance Mexican imports of U.S. agricultural products.

Back at Treasury, Mexicans and Americans broke up into working groups to hammer out the details. The United States agreed to purchase $1 billion of Mexican oil at market prices in a range be-

2

tween $25 and $35 a barrel. Most of it would go to the country's Strategic Petroleum Reserve, the rest to the Pentagon.

Sandwiches were brought in.

Volcker telephoned the heads of the big central banks—Fritz Leutwiler of the Swiss National Bank, Karl Otto Pöhl of the West German Bundesbank, Gordon Richardson of the Bank of England. He wanted them to put up a billion and a half dollars for Mexico through the Bank for International Settlements. The Mexican crisis threatened the stability of international finance; the central banks had an obligation to help. The Fed was willing to put up half the money, $750 million. Mexico had already drawn down its standing $700-million credit line with the Fed.

The Mexicans telephoned the chief executives of the big U.S. banks—Walter Wriston of Citibank, Willard Butcher of Chase Manhattan, Lewis Preston of Morgan Guaranty, Samuel Armacost of Bank of America. The Mexicans reached these men at home. They are required to tell the Fed where they will be during the weekend, in case of an emergency. It was an emergency. Mexico needed for the banks to postpone all debt payments for three months, until an agreement could be reached on rescheduling the credits. They scheduled a meeting with the banks in New York for Friday August 20.

The meetings at Treasury dragged on. The atmosphere was less tense, more workmanlike. There were lawyers everywhere. Some aides fell asleep on the couches in the executive offices.

The meetings went on until 3 A.M. As he was leaving the building, José Angel Gurría Treviño, Silva Herzog's right-hand man, noticed that the hallway lights in the Treasury Building gave off a bluish glow. That was eerie.

Talks continued on Sunday. By 11:30 P.M. the Mexicans and Americans had signed the agreements for the oil deliveries. Treasury would advance the billion dollars from its Exchange Stabilization Fund until DOE (Department of Energy) worked out the details with Pemex. Then the Energy Department would reimburse Treasury. The Mexicans had the money in the bank on Monday morning. Henry C. Wallich, a governor of the Federal Reserve, was landing in Basel, Switzerland, to meet with other central bankers regarding the $1.5-billion credit. It was the routine monthly meet-

3

ing of the BIS (Bank for International Settlements). In seventy-two hours the negotiating partners had mobilized nearly $4 billion in emergency aid. Almost $3 billion of it was from the United States. The Mexican Weekend entered into Washington lore.

On Tuesday evening August 17, Silva Herzog went on national television in his country to explain the crisis. There were a number of problems, he said. Mexico had lost $15 billion in capital fleeing across the border. The country was negotiating with the International Monetary Fund for a credit of $4 billion. It was getting financial aid of nearly $4 billion from the U.S. Government and major central banks. It would boost oil production to earn more foreign exchange. The finance secretary spoke for eighty minutes live without a note.

The Federal Reserve Bank of New York is the most powerful of the twelve Federal Reserve banks. By virtue of its location and activity, the New York Fed in some ways is even stronger than the Board of Governors in Washington. Housed in an intimidating fortress a block away from Wall Street, the New York Fed put its weight behind the rescue effort by providing the Mexicans with a place to meet their bankers.

The seat of power in the New York Fed is the tenth floor, distinguished by a stone floor and oak beams. The executive dining room, located on the tenth floor, is a high, narrow room with massive beams and muted red brocade on the walls. On Friday morning August 20, the tables were removed and chairs set up for 100-odd representatives from commercial banks.

Anthony Solomon, a bearded former Under Secretary of the Treasury who keeps a low profile as president of the New York Fed, introduced Silva Herzog and his team and then quietly retired. The Mexicans explained, once again, that there were a number of problems. Mexico was broke. It wanted a three-month moratorium on debt payments to sort out its finances and to put debt service on a more manageable basis. The country also wanted billions of dollars in new credits to keep its economy going.

The bankers had little choice but to agree. They formed a steering committee to negotiate with the Mexicans. Silva Herzog and his crew picked the steering committee members on the basis of their exposure to Mexico and their demonstrated goodwill. The committee included seven American banks—Citibank, Chase Manhattan, Bank of America, Morgan Guaranty, Bankers Trust, Manufacturers Hanover Trust, and Chemical Bank—and six others—Deutsche Bank of West Germany, Swiss Bank Corp. of Switzerland, Lloyds Bank of Britain, Bank of Tokyo of Japan, Bank of Montreal of Canada, and Société Générale of France.

The Mexicans got on their plane to go back home. It had been a long week. But the call came through at the airport that the bankers' committee wanted one of them to stick around and talk things over. Angel Gurría got out of the plane and spent the weekend meeting with the bankers. Together they formulated a telex to all of Mexico's creditor banks explaining the situation and the need for new money. Citibank's telex operators sent the message to all fifteen hundred numbers in their file of syndication banks. So many of these banks were creditors of Mexico it did not matter if a few who were not received the telex as well.

THE DEBT DISASTER
CHAPTER ONE

❧

1

The world credit crisis officially began on August 20, 1982, when Mexico announced suspension of principal payments on its foreign debt. Mexico was not the first case of a country in trouble, nor, as it turned out, was it the biggest or the worst. Brazil tardily claimed that honor. But the Mexican declaration brought to a head the monetary and financial crisis that had been brewing for more than a decade. It also brought home to the public at large, probably for the first time, the fragility of world finance.

Headlines billed it as the Third World debt crisis, the international lending crisis, the world financial crisis. The media painted lurid pictures of financial collapse. *The Sunday Times* of London headlined one piece "The Day the World Ran Out of Credit." *The Economist* alluded on its cover to Paul Erdman's bestseller about a financial collapse, *The Crash of '79,* with a full-page question, "The Crash of 198?" *Time* magazine titled a cover story on the crisis "The Debt Bomb."

Government authorities equivocated. They tried to say it was serious but not really a crisis. Even as they denied it existed, government officials, central bankers and commercial bankers made the credit crisis the focus of conversation for more than a year. At official meetings in Washington, London, Paris, and Frankfurt; at bankers' conferences in Philadelphia, Brussels, and Honolulu; at

6

cozy symposiums in Davos, Switzerland; Alpbach, Austria; and Ditchley Park, near Oxford, England.

Third World and East European countries together had run up foreign debts of $626 billion by 1982, triple the amount in 1976 and a multiple of the $90 billion in credits in 1971. The Organization for Economic Cooperation and Development, representing the major industrialized countries, minimized the crisis when it published these figures in late 1982. The OECD described the crisis as a problem of a few large borrowing countries—Mexico, as well as Brazil and Argentina, which quickly followed Mexico's lead in seeking help from the International Monetary Fund and a rescheduling of their debt by the commercial banks. Those three countries alone accounted for more than $200 billion of the developing country debt.

The World Bank echoed the OECD theme when it released its annual World Debt Tables in February 1983. Counting different loans and excluding Eastern Europe, the World Bank came up with a lower figure for overall debt—$529 billion.

The World Bank's contention that "there is no generalized debt crisis," like the similar claims by the OECD staff, begged the fundamental question. A system that allows any number of countries—whether two or three or six—to reach the state of Mexico, Brazil, Argentina, and Poland in 1982 is in a crisis. Nor was it just the big debtor countries who were in trouble. Numerous countries with smaller debts also sought relief. By the end of 1982, about forty nations had substantial payments arrears. They avoided formal default only by beginning talks about rescheduling their debts or simply through the indulgence of their creditors. To argue, as the two multilateral organizations did, that the smaller problems present no threat to the financial system, only the bigger ones do, was to willfully overlook the breakdown of a system of commercial bank lending to sovereign nations.

The credit crisis of 1982–83 marked a fundamental change in international lending. From August 1982, when Mexico got the ball rolling, until the spring of 1983, fifteen countries began renegotiating the terms of more than $90 billion in debt owed to commercial banks, because they could not pay off that debt on time. In the twenty-five years up to 1982, there were eighty debt relief agreements, but only thirteen of these were with commercial banks and covered small amounts. The $90 billion under discussion in mid-1983 represented a substantial portion of the $210 billion of total debt those fifteen countries owed to commercial banks.

Those numbers are big enough. The Third World debt crisis was the most dramatic because it directly threatened the world banking system. The whole point of rescheduling, after all, was to keep banks from having to admit that these loans were not being paid off. Banks have to write off loans that are not being repaid, and such write-offs appear as a loss on the income statement. Writing off loans this big could wipe out profits, and eat up the equity capital that represents the final barrier to bankruptcy.

But the credit crisis was more extensive than just the Third World debt crisis. The numbers are even bigger. The U.S. Government alone ran up debts almost as great as all developing countries combined in the period 1973–82. The accumulated budget deficit in those years was $460 billion. The industrial countries as a whole, the OECD, racked up a total $1.25-*trillion* deficit during that period, double the developing countries' total.

Henry Kaufman has made millions for himself and for his Wall Street firm, Salomon Brothers, by correctly anticipating changes in interest rates. His uncanny skill has made him something of a guru on Wall Street. He sometimes moves the market singlehandedly. One of the tools Kaufman uses to assess likely trends in interest rates is a tabulation of world debt. Interest rates are, in the end, the "price" of credit, and it is the law of supply and demand that determines the price, more or less. Using what relatively crude statistics are available, Kaufman calculated that world debt, excluding the Communist bloc, mushroomed by 1981 to $14.3 trillion ($14.3 million millions, or $14,300,000,000,000)! This represents an annual average growth of 15 percent from a mere $3.6 trillion in 1971.

"The debt burden today is awesome and its constrictiveness is permeating our economic life," concluded this guru. Kaufman saw no chance this day and age of adopting the traditional "solution" to debt: massive deflation on the scale of the Great Depression. He did speak darkly, though, of the possibility that "debt deflation overwhelms us." In other words, the depression from a deflating

8

debt bubble might be beyond the power of the authorities to counteract it.

The credit crisis raised specters of the 1930s. Even before Mexico's temporary moratorium, long years of recession and rising debts intimated disaster. In February 1982 the local paper in Hartford, Connecticut, ran a story about the problems of the local savings and loan institution. That same weekend the movie *The Day the Bubble Burst,* was on local television. When the Hartford Federal Savings and Loan opened its doors on Monday, depositors lined up to withdraw $3 million on that day alone, a sum greater than total withdrawals for any month in 1981! The S&L was subsequently merged into another bank, but its situation in February hardly justified the panic among its depositors. Many of them paid high penalties for redeeming certificates of deposit prematurely. It is of the essence of panic, though, that it is logically not defensible.

Among the many scenes televised in the United States to dramatize unemployment, one of the most poignant was the spectacle of 20,000 persons lining up outside an employment office in Chicago on a bitterly cold January morning in 1982 to apply for 3,800 municipal jobs.

By the summer of 1982, it was plain to many that something was out of kilter in world finance. The British Broadcasting Corporation in July aired a special Money Programme on Mexico's nightmare of debt. Just a month later, Mexico's nightmare haunted the world.

Four years of recession and high interest rates, resulting from the fight against inflation, had already pushed unemployment in industrialized countries up to postwar highs. To what extent excessive debt was a cause or a symptom of the malaise is a question economists will argue for decades, but the answer is not so important. A company's demise usually takes the form of bankruptcy—the inability to pay its debts. It is irrelevant at that point whether the demise is due to an adverse economy, bad luck, bad management, or the debts themselves.

A bankrupt company liquidates its assets to pay off its creditors. Countries—whether developing countries with billions of dollars of foreign debt or developed countries with billions of dollars of government deficits—do not go bankrupt, as some American bankers are fond of saying. But they do liquidate assets when they reduce the standard of living of their people. That is the cost of the credit crisis—for Mexicans, for Americans, for everyone affected by the world monetary system, which is to say everyone.

By mid-1982 nerves were frayed within the banking fraternity itself. The respected British newsmagazine *The Economist* published a lengthy special report on international banking with a cover reminiscent of Hieronymus Bosch and the title "Nightmare of Debt." The sober central bankers who convene every month in Basel, Switzerland, at the Bank for International Settlements disquieted the financial markets with their pessimistic observation that $200 billion of international debt was "doubtful" or "potentially doubtful," which is central bank parlance for rotten and maybe-rotten.

With Mexico's moratorium, the culmination of bad news depressed bankers. They spoke of "contagious pessimism." Geoffrey Bell, a debonair British investment banker who manages to keep a tan even in the worst of times, noted the phenomenon when international bankers gathered at the Sheraton Center in Toronto for the joint annual meeting of the International Monetary Fund and World Bank in September 1982. "Those of us going up and down those escalators at the hotel would hear murmurings of Poland, Mexico, Argentina. On the other side would be Massey-Ferguson, Dome Petroleum, and the like. Country and company contagious pessimism," remarked Bell, who went on to make a minor industry out of commenting on the credit crisis.

Bankers stopped believing and international credit contracted. The confidence that had inflated global lending in the 1970s evaporated. It was not so much that a bubble burst, but the debt balloon deflated.

2

Mexico's decision to suspend payments on its foreign debt shocked the world. Morgan Guaranty economist Rimmer de Vries, a sober Dutchman not given to hyperbole, said, "It was like an atom bomb being dropped on the world financial system." Poland's debt of $24 billion was immense, but the debt issue there was a sideline to Solidarity's political struggle, and besides, Poland seemed very far away. Mexico was much closer and $80 billion was much more money. There were no ideological or political issues to obscure the financial disaster.

The waves of debt shock sent tremors around the world. First Mexico, then Argentina, Brazil, Venezuela, and practically every other country in Latin America sought relief from their debt burdens. Earlier Poland, Romania, and Yugoslavia had rescheduled their foreign debts, and things were touch and go for Hungary and East Germany in the East bloc. Meanwhile, some of the biggest and most developed companies in the world shared the plight of the developing countries—International Harvester, Dome Petroleum, and AEG-Telefunken joined Chrysler as bankrupt companies too big for governments to let fail.

Debt became the biggest constraint in public and corporate policy. The United States ran up a record budget deficit of $110.7 billion in 1982, only to find that it would *double* in 1983. The deficit became the focus of debate in financial circles in the U.S. and abroad. Government spending deficits contributed to the fall of Chancellor Helmut Schmidt, the most popular head of government in West Germany's short history. Budget deficits and foreign debts forced President François Mitterrand to abandon many ambitious plans for Socialist reform in France. Debts and deficits changed policies and governments in the small, rich countries of northern Europe, which had set the pace in providing social benefits for their people.

The crisis touches all of us because it touches our money. The numbers are so big they seem unreal. Brazil and Poland and Zaire seem very far away. But billions of dollars of defaulted debt affect the whole monetary system, and so affect the dollars we think we have. The money you think you have deposited in your local bank *does not exist* except as little blips on that bank's computer. You simply *believe* that the bank will give you some dollar bills when you draw on that account. Just as the bank *believes* that you will pay back a loan it gives you for your house or car. That's what credit is all about. The word itself comes from the Latin verb *credere,* to believe. The global financial system rests on a credo that all of us must accept. The debt crisis threatens to put the lie to those beliefs.

11

The credit crisis ultimately affects much that is important in our lives—our jobs, the value of our savings, the security of our retirement, our standard of living, and even our freedom of movement. It is important to all of us not just because it threatens some dire catastrophe like a banking collapse or a stock market crash. It is important also because it affects right now how much interest we pay on our mortgages, how quickly our money loses its value, and how secure our material prosperity is.

Economic troubles in Mexico are not so remote. In testimony given during congressional hearings on the debt crisis, Treasury Secretary Regan pointed out that one out of every eight jobs in U.S. manufacturing industry depends on exports. More significantly, four out of every five new jobs in recent years came from foreign sales. Regan gave as a rule of thumb that $1 billion in exports represented 24,000 new jobs in the U.S. With Mexico's imports from the United States falling off at a $10-billion annual rate in the wake of the debt crisis, fully a quarter of a million American jobs were at stake from the Mexican problems alone.

Big-ticket items like nuclear power plants obviously got shunted to the back burner as public authorities in developing countries ran out of money. This hurt big Western companies like Westinghouse of the United States and Siemens of West Germany. But the crisis affected very little ticket items as well. A dismayed Coca-Cola disclosed that its 1983 earnings would be lower than expected because the protracted debt crisis dampened sales in Latin America.

It was often suspected, although impossible to document, that the high U.S. interest rates prevailing throughout 1983 resulted at least in part from the debt crisis. Real interest rates—the difference between nominal rates and the inflation rate—ran from 5 to 10 percent instead of the normal 2 to 3 percent (let alone the negative real rates that predominated in the 1970s as inflation actually outstripped nominal interest rates). It is the real rates that count. The high real rates of 1983 meant that borrowers, normal Americans who wanted to buy a house or a car, as well as Brazilians, Mexicans, and the rest, paid excessively for credit. High rates also meant exorbitantly high profits for the banks, which they felt they needed in case one of the big debtor countries actually did default. Mexico's problem became the problem of everyone in the United States who wanted to buy anything on credit.

Paul Volcker stands almost as a colossus across the debt crisis. At 6 foot 7 inches, he literally towers over most other financial figures. He wears rumpled, badly fitted suits but his mind is clean and sharp. His big cigar became as much of a trademark in frequent Capitol Hill appearances as Arthur Burns's billowing pipe. As chairman of the Board of Governors of the Federal Reserve System, Volcker was short on tact and long on integrity. A monetary St. George, he set out to slay the dragon of inflation with his visor firmly locked into place. No amount of recession, unemployment, or bankruptcy in the United States or anywhere else in the world was going to distract him from that task. He was firmly convinced that in the long run only a stable currency could support economic growth, employment, and healthy financial structures.

In late 1979, Volcker embarked on a strategy of tightly controlling money supply. This drove up interest rates to more than 20 percent. The policy ushered in a recession with record postwar unemployment, doubled the interest payments of big developing countries who were in the process of doubling their external debt, and cut the annual rate of inflation from more than 15 percent to less than 5 percent by mid-1983.

Volcker spent hours testifying before Congress on the debt issue, and put up with his share of hostile questions and even abuse. One message he tried again and again to drive home was his recognition from the key position that he occupied that the world credit crisis concerned Americans. "In all of this," he said in his statement before the Senate subcommittee on international finance and monetary policy, "the mutual dependency of the U.S. economy and the stability of the international financial system should be apparent. Failure to deal successfully with the immediate international financial pressures could only jeopardize prospects for *our* recovery—for *our* jobs, for *our* export markets, and for *our* financial markets."

Finance ministers, central bank governors, and commercial bankers are making decisions these days that affect our lives in a fundamental way. In a democracy, that is our responsibility. Just as war cannot be left to the generals, debt is too important to be left to the bankers. The issue is difficult, but so are nuclear weapons, social welfare, environmental protection, and other weighty political matters. The credit crisis is a political crisis of the first order, not an obscure problem safely left to the "experts."

It's hard to keep track of a crisis when you're in the midst of it. Reports of these billions of dollars of debt being rescheduled and those billions being lent out start to run together. The numbers are too big to mean anything. The "events" are too arcane. The purpose of this book is to tell the story of the credit crisis of 1982–83 in a coherent fashion, to examine the major problems in their context. The book steps behind the numbers to put a human face on high finance. It is individual men (hardly ever women), after all, who make the decisions to lend or to borrow or to default.

The credit crisis of 1982–83 was only an acute phase of a much more fundamental crisis: the transition from the postwar monetary system to something else. It is a crisis that began more than a decade previously and almost certainly will last throughout the 1980s, and perhaps longer. In narrating the specific events of the 1982–83 crisis, I have tried to show the shape of this fundamental transition. The credit crisis is not a temporary financial problem in the esoteric world of business. The credit crisis is a political problem of the most basic sort. The crisis and its resolution will affect the way we live our lives.

3

Everybody knew the crisis was coming. Academics knew, journalists knew, the countries knew. Even the bankers knew. Especially the bankers knew. It was only a question of time, but they made hay while the sun was shining.

The question was openly discussed in the wake of the oil shock of 1973 and the 1974–75 recession, which everybody thought was bad until the recession of the early 1980s. Emma Rothschild, a British writer who had foreseen the decline and fall of Detroit already in 1973, was warning about the coming debt crisis in 1976 —even while the bankers were congratulating themselves on their success:

All the same, one great crisis is still to come. A prospect of unprecedented peril for hundreds of banks and for the system itself, it promises misery and destruction; and with the most profound political consequences. This is the crisis of the developing countries' debts. . . . The question for the financial system is not whether these debts will be dishonored. Rather, it is an issue of when, and how, and where.

Dire as it sounds, Rothschild's warning fairly fits the crisis that broke in 1982–83. In more moderate language, two Citibank economists argued in *Foreign Affairs* in 1977 that less-developed-country borrowing was a temporary phenomenon. But they conceded: "If the causes (of the borrowing) are persistent and LDCs continue to incur debt as rapidly as in the last three years, many of them may eventually have trouble servicing their debts." They did continue, and they did have trouble.

The economic recovery in 1976–77 and the movement toward equilibrium in capital flows seemed to vindicate the bank economists and undermine Rothschild's arguments. But the lesson of this earlier debate is that growth and equilibrium are also temporary phenomena. An unsound financial structure may hold in a buoyant economy, but the weight of a depression could bring it crashing down. The buoyancy does not strengthen the structure, it just doesn't test it.

Clear-sighted bankers saw this. Two West Germans responsible for the international bond issues of a large bank in Frankfurt were musing one winter afternoon in 1978 about the inevitability of a crash. "It will have to come," said the polished and sophisticated head of the department over a cup of coffee in an elegantly appointed suite. "I don't see how it can be avoided." His younger colleague, less pessimistic by nature, chafed a bit under the other's certitude, but European bankers are too close to history to fool themselves for too long. That's a luxury they leave to their American colleagues, who generally are brash enough to believe that everything will always work out.

Bankers fell victim to a wishful thinking syndrome with regard to developing countries. "Nobody expected the recession to last so long or to cut so deep" was the common plea. Corollaries were:

"Nobody expected commodities prices to fall so far" and "Nobody expected interest rates to go so high"—even though these were the obvious consequences of policies that all right-thinking conservatives, including bankers, were advocating to cope with inflation and the oil shock.

If history has shown anything, it is that there are setbacks. Bankers behaved as if their brave new world of sovereign lending were exempt from history. Even if the recession were not so long, or commodities prices so low, or interest rates so high, it was inevitable that sooner or later something or other was bound to go wrong. To say or believe otherwise was shameful naïveté or cynicism at its most arch. In fact, for the bankers it was neither, but rather a calculated suspension of disbelief. Unlike the reader of fiction, bankers suspended their disbelief not to pass a few hours in another world, but to make a lot of money. Bankers didn't need Emma Rothschild to tell them they were on a disaster course. They knew.

Despite all the protests to the contrary, there was really no excuse for the banks. They knew all along. What astonished them was that the "system" held out so long. At each stage of escalation there was a public discussion about the risks of continued lending to developing countries. After each turning point was passed, bankers breathed a big sigh of relief, patted themselves on the back, toasted the flexibility of the system, and proceeded to push it once again to the breaking point.

It's reminiscent of the rope basket going up to the Greek monastery. The basket was the only access to the monastery, perched on top of a mountain crag. A visitor who was about to be hauled up the sheer cliff wall noticed that the rope attached to the basket was frayed in several places. Concerned, he asked one of the accompanying monks how often they replaced the rope. "Every time it breaks," was the laconic response.

While some bankers may be genuinely naïve, most of the sensible ones not only expected that the system would be pushed to the breaking point, but considered it almost inevitable. In the throes of rescheduling the Polish debt, European bankers were often put out at the hard-nosed attitude of the Americans. The exposure of the U.S. banks in Poland was relatively small; trade had always been a secondary consideration. Polish debt and trade carried much more

16

weight with the Europeans. "Just wait," snarled the Europeans, "until it's Mexico and Brazil who need rescheduling. Then the Americans will sing a different tune." Wait is what they did. Sure enough, the Americans sang another tune. Solidarity was their cry. Save the system. The Federal Reserve lowered interest rates, the U.S. Treasury pulled billions out of its hip pocket, and the Americans couldn't say enough about the importance of sticking together. It was like following a script.

4

Mexico shocked the system, but continued to operate within its framework. Even though the country suspended payments of principal, it continued to pay interest on its loans. Accountants deem that interest payments mean a loan is alive and kicking. The success of the Mexican Weekend seemed to tip the balance in favor of keeping the system intact. If Mexico had decided instead to go its own way, the shock might have been much greater. Here is what might have happened:

President López Portillo, sensitive about his place in history, gambled against a possible military intervention by the United States. As capital flight took on alarming proportions and scheduled debt payments far exceeded available foreign exchange, he took drastic action. On August 1, 1982, he suspended all foreign exchange transactions, nationalized the banks, dismissed the head of the central bank, and fired the finance minister. He declared a state of public emergency requiring his continued presence in office for at least a year beyond his scheduled departure December 1. (President-elect Miguel de la Madrid Hurtado was invited to become vice president, but declined and retired to the sidelines.) Finally, López Portillo announced at a public rally in Zócalo Square that Mexico was unilaterally declaring a moratorium on all foreign debts. From August 1, the country suspended all payments of interest and principal for a period of at least one year. The president, interrupted repeatedly by the cheers of the crowd, announced that Mexico would review outstanding for-

17

eign debt and would repudiate all loans undertaken by corrupt officials that were not clearly in the country's interest.

Bankers in New York and London were stunned. They broke off and canceled vacations to huddle with their lawyers. Paul Volcker rushed to New York to meet with the chairmen of the big U.S. banks at the New York Fed. The governor of the Bank of England, Gordon Richardson, summoned the U.K. clearers and prominent representatives of the Eurobanking community to the hallowed institution on Threadneedle Street.

The markets did not wait, though. Continental European banks, particularly the Germans and Swiss, immediately suspended all dealings in the Euromarket. They canceled short-term lines to all but the biggest banks. Only personal assurances from Walter Wriston, head of Citibank, Lewis Preston of Morgan Guaranty, and Willard Butcher of Chase Manhattan that matters were under control kept them from cutting off even the biggest U.S. banks.

American investors had no such personal assurances. López Portillo's announcement was hardly on the ticker before sell orders began to flow into brokers' offices. Large blocks of bank shares were put on offer and prices went into free fall. Market operators and institutional investors could see no percentage in a Mexican default, even if authorities were able to keep the banks from failing altogether, as presumably they would. Most of the money center banks had about half of their capital out in loans to Mexico. Even if the Fed gave them some leeway in writing off the debt, the Mexican default was bound to wipe out profits.

The shock waves went through the whole market. Volume picked up and the Dow Jones average of thirty industrials dropped forty points in half an hour.

After fruitless efforts to reach Mexican authorities, Treasury Secretary Donald Regan appeared at a hastily summoned press conference to announce that there was no danger to U.S. banks or the U.S. financial system from the Mexican default.

Volcker and bank executives were discussing ways to treat the Mexican loans so that capital and earnings of the banks would not be mortally impaired. The Fed was ready to discount notes from the big banks in whatever amount was needed. "These banks," said Regan grimly, "simply will *not* be allowed to fail." The President was informed. Intense diplomatic efforts were under way to determine the implications of Mexico's announcement.

The Euromarket was already unraveling. The run on interbank deposits had already technically bankrupted consortium banks whose sole source of funding consisted of these deposits between banks. Those in London quickly appealed to the Old Lady, as the Bank of England is called. The Bank equivocated, and tried to reach the parent banks of the bigger consortiums. They were not too pleased with what they heard. The parent banks were not about to make any commitments to bailing out these consortiums until the extent of the crisis and their own exposure was clearer.

Alarmed by the stock market reaction to the news, European banks decided that Wriston's assurances weren't good enough and began yanking funds from the big American banks. European corporations and then Arab monetary authorities began following suit. The U.S. banks started to offer higher interest rates to keep the deposits in. Panic bidding pushed the London interbank offered rate up at an unprecedented pace, lifting it five full points in an hour.

The move in interest rates pushed the stock market lower. The Dow had lost 100 points in two hours. A quorum of the New York Stock Exchange board of directors met hurriedly and decided to close the market early.

The news that the Big Board was closed spread like wildfire. Bulletins interrupted television and radio programs, afternoon editions of the newspapers carried full-page headlines, and it was a "Have you heard the news?" topic of conversation. This firm evidence of impending catastrophe overwhelmed the vague assurances of the Treasury secretary. With only an hour left until the banks closed in New York, lines began to form at tellers' windows, snaking around the cordons through the lobbies and finally out into the streets. People knew all about deposit insurance, but instinct dictated that if a lot of banks were in trouble not even the Federal Deposit Insurance Commission could handle all the claims promptly.

As big depositors took their money out of American banks, they shifted the funds to Europe and exchanged dollars for Ger-

19

man marks, Swiss francs, and even British pounds. The European banks were far less exposed to Mexico than the American banks and the European economies far less dependent on the Mexican market.

The Fed began to make good on Regan's promise and pumped dollars into the banks to replace the departing deposits, but that only fueled the outflow. The dollar plummeted against the German mark, falling 30 pfennigs in a half hour to 2.20 marks. By 2 P.M., as volume in currency markets increased, the dollar had dipped below 2 marks. The Bundesbank, the West German central bank, intervened to support the dollar. It bought $3 billion in twenty minutes, then quickly realized that its intervention was having no effect at all. The market was not paying any attention to central bank signals. As the dollar continued its fall, the Bundesbank ordered German banks to suspend all foreign exchange trading. An intense phone call from West Germany's chancellor, Helmut Schmidt, to Luxembourg's premier, Pierre Werner, quickly halted all trading by the big German subsidiaries there. Swiss National Bank president Fritz Leutwiler quickly copied the Bundesbank action, and Paris and London followed suit. Within an hour foreign exchange trading had all but ceased, but only after the dollar had lost a third of its value against other major currencies.

By 3 P.M. New York time all financial activity had ground to a halt. Most people in the United States were only vaguely aware that the Mexican president had said something inimical to American interests. Outside New York, even the early closing of the stock exchange was little more than a diverting novelty. But the White House, now turning its full attention to the crisis, announced that President Reagan would address the nation at 9 P.M. Eastern Daylight Time to explain the consequences of the Mexican default.

The lions of Wall Street, as the major corporate law firms are affectionately known, were hastily drafting papers to attach Mexican bank deposits and property. Since Mexico was already in arrears on several loan payments, it was a technicality to officially declare the country in default, and that was the first step for the lawyers.

López Portillo followed up the morning speech with a televised address that evening. He repeated his measures and the reasons for them and called for national solidarity. He went further and appealed for other Third World nations to seize the moment to follow Mexico's example and to throw off the yoke of economic imperialism. López Portillo recalled his predecessor, Luis Echeverría, from retirement and announced his immediate departure on a round-the-world trip to win support for the Mexican initiative. Following emergency conferences earlier in the day, Argentina answered on cue with its own unilateral moratorium. The country was still smarting from the Falklands dispute, had not yet set accounts straight with British banks, and had no idea how it was going to meet its debt payments anyway. A debt moratorium would rally public opinion and perhaps restore the government's authority. General Reynaldo Bignone, the Argentine president, suggested Buenos Aires as the site for a Third World conference on trade and finance, to set up a world monetary system free of American domination. He invited industrialized countries to attend as well.

In his address to the nation, President Reagan concisely related Mexico's action, but told the American people that there was no need to worry. The full resources of the government and Federal Reserve were adequate to support the banks who were heavily exposed.

As trading opened in Tokyo, at 9 P.M. EDT, the yen shot through the roof. Japanese banks had extensive loans in Latin America and Japan had nurtured trade ties to the region, but its connection paled by comparison to U.S. involvement. Japanese authorities intervened heavily to brake the yen's rise, because keeping the currency's value low is a key part of Japan's trade strategy. Finally, an hour and a half and $12 billion later, the Japanese, too, shut down all currency trading. By the time the Pacific banking centers of Hong Kong and Singapore were open for business, foreign exchange trading had ceased. What picked up steam was trading in gold. Bullion had already jumped $40 an ounce in London to $382 at the fixing. In thin Asian trading, gold quickly tacked on another $100. Bid and offered rates widened and traders began to deal more cautiously. Demand for

21

gold skyrocketed once Middle Eastern financial centers on the Persian Gulf woke up. The market ground to a halt for lack of sellers. The price had nearly doubled from the previous day to $650.

By the time the sun got around to London again, international financial and money markets had gridlocked. Banks opened their doors as usual; there was no panic or unusual activity among retail depositors. Phones were ringing off the hook, though, with inquiries from corporate financial officers. Airlines already were canceling cargo flights because of the disruption in the smooth flow of credit documents.

Central bank governors agreed in a series of phone calls to keep foreign exchange markets closed. They called an emergency meeting at the Bank for International Settlements in Basel, but only for the next day, because the United States had to clarify its position further.

In just eighteen hours, López Portillo's announcement had thrown a wrench into the creaky machinery of international trade and finance. In succeeding weeks, other Latin American countries, including, after some hesitation, Brazil, joined Mexico in declaring a moratorium on foreign debts. Practically all of the twenty largest banks in the United States were technically bankrupt, but the Fed directed that all Latin American assets be sequestered in a special account. The U.S. recalled its ambassadors from Latin America, but ruled out military intervention. Courts across the United States had impounded planes, ships and shipments of the countries, but their value was insignificant compared to the outstanding debt. Court orders froze nearly $19 billion in bank accounts of these countries, but even that sum hardly offset the $250 billion included in the moratorium.

The Buenos Aires Monetary Conference was pointedly scheduled for September 6, to coincide with the long-planned joint annual meeting of the World Bank and the International Monetary Fund. Foreign exchange markets remained closed throughout August, eventually creating hardships for tourists because banks were obliged to ration currency exchange and, toward the end of the month, to halt it altogether.

A steady stream of official reassurances, plus the continuing semblance of normality, kept the public from panicking. Stock markets reopened but were hit steadily by selling, interrupted occasionally by a hopeful market consolidation.

An emergency meeting of finance ministers and central bank governors from the ten biggest Western countries, called the Group of Ten, attempted to come to grips with the crisis. Treasury Secretary Regan made a special appeal to Arab oil exporters aligned with Washington to observe a standstill in their financial holdings. They had little choice, anyway, with currency markets closed, and so the Arabs assented. The Europeans balked, though, at the American suggestion that they pool $20 billion in their currencies to support the dollar in order to reopen currency markets. Such support would be inflationary for their own currencies, they argued, and besides would be woefully inadequate given the pressure on the dollar.

France and Sweden announced their intention of attending the Buenos Aires conference. At the G-10 meeting, they maintained that the industrialized countries could not ignore the conference or run counter to it. The Kremlin gave cautious support to the Mexican initiative, but remained noncommittal. At the same time the Soviet Union began intense secret negotiations with Brazil and Argentina to trade gold and oil for grain. Pending the monetary conference, Mexico, Brazil and Argentina signed a series of bilateral trade agreements for raw materials. Accounts were settled in a "clearing dollar," a bookkeeping device with no direct connection to the U.S. dollar. Yugoslavia became the first non-Latin American country to join the debt moratorium. It encouraged the nonaligned movement of Third World countries to support the Buenos Aires conference.

The United States soon found that it had no political or economic levers to threaten or cajole Latin America back into line. Oil shipments from Mexico and Venezuela ceased and shortages began to occur in some parts of the United States. The government did not tap the strategic oil reserve but let prices rise. Eventually gasoline was rationed. Coffee prices doubled and sugar began to get more expensive.

The Fed continued pumping money into the banks, but Congress, recalled in emergency session, could not agree on a bill to establish an Emergency Debt Stabilization Agency backed by the government to take over the Latin-American loans from the banks and bridge the huge gap in their balance sheets. Bank shares remained suspended on the stock exchange.

Now you can play the game, too. From this point on you can depict the world economy entering a deflationary spiral like that in the 1930s. Complete financial collapse leads to massive decline in production which results in widespread unemployment, protectionist trade measures, and a trend to economic autarky. Or, if you like the exotic twist, you can opt for a period of hyperinflation. Price rises running at an annual rate of 500 or 1,000 percent lend a certain zip to business. Of course, a hyperinflationary bubble eventually bursts, and then you proceed to a deflationary spiral, as before.

To play the game seriously, though, requires an extraneous catalyst. After all, there is more going on in the world than just business. Suppose at the juncture we left Congress something exciting happens: King Fahd of Saudi Arabia is assassinated, or the pope. Suppose the Soviet Union invaded Iran, or Castro launched a full-scale invasion of El Salvador.

5

The Wall Street Journal sketched another disaster scenario. The *Journal* described a trillion-dollar global banking failure in eight scenes, beginning with the collapse of a property finance company in Hong Kong and ending with the insolvency of a local bank in Youngstown, Ohio, twelve days later. This scenario, too, depicted the key role of the interbank market, the vulnerability of consortium banks, the potential recalcitrance of Argentina, and the final grip into Middle America.

The problem with any scenario depicting a possible financial collapse is that it is superfluous. The credit crisis of 1982–83 did not threaten to bring down the postwar system of international finance. *The crisis was itself the collapse.* It was the final stage in the slow disintegration of the system that began in the 1960s.

The truly disturbing thing about the scenario sketched above, or that in *The Wall Street Journal,* was that much of it actually happened. The only difference was that quick official action preempted a financial panic. But that was successful only because the authorities maintained certain fictions. The liquidity crisis of 1982–83 and the official response to it were not the end of the story. The crisis will be working itself out for the rest of the decade. Some catalyst may make it more acute and speed up the process. There is no "solution" to the crisis in the sense of repairing the system, because the crisis represents a transition from one way of arranging the world's business to another way that we don't know yet. The only question is whether we can mitigate the pain of the transition.

Many of the worst things in the scenarios actually happened. Bankers, backed by the central banks of the industrial countries and their front organization, the International Monetary Fund, succeeded at first in preserving the fiction that the old order was continuing to function. But that is in fact the fiction, rather than the hypothetical scenarios. It is only a question of time before acknowledged reality catches up with the underlying facts depicted in the scenarios.

The developing countries will eventually realize that most conceivable sanctions that would accompany a full-scale debt repudiation have already been visited upon them in the course of the "rescue" mounted on their behalf in 1982–83. A debt repudiation, so the traditional warning goes, would shut a country out of the credit markets for a generation. But these countries are effectively shut out already. The bigger debtors—Mexico, Brazil, Argentina—do get new credits as part of the rescue program, but the new loans go almost exclusively to pay interest on the old ones. The countries get no benefit from these new credits. They only increase the amount of debt they somehow have to pay interest on next year.

Without credit, runs the standard warning, the developing countries could not pay for their imports, could not finance their exports. But how much greater impact could that have on Mexico than the "stabilization program" which cut the country's imports by two thirds in the first half of 1983?

Developing countries large and small already lacked trade finance in the summer of 1983 and were turning increasingly to

25

trade by barter. Counter-trade, as it is now called, enjoyed a renaissance as Indonesia swapped rubber for railway cars from Canada, the Soviet Union bartered natural gas for German technological know-how, Iran traded oil for New Zealand's lambs, China exchanged frozen pork for French capital equipment, Jamaica purchased Chrysler cars with bauxite, and Ecuador bought British aircraft with bananas.

The lending carrousel of the seventies had careered to a halt. Many developing countries were no longer creditworthy by definition, because they could not get credit. Only the prospect of outright disaster forced the banks collectively to lend any new money to countries in trouble. The banks were waiting for the first chance to close the credit windows altogether. George Soros, who has been called "the world's best money manager," described this vicious circle in a pessimistic analysis distributed by investment bankers Morgan Stanley & Co. in mid-1983: "If it takes the threat of a breakdown to induce collective action, while collective action is necessary to avoid a breakdown, it follows that we shall hover on the verge of disaster for the indefinite future."

Friedrich von Hayek, a conservative Austrian economist who won the Nobel Prize in 1974, described a new crash as inevitable. In a gloomy interview with a French magazine, the economist said the crash will come sooner or later, and it would be better if it came sooner. Asked how he would advise President Reagan and other heads of state, Hayek responded: "I would tell them: Face up to it. Dare to confront the crisis. Do it as soon as possible. If you delay the crisis another twenty years, it will be even worse. In the world's interest, let it break down now." One of Hayek's distinctions was that he correctly predicted the 1929 crash. But the then eighty-three-year-old economist did not think he would see the new crash in his lifetime.

6

There was no mystery in the credit crisis once it came. The causes were clear. Some analyses delved more deeply into underlying economic factors, but there was a consensus about the immediate causes of the developing country debt crisis. These were the prolonged recession in the wake of the second oil shock in 1979, the high level of interest rates, and a sharp downward swing in volatile commodities prices.

When OPEC raised oil prices, it drew money out of the economy that would otherwise have been spent on other things, like machinery or automobiles. This had a depressing impact on a national economy. The first time around, in 1973–74, governments of industrial countries largely counteracted this depressing effect by increasing the amount of money available so that they could both pay for the oil *and* buy machinery and automobiles. But any increase in the supply of money that is not accompanied by a commensurate increase in goods creates inflation. The second time around, when OPEC doubled prices in 1979–80, governments decided to fight the inflation rather than the depression. The United States and Britain set the pace. Monetary authorities not only did not accommodate the new charges with new money, but actually decreased the amount of money available. OPEC drew off huge amounts of money from the Western economies and they deflated. The recession following the first oil shock was mild and quickly over. The recession after the second shock went much deeper and lasted much longer, because the amount of money involved was bigger and government policies actually exacerbated the depressing effect.

In the four years from 1979 to 1983, Western economies had their ups and downs. The end effect was that the United States and West Germany were producing at 1979 levels in early 1983, while Japan and other countries were only slightly higher. After four years, the biggest economy in the world had not grown an inch in real terms. Industrial production itself actually declined to 1976 levels. The effects, especially on unemployment, were grave.

A depressed economy requires less from abroad. Imports by the twenty OECD countries declined. World trade stagnated in 1980–81 and then fell in 1982.

The recession *did* bring down inflation. In the United States, inflation plummeted from double digits to below 5 percent. But interest rates, which had shot up to 20 percent, came down much more slowly. The so-called "real" interest rate skyrocketed as the gap between the inflation rate and the nominal interest rate widened. The real interest rates on dollars went from zero or even negative in the 1970s to more than 10 percent in 1981–82!

The impact on developing countries was shattering. They had been bubbling along in the 1970s borrowing as much money as they wanted. With inflation rates sometimes exceeding interest rates, they actually made money by borrowing for a time, and usually paid little or nothing in real terms for their credits. At the same time they increased their foreign currency incomes, because commodities prices rose sharply. Prices of all primary commodities went up after the oil shock in the general panic about the scarcity of natural resources and the power of producer cartels.

Commodity prices increased 25 percent a year on average in dollar terms through 1979 and 1980. Then they fell, dropping 33 percent from their peaks by the end of 1982. Commodities are major exports for developing countries. The beef that Argentina exports fell from $2.25 a kilogram in the second quarter of 1980 to $1.60 by the end of 1981. Sugar from Brazil and the Caribbean fell from 79 cents a kilo to 27 cents by 1982. And copper, a big-ticket item for the likes of Chile and Zaire, fell from $2.61 a kilo to $1.66.

Industrial countries bought less from developing countries and paid less for what they bought. At the same time these heavily indebted countries, now earning less, had to pay much more interest than they were used to on their debts. Recession precipitated the debt crisis in 1982. But the debt crisis took place because there was so much debt. Most of that debt had accumulated in the preceding decade. The deeper origins of the crisis lie in the much more fundamental trends described in the next chapter. The most obvious of these is the sharp imbalance in international payments caused by the oil shock in 1973. Even before that, though, the collapse of the postwar system of fixed exchange rates in 1971–73 removed the last vestiges of discipline and control in the international monetary system. It was in this environment that the Euromarket grew up. The Euromarket, that agglomeration of money existing outside of time and space, is the "place" where the debt crisis happens. These three factors—"recycling" of OPEC surpluses, floating exchange rates, and the growth of the Euromarket—created the conditions for the world credit crisis.

THE
MONEYCHANGERS
CHAPTER TWO

———❦———

1

Mohammed Abalkhail does not appear menacing. Sitting in his Riyadh office with his feet hardly touching the floor, in fact, he seems almost elfin. Yet this is the Arab who as finance minister of Saudi Arabia is responsible for upward of $150 billion of liquid assets accumulated in the ten years after OPEC quadrupled oil prices. In thrillers, it is the Abalkhail figure who brings the Western banking system to its knees by shuttling around Saudi Arabia's immense deposits.

The real Abalkhail complains about the headaches he gets from trying to balance the Saudi budget. True enough, the kingdom whose history sounds like a tale of Scheherazade earns a lot of money selling oil. But with a little thought, it has figured out how to spend a lot of money, building the world's biggest airport and university, buying jet fighters and tanks. Of course, a finance minister does not have to worry too much about a small budget deficit if he has $150 billion in liquid reserves. Abalkhail might indeed withdraw a few deposits to cover the deficit, but not in order to cripple the world financial system. Saudi Arabia, in the end, is banking on that system with a faith few others could claim. They have nothing to gain from a collapse of the banking system, and $150 billion to lose.

Abalkhail is a technocrat of indeterminate age. A graying mustache, the only hair visible in Arab dress, belies the youthful features and demeanor. Typically, he is very polite. He has a habit of not finishing his sentences, which is perhaps a polite way of letting you draw your own conclusions, or a polite way of keeping his options open. Less prominent than the oil minister, Ahmed Zaki Yamani, Abalkhail is, like him, one of the few non-royals entrusted with major responsibility by the Saudi ruling family.

Saudi Arabia has consistently opted for short-term investments with its oil wealth. Kuwait, by contrast, has invested in shareholdings and whole companies in Europe and America as part of a long-term trading and industrial strategy. Saudi Arabia, meanwhile, has avoided large acquisitions and instead bought U.S. Treasury Bills and put money in short-term Euromarket deposits. The idea is to have the money available in case the kingdom needs it. Saudi Arabia's reserves are like the foreign exchange reserves kept by any other country, only they happen to be much larger.

With that much money, Abalkhail's main concern is to keep it safe. Like any sensible investor, he does not want to put all his eggs in one basket, but to spread the risk by depositing his funds in several banks. On the other hand, you can spread the risk only so far. Each bank itself should be a reasonably safe bet. The Saudi Arabian Monetary Authority, the central bank agency under Abalkhail's tutelage, has drawn up a famous list of banks it will deposit funds with. The list remains confidential, but informed estimates show about sixty banks. These are almost exclusively the big private banks in industrialized countries, who have an equity base large enough to take the size of deposits SAMA wants to make. The bank's financial standing, and its home country's economic standing, seem to be the only criteria. SAMA reportedly kept its link to Banque Bruxelles Lambert of Belgium even while that bank was on the Arab boycott list. One Middle Eastern publication explained that only two Arab banks were on the list, and then only because the Saudi Arabian Government had a substantial shareholding in the banks. Otherwise, Arab banks are not big enough or seasoned enough for SAMA deposits.

Abalkhail and his colleagues are cautious. They ceased dealing with Banco do Brasil as that country's financial situation grew precarious. They even reduced their deposits in Canadian banks as Canada's economy became critical and the banks themselves were threatened by large losses from Dome Petroleum.

Walter Wriston was America's premier banker even when David Rockefeller was chief executive of Chase Manhattan. He was not the scion of an oil millionaire nor the easy target of conspiracy theorists, like Rockefeller, but Wriston was the strongest and smartest personality at the head of a big bank, and that bank was the most dynamic and in the end the biggest bank in the country.

Walter Wriston wrought not only Citibank, but also American big banking, and to an extent world banking, in his image. He pushed Citibank's expansion with a single-mindedness and self-confidence that approached the demonic. But often enough, Wriston came across simply as a glorified vacuum cleaner salesman, a small-town smooth-talker whose only goal in life was to make a buck.

The worries of the debt crisis and the challenge of crumbling U.S. bank regulation coming at the same time taxed even Wriston's formidable abilities. A tall man with a pointed head and prominent ears, he always betrayed a nervous manner. Nearing retirement, he got even twitchier. A European banker who met with Wriston shortly after the Mexican package was agreed to caricatured the Citibank chief with a spastic jerk of the head and uncontrolled blinking. "He used to be so smart," commented this longtime acquaintance. Wriston's perception of reality, at least as reflected in his public statements, became so one-sided during the debt crisis that he began to lose credibility. Lord Lever called him the fairy of world banking for his obsessive optimism.

Citibank is a world apart. It has its own language, its own hierarchy and its own values, and respects little else. Citibank is everywhere. A visitor can come into a strange city or country, confer with the local Citibanker, and see the new place filtered into Citibankspeak. It is a world view more homogeneous even than that of the U.S. Foreign Service, because it is even narrower.

One of the bank's area managers in Europe provided an insight into the character of the successful Citibanker with an anecdote about his childhood. His family was living in North Africa at one stage when the young banker-to-be discovered a cache of Confederate money at home. Playing the ingenue, he traded the worthless bills with some cagey Arabs who gave him local currency at a rate far lower than dollars normally fetched. But the Arabs accepted the Confederate bills as real U.S. dollars. "They thought *they* were cheating *me*," recalled the Citibanker with a smug grin.

Citibank wants to make money. That is all it wants. That is a fair objective for a private firm. To make money, Citibank will expand aggressively into new business, new locations. Finding New York too small, Citibank spanned the globe. With that conquest behind it, the bank set its sights on the land of the free and the brave. The bank lobbied and bullied its way through borders set by the McFadden Act, which forbids interstate branching, and the Glass-Steagall Act, which separates commercial and investment banking. If Walter Wriston gets his way, Citibank will be everywhere in the United States that is profitable, and in every line of financial service—banking, insurance, stockbroking, and underwriting.

One woman aptly described him as a very intelligent toad. Antonio Delfim Netto was a very hardworking toad at any rate. Brazil's superminister arrived at the office at 6 A.M. to begin his round of documents, conferences, and crises for the day. A self-made man of Neapolitan ancestry (Delfini was the original name), Delfim is a short, well-groomed man of fluctuating girth. Long on self-confidence, Delfim was a source of admiration and irritation within Brazil and abroad during his first stint in government, 1967–74, and upon his return in 1979. He got a lot of credit for Brazil's economic miracle of rapid growth and development in the earlier period. But his credit was wearing thin during his second tenure as Brazil's roller-coaster finances took increasingly sharp dips.

As planning minister, Delfim effectively controlled Brazil's economy. Brazil's debt situation caused a minor panic among international bankers as early as 1980. Delfim reassured them by abandoning his former policies of growth at all costs in favor of economic austerity and monetary restraint. He made them feel even better by accepting interest rates much higher than formerly tolerated in Euromarket loans and significantly above what countries like Mexico were paying. Also, Delfim and his crew made an ostentatious effort to stagger the terms of their loans, including those of government agencies, so that they would not all fall due at once. This was in marked contrast to Mexico and other developing countries, who only loosely coordinated their public sector borrowing.

Delfim tended to be somewhat smug about Brazil's debt management. Wriston bestowed an almost paternal accolade on the planning minister when he put arm around Delfim's shoulder at a bankers' meeting in Switzerland and told the assembled financiers how "proud we all are" of what Delfim had accomplished. That was before the Mexican debt shock. The pride turned quickly to irritation later when Delfim's smugness came across as arrogance. He alienated a lot of former backers by maintaining far too long into the 1982 crisis that Brazil had no problems, and then, when the problems were imminent, by implying that it was the bankers' fault and their responsibility.

A man of immense energy, Delfim fairly crackles in an encounter. He is sober and serious as only an Italian can be. He thrives on power and enjoys his work. A former colleague on the faculty of São Paulo's university, where Delfim taught economics for thirteen years, remarked, "He really is what he looks like, a fat, happy guy."

Three men who make the world go 'round, Abalkhail, Wriston, and Delfim, incarnate "recycling." Abalkhail is the main proponent of depositing surplus funds earned from oil exports with the major international banks. Wriston has led commercial banks into sovereign lending on a major scale. Delfim's confidence in Brazil's future prompted him to run up the world's biggest foreign debt. Whatever economic logic there is in the recycling of capital flows that followed the oil shock, the system developed because these intelligent, ambitious men decided to invest and lend and borrow. It developed also because other intelligent, ambitious men in Western central banks and governments decided not to do anything to cope with an unprecedented transfer of wealth.

The system worked. Saudi Arabia managed to hold the erosion of its assets to a minimum while keeping flexibility of action. Citibank became the preeminent bank in the world and made lots of profits. Brazil developed its economy, increased its exports and improved the overall standard of living. Abalkhail and Delfim had to accommodate their policies to the governments they worked for, and even Wriston had to pay some heed to potential pressure from stockholders and his board, but the influence of these powerful personalities largely determined what happened to a good deal of the world's money. Finance does not follow some abstract law of nature. It is not a theoretical economic consequence. Finance is the result of decisions by intelligent, ambitious men in pursuit of wealth.

2

When the OPEC countries quadrupled oil prices in 1973–74, they altered the world's capital flows. They earned much more money than they were used to, and importing countries paid a lot more for oil than they were used to. It took everyone a while to adjust to this sudden change. In the meantime, the OPEC countries collected a lot more money than they could spend, and the other countries spent a lot more money than they collected in foreign transactions. International payments of individual countries no longer balanced: In economic parlance, the oil producers were running a surplus on their balance of payments and the other countries were running a deficit.

The sums involved were enormous. In the period 1974–79 alone, before the second wave of oil price hikes, the OPEC countries ran a balance-of-payments surplus of about $220 billion. The twenty industrialized countries grouped together in the OECD registered a deficit of $100 billion, keeping to round numbers. The non-oil-producing developing countries, called NOPECs by some, ran a deficit of $150 billion in the six-year period. In 1981 the NOPECs registered a deficit of $100 billion for that single year alone.

Deficits have to be financed. If your monthly household bills exceed your income, you have to dip into the savings account or go to the finance company. The developing countries had no savings, so they had to borrow. Their deficits were of such magnitude that the only source of funds big enough to finance them were the oil surpluses themselves. But OPEC countries did not want to lend money directly to the countries who needed to borrow, especially not to the developing countries. So they deposited their money in the big international banks. These banks suddenly had a lot more money to lend out, but there was not much demand for loans in industrialized countries because of the recession caused by higher oil prices.

So the banks started lending the money to those who needed it—the oil-importing developing countries who were running big balance-of-payments deficits. They could use the funds to meet their foreign payments and so continued to grow economically. The process came to be known as recycling, because money went in a closed cycle like the water in a fountain. The oil-importing countries spewed out the money, which was collected by the OPEC countries and funneled into the banks, which pumped it back into the importing countries so they could spew it out again. As the process continued, the OPEC countries accumulated assets in the form of deposits on the books of the international banks, and the importing countries accumulated liabilities in the form of debts on the books of the international banks.

Recycling normally refers to this process of transferring the payments surpluses of oil-exporting countries to oil-importing countries, to finance the trade deficits caused by the higher price of oil. But recycling also took place at a more basic level. The oil shock diverted trade flows as well as capital. The most important form of this fundamental economic recycling, often overlooked, was the purchase by the newly rich Arab countries of goods and services from the industrialized countries. Capital goods suppliers, construction companies, engineers from the United States, Japan, and Europe profited from the building boom in the Near East and North Africa. OPEC countries mounted such ambitious development programs that they threw Western estimates of payments surpluses out of kilter. The underpopulated Arab countries spent a far greater portion of their oil income than generally forecast. Poor countries in southern and Southeast Asia also benefited by supplying thousands of workers to the thinly populated OPEC countries in Asia Minor.

In the wake of the oil shock, developed countries could afford to dampen growth because of the diversity of their economies and the sophistication of their social welfare systems. Most industrial countries were able to cut imports and conserve enough energy in the space of a couple of years to eliminate the payments deficits following the sudden increase in oil prices.

Another way of adjusting for industrial countries was to increase their exports to the developing countries. The poor countries were able to continue buying things from the rich countries thanks to the credits so helpfully supplied by the Western banks. By continuing their economic growth, financed by bank credit, the developing countries took upon themselves the burden of the payments deficit. The developed countries transferred their deficits to the developing countries.

A recent study by two British economists shows that the relationships of the non-oil-exporting developing countries remained as oppressive after the oil shock as before. Trade deficits with OPEC countries, while always important, fluctuated sharply in the years after 1973, rising to as much as three fourths of the overall deficit, but then declining again to two fifths. In the four-year period 1974–77, the NOPECs trade deficit with OPEC countries totaled $75.5 billion. At the same time, it was $63.5 billion with the industrial countries as a group. Oil payments counted for more than half of the overall deficit, but the shortfall in trade with industrial countries was still very substantial. The largest collective deficit, in fact, was with Japan, at $30 billion! The remaining countries in the top ten, in order, were Saudi Arabia, France, Venezuela, Iran, Kuwait, West Germany, Nigeria, United States, and Iraq.

Denis Healey, a former Chancellor of the Exchequer in Britain, recalled that the International Monetary Fund urged the industrial countries early in 1974 to finance their oil deficits by borrowing instead of deflating. But these governments reduced domestic demand, eliminating their deficits and in effect shifting them to the relatively defenseless group of non-oil-exporting developing countries. These had no alternative but to finance by borrowing, even though their less developed financial structures were ill suited to such an undertaking. As Healey, writing at the end of 1979, noted prophetically, "The non-oil developing countries from now on will have to bear a disproportionate share of the resulting deficits, will suffer very badly from deflation in the industrial countries, and will risk facing new barriers to their manufactured exports. Moreover, they may find it less easy than before to finance their deficits." He was right on all counts.

In the end, the developing countries had to finance not only the shortfall from oil imports, but also that from their trade with industrial countries. They had to borrow to cover their own deficits, and then borrow more to take over the industrial countries' deficits. The industrial countries, in short, "recycled" their deficits to the developing countries. This economic recycling is as important as, and more sinister than, simple financial recycling. The press has largely ignored this basic type of recycling. Yet it is the key to understanding why the plight of developing countries now is not due simply to mistakes on their part and why industrial countries are obliged in justice to find a solution to the debt problem.

3

A high-level conference in Bretton Woods, New Hampshire, agreed in July 1944 on how to run world finances once the war was over. The conference followed three years of intensive work by economic experts—John Maynard Keynes was the foremost among them—and aimed to avoid the problems that had led to the Great Depression and World War II itself. The new system, never implemented fully in Keynes's conception, functioned more or less successfully for two decades. By the mid-1960s, it began to run into trouble. The system was based on the strength of the dollar, which was backed by the political, military, and economic hegemony of the United States. Linking the dollar to gold was supposed to discipline the United States while giving further backing to the dollar.

By 1971, in the wake of the Vietnam war, the political, military, and economic prowess of the United States was not what it used to be. Nor was there much discipline. The United States could not finance the war, increase living standards, *and* fulfill its role in the

37

international monetary system. The war led to heavy deficits, excessive consumption led to inflation, and both of these made the dollar less trustworthy. Something had to give, and that was the world monetary system. In August 1971, President Richard Nixon unilaterally decoupled the dollar from gold. It was the death knell for the Bretton Woods system. Fitful attempts to keep exchange rates fixed to the dollar failed because there was no external discipline for the U.S. currency. In 1973 the major Western governments abandoned fixed exchange rates altogether.

Currency rates "floated." Like so much flotsam on top of a rough sea, currencies were tossed up and down by huge capital flows. Like sorghum or pork bellies, dollars, pounds, marks, and francs became a bulk commodity that traders bid up and down according to the vagaries of demand and speculation. Money, which economic textbooks once described as a "store of value," became valueless in international transactions. Supply and demand determined its value.

Currency gyrations turn values on their heads. An American in Paris in 1979 who worked for a French company and got a salary of 200,000 francs had something to write home about, because his French franc salary was the equivalent of $50,000. But the franc declined in value against the dollar, dropping from four francs to the dollar to seven francs to the dollar in 1982. Now the American's salary was reduced to the equivalent of $30,000, and he was writing home about the unfairness of it all (or more likely going home). A compatriot who was paid in dollars meanwhile would have felt disadvantaged with a salary of $40,000 in 1979, because that was only the equivalent of 160,000 francs. But he felt very good by 1982 because his dollar salary was worth 280,000 francs. Magnify these swings by millions and you see the problems facing corporate treasurers of multinational corporations. It's impossible to project cash flow when extraneous events like exchange rate swings can double or halve your numbers in a matter of months. Even forward transactions to lock in a certain currency rate, a device called "hedging," only mitigate the effect of swings.

There's no secret formula for anticipating currency movements. *Institutional Investor,* a magazine catering to international bankers and treasurers, emblazoned a dramatic warning across its cover in

September 1981: "The Coming Decline of the Dollar," based on a commentary by C. Fred Bergsten, a former undersecretary of the Treasury who is an acknowledged international expert on foreign exchange. The dollar didn't decline that fall, or even the next fall. Any eventual decline would make Bergsten's prediction true, but that type of forecast is not very helpful if you're trying to decide what currency to put your money in or to project income from foreign subsidiaries.

Currency distortions worsen what is called the terms of trade. Countries buy things with money, but they earn their money by selling other things. If the things they sell decline in price, while the things they buy increase in price, they have to sell more of their own products to buy the things they need to import. Their terms of trade have worsened. When it comes to commodities, prices actually do rise and fall depending on demand. But big changes in currency rates can aggravate these price swings, which are bad enough in themselves. President Julius Nyerere of Tanzania gave just one example of his country's deteriorating trade position. To buy one seven-ton truck in 1981, he said, Tanzania had to produce four times as much cotton, or three times as much coffee, or ten times as much tobacco, as it did five years earlier to purchase the same vehicle. Of course, Tanzania most likely is not in a position to use its cotton income to buy seven-ton trucks; that money goes for interest payments.

Floating exchange rates would make a mockery of free trade, if such a thing existed. In theory, free trade allows an international division of labor according to competitive advantage. That means that whichever country produces this or that most efficiently will successfully export it to other countries who will stop producing this or that and devote their time and energy to some other product where *they* have a competitive edge.

Whatever the other problems, volatile exchange rates distort trade flows. Japan may indeed have the world's most efficient steel plants, but its commercial success is due partly at least to keeping its currency, the yen, undervalued. A currency is undervalued when its exchange rate against other currencies is lower than its domestic purchasing power indicates. If a gallon of milk costs $1 in Japan according to the yen-dollar exchange rate, but costs $1.50 in the

United States and Europe, the purchasing power test suggests that the yen is valued too low. If practicable, an American would begin buying his milk in Japan. That's not practicable, but steel bars are not so perishable.

Floating exchange rates increased the volatility of export prices, interest rates and most other monetary values. Whether a better system was available or not, floating currency rates certainly contributed to the credit crisis.

Monetary authorities argued throughout the 1970s that the huge transfers of money generated by the oil shock made a return to fixed exchange rates impossible. Fixed rates are inflexible by definition, but the sudden shifts in international payments required a good deal of give in the system. But that give made it difficult for everyone from the treasurer of IBM to the finance minister of Brazil to calculate ahead of time how much he has to pay for what.

4

The debt crisis could not have taken place without the Euromarket. This market without a country, this free-floating loan exchange, was the "place" where Abalkhail deposited his money with Wriston and Wriston lent it to Delfim. American banks, European banks, Japanese banks all lent a large portion of their money through the Euromarket. Mexico, Brazil, and Argentina all borrowed their money through the Euromarket. There was no regulation, no central bank, no interference. The Euromarket provided the loan techniques, the institutions, and the freedom for recycling in a world of floating currencies. To understand just how the debt crisis came about, it is necessary to look at this arcane world of Eurocurrencies and syndicated loans.

The Euromarket was a bit like Oz, a land of wealth where your wishes come true. For companies and countries with extra cash, the Euromarket was an investors' paradise. Assets were liquid, anonymity reasonably sure, and returns high. For a borrower, it was a cash machine. The market mobilized millions of dollars overnight, with only a few telexes and no red tape. For the banks it was best of all. They felt as if they had come home. In the Euromarket, banks operated without any supervision or direct regulation. They conducted massive wholesale business, yielding generous cash flows offset by only marginal overhead.

Unlike Oz, the Euromarket was on this side of the rainbow. There was no wizard, but there were some clever conjuring tricks. One was the medium-term syndicated loan on rollover basis. In the past, banks extended short-term loans in the form of credit lines to their corporate customers, while making a variety of overdrafts and loans to their private customers. Or banks backed commercial transactions, which normally liquidated themselves in a matter of months. The nature of a bank's deposits kept loan maturities short, for prudent banking meant that deposits and loans should fall due in reasonably similar amounts so that the bank would have funds to pay off a depositor who decides to withdraw. A short maturity minimized other types of risk as well—the danger, for instance, that the borrower would go broke, or that interest rates would take an unfavorable turn.

The syndicated loan extended maturities while keeping risks low. In a medium-term loan, the banks committed themselves to a credit over seven or ten or twelve years. This gave both borrowers and lenders a greater certainty in planning. To minimize the interest-rate risk, though, the banks rolled over the loan every six months. That is, they set a new interest rate for the borrower on the basis of what it cost them to obtain funds. Banks cut the risk on the credit itself by spreading the loan among several institutions. A bank can make a $10-million loan to a customer by getting four other banks to join in, so that each of them lends only $2 million. If the customer goes broke, it is better to lose $2 million than $10 million. On this principle, banks formed syndicates ranging anywhere from a handful of institutions to 160 banks for France's $4-billion loan in the fall of 1982.

The dazzling simplicity of the syndicated loan blinded lenders and borrowers both to a couple of major flaws. The bankers did not remove the interest-rate risk by floating the rate, they simply passed the risk on to the borrower. When a credit carries a fixed interest rate, both the lender and the borrower know what they are in for during the life of the credit. A change in market rates during that period works to the advantage of one or the other. A borrower

41

feels good if interest rates go up because he has locked in a cheaper rate, while the banker feels good when rates go down because this loan continues to bring a higher return. Borrower and lender split the risk that rates will change. With rollover credits, the bank has virtually no interest-rate risk. Its return is a spread fixed over the cost of funding. The bank sacrifices the chance for extra profit with a favorable turn in rates, but you have to take the good with the bad.

The borrower, meanwhile, is at the mercy of the market. He has no control over what he will pay for his credit. The art of the debt manager traditionally was to stagger maturities and sources to achieve an average cost of funds that could be projected in a five-year financial plan. That is impossible with floating-rate credit. The borrower has to pay a spread above banks' funding cost, which is generally represented by the rate of interbank transactions in London, the famous Libor (London interbank offered rate). This rate can register huge fluctuations, like its rise from 10 percent in summer 1980 to 17 percent by the end of that year. Suppose you got a car loan from your bank at 10 percent and six months later the bank raised your car payment by half because the rates had gone up!

The other major flaw hit the banks. Syndication lessens an individual bank's risk in any single credit. But it also attenuates the control of the bank over the borrower. This is especially true when sovereign countries are the borrowers, because they do not like to concede any control anyway. By spreading the risk, the bank reduces any eventual loss but dilutes the relationship with the customer. Normally, banks play the bully. They dictate the collateral, the terms, and anything else they feel necessary to keep the borrower sound. But a syndicate manager has no such sway. The borrower operates as a free agent on an open market. One consequence is that the bank can no longer set certain conditions on a loan. A principal condition of normal loan agreements is a limit on the overall indebtedness of the borrower. In the case of a sovereign borrower on the Euromarket, this condition is not practical.

A borrower may have a perfectly acceptable level of debt when a seven-year loan is made. Two or three years down the road, the overall debt may have swollen to unmanageable size, but the syndicate making the original loan had nothing to say about it. Obviously, though, the risk has become much greater than when the credit originally was granted.

Risk from syndicated loans accumulates in another way as well. Sovereign borrowers are limited in number and come to the market often. A bank spreads the risk on a first loan by syndicating it. For sheer lack of other clients, the same bank may join a second syndicate for that same borrower. The bank's exposure in the original $10-million loan was $2 million. If it takes on the same amount in the second syndication, its exposure grows to $4 million. After a few more loans like this, the bank has $10 million of loans to that one country on its books—just as much as if it had made the original $10-million loan by itself. Leaving aside the fact that a succession of different terms may have improved the overall yield to the bank, the fact remains that its credit risk has reached the level it sought to avoid by syndicating in the first place. Syndication spreads the risk, but the continuous interaction of a limited number of operators in the Euromarket concentrates it.

5

Bankers are money salesmen. Beneath the polished veneer and expensive suit lurks a huckster. Foreign assets of U.S. banks quintupled in the period 1965 to 1980. The explosive growth of international banking expanded the ranks of traveling salesmen. Like their counterparts who ply the Interstates in station wagons to peddle vacuum cleaners, these jet-set salesmen demonstrated a remarkable stamina. They could rise at 4 A.M. to catch an early plane, shrug off transatlantic jet lag, even go from the airport in Sydney after twenty-eight hours in the air directly into negotiations with the finance officer of New South Wales. Senior bankers would routinely circumnavigate the globe, making their pitch along the way.

Money is more or less the same, but the price—the interest rate —can be competitive. As the pin-striped salesmen crowded each other in Interconti hotel lobbies and the reception rooms of finance ministers, the price of credit went down. The so-called margins— the spread above the cost of funding—declined from at least one percentage point down to a half point. Downward pressure soon crumbled this barrier and deals were made at 3/8 and occasionally even 1/4. The Americans were the first in the field, but as the Japanese, Europeans, and Arabs joined the game in turn, the going got tougher. Competition tended to clump the bankers together, like four gasoline stations locating at the same intersection. Propinquity leads to price wars. International bankers, to change the metaphor, formed into roving bands of money gypsies, descending on any town where there was a whiff of borrowing need. Certain borrowers or groups of borrowers enjoyed a vogue, and the money bazaar moved in.

The deals got to be bigger, better organized, more intricate. Loose affiliations grew between the banks in syndication. An unwritten code regarding reciprocal invitations to deals came into effect and weighed in the bank's final decision: You scratch my back, I'll scratch yours. Loan agreements became standard and were programmed into word processors. As the routine became more efficient, the pace quickened. Telexes came clacking into the banks' message centers one after another. How much are you in for in this deal with the Mexican electricity commission, the Spanish railroad authority, the Brazilian development bank? Details of individual projects were sketchy, the terms were not: margin 1/2 to 5/8, commitment fee 3/8 (to pay the banks for keeping the money ready), participation fee 3/16 for amounts above $5 million. The bank putting together the syndication may have had a long relationship with the borrower, or may have a domestic manufacturing customer who is delivering turbines or rail cars for the project to be financed by the loan. More often, though, the organizing bank had made a bid against other syndicate managers and had come in lowest. None of that really mattered. The relevant question was simple: How much are you in for? Please reply within a week, or in twenty-four hours. The decision turned not only on the credit rating of the borrower, but the chances for domestic customers to export something for the project, the overall relationship to the government in question, and subtle alignments among the banks. There were so many credits to decide on. "How could we possibly have studied each one closely?" demands the syndications manager at one of the world's five biggest banks, in a reflective post-Mexico mood. "It was what I call 'receptionist banking,'" recounts another. "When you went out to lunch you could have told the receptionist to watch the telex and take $5 million of any deal offered."

What could be simpler? Answer a telex, dispatch an officer to a signing ceremony, and fly your flag on a tombstone, those deliberately dull financial ads that list the banks involved in a loan. It was called "telex and tombstone banking," and for a long time it was an easy way to make a lot of money.

6

The key to understanding the Euromarket is currencies. Currencies are like casino chips. When you want to gamble in a particular casino, you buy their chips at the door, place your bets, and cash in your winnings when you leave. The chips are not usually good for much outside the casino, so there is no point in taking them out. This was generally the case with currencies, too, until the 1950s and 1960s. China and the Soviet Union, suspicious in the chilly climate of the Cold War, did not want to deposit their dollars in the logical place for them—that is, U.S. banks. U.S. regulations designed to keep dollars from leaving the country actually encouraged American banks and companies to earn higher returns by keeping dollar deposits abroad, particularly in Europe. The dollar, in fact, is one casino chip you can play with in a lot of clubs. Other currencies, too, are convertible: like the "convertible" chips of casinos where the house always has the backing to cash them in, "convertible" currencies are those that are worth something outside their own country.

Eurocurrencies are simply national currencies held outside their country of origin. There are Eurodollars, Euromarks, Eurofrancs, and so on. Almost by definition, only convertible currencies can qualify for this designation. The Euromarket is the free-floating exchange, gravitating more or less toward London, of Eurocurrencies. Eurocredits are syndicated loans funded by Eurocurrencies. Eurobonds are, broadly speaking, those offered outside the country of the currency they are denominated in (although there are various hybrid versions).

The Euromarket grew up in London and other European finan-

45

cial centers. The market makers were branches of U.S. banks, European banks, and joint-venture or consortium banks especially established for the purpose (Eurobanks). The prefix Euro- stuck, even as the market expanded around the world. A brave attempt to introduce xeno-, the Greek prefix for "foreign" (as in xenophobia), failed. Bureaucrats prefer to speak more precisely of international money and capital markets, but Euromarket remains the colloquial expression.

The Euromarket basks in endless sunlight. Trading passes on among money centers girdling the globe—Zurich, Frankfurt, Luxembourg, London, New York, San Francisco, Tokyo, Hong Kong, Singapore, Bahrain. There is no Big Board or ticker as in stock exchanges, no money pits like the commodities pits in Chicago, no space-age trading floor dominated by television display screens as in options markets, no face-to-face contact. Trades take place in an electronic ether. Deals are done on the telephone or the telex or the cathode ray tube in the trader's office. Billions are shunted around from one bank's computer to the next. Eurodollar bills do not exist. Eurodollars are blips on a magnetic computer tape. The Eurodollar, in fact, is a fiction. It is completely fungible—i.e., exchangeable—with any other U.S. dollar. Constant arbitrage with the domestic money market keeps interest rates largely parallel and allows supply and demand for funds to function in the market as a whole. In the end, every Eurodollar comes home to roost and becomes a deposit in an American bank, because that is the only place a dollar really exists. The Eurodollar market is a closed circuit. As boundaries between dollars and Eurodollars blur, it is more accurate to speak of the internationalization of capital markets than of the international capital market.

7

The Euromarket radically changed the way banks do business. The banks are the whole show. They and they alone determine who gets credit, how much credit there is, what the terms are. In the initial rush of competition, banks forgot their manners, their prudence, and their rules. And nobody slapped their wrists. There are no exchanges, no regulators, no central bank, no laws.

Price information, for instance, which is necessary for any market to function, is supplied exclusively by the banks. Reuters went from being just a competent news agency to cashing in as a rich multinational when it hit upon the genial idea of letting banks pay to have their currency and bond rates distributed via Reuters' network of screen displays. The market is made by the simultaneous bids and offers of the Eurobanks. The screen is the window on that market—an electronic exchange floor. The deals themselves are usually made on the phone or telex.

The changes in banking went much deeper. Credit used to be something confidential. Banks used to be discreet. The Euromarket eroded this tradition. First of all, the market was new and competitive. In the domestic markets of the big industrial countries, financing relations were relatively mature and stable. Morgan Stanley and Chase Manhattan had their customers, and shifts were the exception. The Euromarket was a free-for-all. Competitive edges were much smaller in a growing market. There were fewer established loyalties, and there were many new customers. Most notable, after the oil shock, were the big developing countries, who felt free to pick and choose their bankers. A tailor to cut the suit to measure seemed expensive when there were so many well-fitting suits to take off the rack. The model was no longer the discreet talk between the merchant and his banker, but the open quest of a customer for the best deal in town and the open response of bankers to offer him just that.

The syndication of credits eroded discretion. William F. Low, an enterprising young Scot who launched one of the early newsletters covering the Euromarket, became notorious for rummaging through the wastebaskets of banks' telex rooms to find the carbon copies of invitations to a syndication. The telexes contained much more information about a deal than bankers, still under the influence of traditional practice, were willing to publicize at that time. Eventually it became impossible, and even undesirable, to keep a lid on this information. The agencies, newsletters, and financial papers began carrying full details of Eurocredits—maturity, interest

47

rates, fees. Such transparency keeps terms finely honed, but robs both borrower and lender of any confidences.

Other banking virtues degenerated. When most of us go in for a loan, we have to supply collateral. For a mortgage, obviously the collateral is the house; for a car loan, the car. If we fail to keep up payments on the loan, the bank forecloses and takes the house or car away from us. Classic. Eurocredits, on the other hand, are mostly unsecured. Interbank loans, credits to big corporations and to sovereign countries, usually have no specific collateral. In the case of sovereign countries, the Eurocredit resembles the type of loan the rest of us get through a credit card. The collateral for a credit card really is your personal income. Credit card operators inquire about your income and set a credit limit accordingly. They also ask for details of other obligations you have, because these are also claims on your future income. But Eurocredit managers do not ask this question, or at least do not ask for sufficient detail to judge creditworthiness by balancing the borrower's income against other claims on that income.

Two other differences make a sovereign Eurocredit riskier than a credit card. A sovereign country can experience a sharp drop in income resulting from lower commodities prices or a recession, whereas most credit card holders can count on maintaining their income. Second, a sovereign borrower can see its interest rate double *on credits it has already used.* Most credit cards charge usurious interest rates to begin with, but they raise them only with notice and only on *new* credits. The credit card holder has the choice to refrain from incurring new obligations in view of the high rates. The sovereign borrower is not so lucky. In fact, he often has to borrow more money at the high rates just to pay the increased interest on his old credits.

The lack of collateral in Eurocredits is one of the things that make banks so edgy. They tend to travel in herds, seeking some comfort in company for their lack of hard security. This behavior is unconscious, because there is surprisingly little reflection among bankers about the impact of the Euromarket on traditional banking principles. Karl Otto Pöhl, the gregarious president of the West German central bank, unwittingly betrayed this latent schizophrenia in a remark about the central bank bridging loans to the Latin

American countries. Pöhl had authorized the Bundesbank's contribution to these loans on his own authority, because the central bank is allowed by law to engage in "banking" business as well as central banking. "But if it's banking business, I want to see collateral," expostulated Pöhl. Catching himself, the central banker had the good grace to chuckle. It was precisely the failure of commercial banks to observe banking's basic precepts that made it necessary for the central bank to get into "banking" business with Mexico, Brazil, and Argentina.

The Euromarket represents a new phenomenon that has scarcely been recognized as such. The market that was born almost accidentally became unintentionally the instrument for mounting the largest international financing operation in the history of the world.

While there has been much discussion about the theory of Euromarkets, very little attention has been paid to the practical consequences of the way banks do business and the long-range impact of ad hoc practices on money and capital flows.

The most notable historical instance of capital transfer prior to the postwar period was the financing of development in the Americas by European capital at the turn of the century. But this finance was in the form of direct investment in projects or in bonds subscribed by nonbank investors. When defaults occurred, as they frequently did, individual investors were left holding the bag. They lost their money. Eurobonds are the latter-day equivalent of these foreign bonds. The lending to developing countries, however, is something different, because it consists mostly of syndicated rollover credits. It is the banks who make the loans. In the case of default, they are the ones left holding the bag, but the money they lose is not theirs. It is somebody else's (yours and mine, for instance). Banks have always made loans, of course, and these have gone bad often enough. But this is the first time in history that banks have been the intermediaries in a capital transfer on this scale.

It may seem logical that a loan is a loan is a loan, and once a bank knows how to evaluate a credit risk, it should be able to make a loan to anybody. Because it seemed so logical, the Euromarket grew up and took over recycling. It seemed perfectly natural that banks, who make loans to you and me and the companies we work for, should make loans to Brazil and Zaire and Poland. But there's a world of difference between a $1-million line of credit to XYZ Corp. and, for example, Citibank's $4.3-billion exposure in Brazil.

Alexandre Lamfalussy, the dapper chief economist at the Bank for International Settlements, makes the point: "Banks have had a hundred years to learn how to make a loan to the butcher on the corner. They've had only ten years to learn how to evaluate a sovereign risk." There's only one way to learn and that's the hard way. But it's hard on all of us, because banks are intermediaries. Just as they pass on one person's savings to make another person's loan, they pass on their costs in learning how to make sovereign loans to the rest of their customers, in the form of higher charges and higher interest rates on loans and lower interest on deposits.

If a bondholder goes bankrupt because a borrower defaults, it's too bad for him. But if a bank approaches insolvency because of a borrower's default, it is a matter of public concern. This consequence, which became painfully obvious with the onset of the debt crisis, was clear from the moment banks began making loans to sovereign countries.

8

The lack of a central exchange or central bank in the Euromarket has two major consequences. One is that it is very difficult to compile statistics on the market, because there is no natural compiler. Major central banks regularly publish voluminous accounts of what's going on in domestic credit and capital markets. They have well-oiled reporting channels from banks and other participants to report the raw data that enable the central bank to publish analytic statistics. These numbers are big, but reassuringly finite. The *Federal Reserve Bulletin,* published monthly, can readily tell you, for instance, that U.S. banks had assets of $1.8 trillion at the end of 1982, or that there was a total of $1.6 trillion in mortgages. The Bank for International Settlements in Basel, which is commonly known as the central bank of central banks, comes closest to being a natural reporting institution for the Euromarket. The BIS does indeed provide the most authoritative information about the market, but the statistics have shortcomings. The numbers are reported indirectly by the central banks to BIS and are not always of the same quality or thoroughness. Although the important trading centers are included, many others are left out. The time lag in reporting is very long, between four and seven months, which makes international banking seem like trying to land a space capsule on the moon while Houston Control works out the coordinates on an adding machine. The analytical breakdown is inexact, and makes the figures at best a guide to what's going on rather than an exact indicator.

Still, the BIS statistics have earned a certain affection because they are the best there is to measure the Eurocurrency market itself. Other statistics, compiled by the International Monetary Fund, World Bank, Organization for Economic Cooperation and Development, treat capital flows more generally. Only the BIS gets reports, indirectly, from the banks. All other estimates on the size and structure of the Euromarket draw on this reporting base. The most widely recognized estimates are those published monthly by the prestigious New York bank Morgan Guaranty. According to Morgan, the gross size of the Euromarket topped $2 trillion by the fall of 1982. Nearly three quarters of that represented transactions between banks. About $575 billion were in credits to nonbanks. But none of these statistics are refined enough or fast enough to catch a buildup of short-term credits (those lasting less than a year), which is exactly what precipitated the Mexican payments crisis. No single agency or bank has firsthand information on all types of credit— bilateral, military, export, Euromarket, medium-term, short-term. Oddest of all, perhaps, is that until the crisis itself, only a few central banks had any idea of the overall involvement of their commercial banks in international loans. The business is spread out in a number of branches and subsidiaries throughout the world, so that a total would appear only in consolidated accounts. Many European countries have not required banks to submit consolidated accounts. This shortcoming had been discussed for years, but only with the Mexican crisis did European central banks get serious about requiring consolidated bank accounts.

Information is control, and control is one thing the Euromarket lacks. This is the other major consequence of not having a central authority. Bankers, of course, resist any moves to control the Euromarket, because they like the freedom of action. They do not exactly have to twist the arms of the regulators to win agreement. Various halfhearted attempts to mount controls on the Euromarket have quickly foundered on relatively flimsy excuses.

A move by the United States in the late 1970s to impose reserve requirements for Euromarket deposits failed to gain any momentum. Central bankers weakly contended that unless all Euromarket centers agreed to the requirements, banks would simply do their business in the centers that do not have the requirements. (Reserve requirements are the minimum fractions of customer deposits that banks have to keep without interest in the central bank.) But, as the Scandinavian central banks have shown, where banks do business can be effectively controlled by requiring licenses for foreign operations. Regulatory authorities could simply deny their banks a license to operate in a center that did not agree to an international reserve requirement. The merits of reserve requirements are debatable. Given the far-flung nature of existing bank networks, such a licensing requirement would be difficult to grandfather in. The point is that bank regulation is really a case of finding a way when there is a will. At least until the 1982–83 crisis, central banks were not able to muster the will.

These three developments created the environment for the world credit crisis. The oil shock, with its massive diversion of trade and capital flows, eventually generated the debt shock. The oil shock had such an impact because the monetary discipline established by Bretton Woods had collapsed. The existence of a large and uncontrolled market in Eurocurrencies magnified the shock. The debt shock precipitated a totally new type of crisis.

"NOT A VERY
EXCITING NUMBER"
CHAPTER THREE

————◈————

1

The debt crisis of 1982–83 was unprecedented. International debt had reached proportions scarcely imaginable before. Funneling billions of dollars of credit through a few financial institutions made the whole situation that much more acute. Debtors had the possibility of holding the Western world hostage. The problem was partly the size of the debt and the countries' difficulties in repaying it. But the position of the lenders was what galvanized concern in the industrial countries.

Credit to developing countries in the nineteenth century, for example, was channeled through a broad spectrum of private investors who bought shares or bonds in railroads and mills in North and South America, Russia or China. Banks organized these loans and underwrote the issues. They even bought securities for their own account. Argentina's financial troubles nearly bankrupted the renowned British merchant bank Baring Brothers in 1890. Baring's was on a par with Rothschild's in England. Its threatened collapse was like the teetering of a National Westminster Bank or Chase Manhattan today. Only a massive rescue mounted by the Bank of England kept Baring's afloat. The supply of "busted" bonds—those left over from nineteenth-century defaults—is so great and diversified that a new hobby has grown up in the last few years of collecting and trading them, like stamps.

Herbert Feis, a historian and State Department adviser, recounts the boom in European investments abroad in the period 1870–1914 in his classic 1930 work. He routinely includes notices of default. A Portuguese default in the 1890s (an early evidence of Brazilian money problems) "incensed financial circles," recounts Feis baldly. "After the Turkish bankruptcy in 1876," he relates, "the London market tended to refrain from further reliance upon the credit of that country." British capital became disillusioned with European borrowers after further defaults from Spain and the Balkan countries. Investors then favored the new worlds abroad. But by the end of the century these investments, too, halted in "balked disappointment":

> The rapid extension of agricultural production brought falling food prices and financial distress in the newly opened areas. The speculative land and mining booms ended in a violent smash, especially in Australia. Many of the railroad systems of the United States, financially mismanaged and plunged into headlong competition, ceased payment on their bonds. Economic and financial maladjustment in Argentina ended in default upon all the securities of that government; while revolution and currency troubles in Brazil seemed to make further losses of the same sort inevitable.

Charles P. Kindleberger, a professor at the Massachusetts Institute of Technology, has made a hobby of studying financial crashes. He published a study of monetary disasters with the charming title *Manias, Panics and Crashes.* He lists manias of foreign lending taking place in 1808–10, 1823–25, 1856–61, 1885–90, 1910–13, and 1924–28 that were all followed by "revulsions." Classically, in Kindleberger's analysis, some outside shock, a displacement, ignites lending fever that invariably snaps with default. "Boom loans are undertaken on the upswing, defaulted at the peak, and refunded in the next upswing, which may also lead to new borrowing." This is a pattern, Kindleberger maintains:

In short, productive loans in the developing countries are not very productive and do not stay long out of default, for several reasons: the lending occurs in bursts, often called "manias," which are precipitated, if not caused by some shock to the system (the displacement), whipped up by euphoric excitement, overdone, with the borrower typically getting less than it is committed for, and being forced to suspend debt service in the next recession.

Particularly sinister are recycling loans, which closely resemble the loans made a half century earlier for war reparations. Typically, these go to finance consumption and only postpone default. "The problem of developing country debt today," Kindleberger wrote in 1981, "is rather that the loans to developing countries, and even those to Britain, France and Italy in the last three and a half years, have been used to finance consumption, and that the recycling which has postponed default cannot continue indefinitely."

Banks stumbled into sovereign loans by accident. In the heyday of postwar economic expansion, banks had enough to do financing domestic industry. American banks were big enough and strong enough to follow U.S. industry abroad, particularly to Europe. U.S. payments restrictions further encouraged their international expansion. But the bulk of their business was still the classic commercial and industrial loan.

The postwar decolonization process extended into the early 1960s, creating new developing countries. External finance came through bilateral government aid, first from the former colonial power, supplemented by credits from the multilateral financing agencies. Older developing countries, like those in South America, received capital by means of direct investment as U.S. and, later, European multinationals built facilities in these countries. American banks followed the companies. They soon got involved in the local market, bringing new services and expertise to the local economy. A useful synergy developed. The banks, like the industrial companies, expended into a new and growing market. The local economy got a window on the world. Economies boomed. Brazil, the biggest country in Latin America, grew at an average annual rate of eleven percent in the period 1968–73. It was simply the most prominent example.

U.S. banks began reaping profits on a scale that relegated their domestic operations to second place. By the 1970s Chase, Citibank, and Bank of America were making more than half their profits abroad. These banks set up branches in every corner of the globe, becoming world banks whose headquarters happened to be in New York or San Francisco. Young, ambitious executives circulated among these branches, aggressively enhancing the greater glory of their banks while making their own career. The banks had regional desks like the State Department and accumulated a similar pool of expertise in their international corps.

By the 1970s, the American banks employed their expertise more and more to finance developing-country growth. What's good for Brazil was good for General Motors. Growth in the big developing countries outpaced official aid flows, which increased only slowly in real terms. Government agencies mounting big infrastructure developments, state-owned basic industries increasing capacity, newly nationalized natural resource developments—all these state borrowers turned with greater frequency to commercial banks for finance.

When the oil crisis came in 1973–74, the question was whether the shock would interrupt this upward surge. For a while it continued. Developing countries borrowed the difference. The new question was: How long could they go on borrowing before the debts themselves braked economic growth?

2

Three cases in the latter half of the 1970s gave, or should have given, ample warning to bankers of the tribulations that lie ahead. They seemed *sui generis* at the time. In retrospect, though, it's clear that they foreshadowed what was later to become a pattern—sudden liquidity crisis, practical default, ad hoc rescue efforts involving the International Monetary Fund, commercial banks, and Western governments. Zaire, Peru, and Turkey created difficulties that pale in comparison with later cases like Poland, Mexico, and Brazil. But these earlier cases caused headaches aplenty to monetary officials and bankers at the time. They seemed to be dangerous and frightening aberrations, upsetting the established order.

The worst fear at the time was that of setting undesirable precedents. This betrayed the shortsightedness of the bankers. They were too worried about certain "solutions," like postponing or delaying payments, giving ideas to other debtors. Instead, they should have looked more closely at the reasons for their trouble.

Zaire, Peru, and Turkey were marked by crass examples of corruption and economic mismanagement. But bankers should have seen that a credit system which allowed corrupt or mismanaged countries to amass billions of dollars of bank debt was a vulnerable system.

What distinguished these cases from other critical financial situations in the 1970s, like those of Argentina, Brazil and Mexico, was that the banks were already heavily exposed and didn't want to increase their commitment. The big Latin-American nations succeeded in getting more bank finance to resolve their financial problems. For Zaire, Peru, and Turkey the problem arose because the banks were not willing to give them any more loans. The same reluctance of the banks, on a bigger scale, overtook the "Big Three" too, only much later.

The banks cut their rescheduling teeth on these early cases. Resolving the situations in Zaire, Peru, and Turkey involved what was then an unprecedented deployment of manpower and brainpower.

Zaire, the former Belgian Congo, is a huge country rich in natural resources. The possibilities blinded the bankers. After the harrowing three-year attempt "to prevent commercial banks from calling a default a default, and to induce them to talk about rescheduling without calling it rescheduling" one exasperated banker cynically commented that "Zaire is a country with enormous potential, and it'll still be a country with enormous potential in one hundred years' time."

The trouble started in June 1975 when Zaire stopped paying any principal or interest on its $700 million to $800 million of commercial bank debt. Citibank took the lead for the nearly one hundred banks with credits to Zaire, and rejected the country's request for a

57

moratorium or rescheduling. The Citibankers argued that such a step would encourage the likes of Peru, Turkey, Pakistan, and Sudan to do the same. They missed the point, of course. Pretending that rescheduling or default was not possible did not make it possible for any of these countries to pay their debts. In succeeding months, all of these other countries were rescheduling their debts by one means or another.

Because the amount involved was relatively small, the bankers were more concerned about precedents than about the actual loans to Zaire (or than they were about Zaire's welfare). It took them nearly a year to put together a proposal for Kinshasa. In the meantime, official creditors—that is, governments—meeting in the Paris Club agreed in mid-1976 to reschedule another $800 million that Zaire owed to them. That agreement fell apart in just one month, when Zaire missed its first payment.

By the end of the year the banks had agreed to restructure the $375 million of unguaranteed bank debt. Citibank proposed to raise a new credit of $250 million on a "best efforts" basis on two conditions: first, that Zaire reach an agreement with the International Monetary Fund on restoring economic stability, and second, that the country pay foreign exchange to cover its interest arrears into a blocked account in the Bank for International Settlements. The bankers wanted to see a minimum of $130 million in this account before making the new loan. Zaire eventually paid in as much as $80 million.

Two invasions from Angola into the Shaba province slowed down these negotiations. The IMF agreed in March 1977 to lend Zaire $90 million, but rescinded that loan in November after paying only the first tranche of $33 million. (*Tranche,* the French word for "slice," refers to the first installment of a credit.) The loan was restored in February of the following year when Zaire agreed to put an IMF appointee in the central bank to run the nation's monetary affairs. The second Shaba invasion postponed the arrival of this gentleman, a retired Bundesbank official named Erwin Blumenthal, until August. That same month Zaire drew $18 million out of the supposedly blocked BIS account, which put paid to Citibank's plan to get new money from the banks.

Many bankers felt that the Citibank scheme, masterminded by

Irving Friedman, then a senior vice president at the bank, had been a wild-goose chase. Many of the other bankers involved in the talks felt that Friedman's deal was "cosmetic nonsense." They point out, for instance, that the $250 million loan corresponded exactly to the amount of debt service Zaire had through 1978. The new loan would not be going to finance new economic growth, they surmised, but simply to pay off old debt. It amounted, as far as they could see, to a rescheduling no matter what it was called.

Friedman, a thirty-year veteran of the IMF and World Bank, takes credit for inventing country risk analysis in commercial banking. At the time he fancied himself as a sort of Henry Kissinger of the monetary world, shuttling around the globe in pursuit of diplomatic settlements to knotty problems. He was probably more right than he knew, because his proposal was as much a solution for Zaire's financial problems as Kissinger's solution in Vietnam was the right way to peace with honor.

Citibank chairman Walter Wriston, a master at half-truths, set the tone of arrogant optimism that he would continue a few years later with bigger rescheduling cases. Speaking to *Euromoney* of Citibank's $40 million exposure in Zaire, Wriston said, "If we lost our total unguaranteed portion in Zaire, that would be a third of what we wrote off on the Penn Central. That's not a very exciting number, but people seem to get excited about it." Those excitable people probably had the problem of precedents in mind just as the bankers did. Wriston never talked so casually of writing off total exposure in Brazil or Mexico.

By the 1982 crisis, most banks had written off their Zaire exposure completely. They saw the country as a basket case. Rumors circulated in Brussels that summer that Zaire's president-for-life, Mobutu Sese Seko, had billions salted away in Swiss bank accounts.

A cover story in *Institutional Investor* at the time called the Zaire negotiations "the toughest, most complex and most exhausting set of negotiations between a sovereign government and its creditors in years." The longtime vice chairman of Citibank, G. A. (Al) Costanzo, agreed. "Zaire is the most difficult case we could have picked out," he said. "If we can do it for Zaire, we can do it for anybody." He, too, may have been righter than he knew. The attempt did not work in Zaire; it has yet to work anywhere else.

Following the slow death of the Friedman initiative, Zaire lurched on in a financial limbo. A $1.2-billion IMF program worked out in 1979 led to a single payment of $200 million in 1980 before the IMF suspended the program because Zaire failed to meet the targets for cutting the budget deficit. In October 1982 Zaire paid only a fraction of the interest due to banks and prompted new discussions. Typical of the problems faced by many African and other developing countries was the decline in Zaire's export income in 1981. It fell to $1.4 billion, from $1.9 billion in 1980. Unfortunately, both the IMF program and a Paris Club rescheduling in July 1981 were based on export income remaining the same.

But Zaire has one big problem that is not so typical elsewhere, at least not to the same measure it has been in Zaire. Corruption, by all accounts, reaches an intensity in Mobutu's Zaire that goes beyond shame and almost beyond imagination. The Brussels rumors speculated that the president-for-life's personal fortune in hard currency amounted to about the sum of the country's entire debt—about $5 billion. (Zaire *does* keep its debts to Swiss banks current.)

Most germane for the bankers was Erwin Blumenthal's bitter assessment of prospects in Zaire. Having practically fled Kinshasa in 1979 after a frustrating year of trying to bring order into the chaos, Blumenthal wrote in 1982, "There is no, I repeat, no chance that Zaire's numerous creditors will recover their money." The disillusioned central bank official ventured that Mobutu and his cronies were cynically calculating that Western governments and banks would continue to up the ante to avoid declaring a default with all it would entail. By the end of 1982, most banks had written off their Zaire exposure completely, having given up hope of ever getting back a cent. They had come to the same conclusion as had the hapless Blumenthal.

With the arrival of the full-fledged crisis in 1982, Zaire had plenty of company in Africa. At least forty low-income countries, the bulk of them on that continent, were reported in arrears on their public debt. The *Financial Times* said the month after Mexico's moratorium that the outlook for developing countries reached "to the deepest gloom for the most poverty-stricken primary commodity producers. The worst-off region seems to be sub-Saharan Africa."

60

A $150-million syndicated loan planned for Ivory Coast had the bad luck to be announced just one day after Mexico's bombshell. The attempt by lead manager Bankers Trust to assuage potential lenders with a meeting of World Bank and IMF experts backfired when that meeting gave rise to speculation in the financial press that Ivory Coast was a candidate for rescheduling. The loan languished and was completed only after the French Finance Ministry pressured its state-owned banks to join the Euromarket syndication. Ivory Coast, a prosperous country by African standards, was still sitting well compared to some others.

Sudan had to suspend imports even of medication. The huge country, which straddles Arab and black Africa, had to go back to official and commercial creditors alike to reschedule the $3 billion external debt it had just rescheduled in 1979.

Lack of foreign exchange had unexpected effects. In November, British Caledonian canceled its flights to Sierra Leone because it had £3.5 million tied up uselessly in that country's local currency. Tanzania coughed up $15 million due to the World Bank after an official from the Washington institution pointedly reminded President Julius Nyerere about the implications of defaulting on Bank repayments. The World Bank likes to boast that it has never had a default. It had suspended further funding of forty-three development projects until Tanzania saw the light.

The other Bretton Woods institution, the International Monetary Fund, cracked down on a number of African countries in the wake of Mexico. Zambia, Zimbabwe, and Kenya pushed through major devaluations to secure or restore IMF standby credits. Uganda was an economic shambles after Idi Amin's dictatorship. Under President Milton Obote, the country embraced the IMF. The Fund's representative occupied an office down the hall from the governor in the country's central bank, and the Ugandan economy was completely under his tutelage.

For its part, Ghana agreed to an IMF program in 1981, but backed out after President Hilla Limann was overthrown. In the ensuing year, a passionate public debate tilted toward going it alone and rejecting the model of docility set by Uganda.

Ghana has always been prickly. Nkrumah irritated Western

policymakers during his fifteen-year rule by his flirtations with the Eastern bloc. When he was overthrown in 1966, the country turned to the West. In a major policy decision, the new government bravely declared that Ghana would honor the considerable amount of debt Nkrumah had run up. This included a whopping $580 million in suppliers' credits (compared to less than $100 million in official medium- and long-term credits). Suppliers' credits are those extended by Western exporters or their banks, usually under the guarantee of the Western government, to finance sales to the developing countries. Before the growth of the Euromarket and syndicated loans, they were the main type of commercial loans made to developing countries.

Ghana hoped to capitalize on the goodwill from the homage to Holy Contract, in its decision to honor Nkrumah's debts, even though many of the supplier credits were the result of high-pressure sales techniques by Western exporters. But successive reschedulings failed to reduce Ghana's debt burden to manageable proportions. Following another coup in 1972, Ghana threatened outright repudiation of part of the commercial debt. All principal payments rescheduled in previous agreements were postponed once again, on the best terms ever: eighteen years with eleven years' grace, at only 2.5 percent interest. The author of an exhaustive study of Ghana's debt struggles, titled *Development and the Debt Trap,* draws the obvious conclusion: "While no one can say with certainty what would have happened had Ghana reneged on its debts in 1966, there may be a moral for other countries in the creditors' reaction to Colonel Acheampong's declaration in January 1972 that Ghana was repudiating a part of the debt and unilaterally rescheduling the rest. Western governments have since then offered Ghana by far the most generous settlement package it has yet received."

3

After Zaire, Peru gave the second big warning in the mid-1970s. The amount at stake was relatively small. Still, the $3 billion of debt Peru had amassed by the end of 1975, two thirds of it owed to banks, seemed large at the time, especially in view of the country's size. Peru worried the bankers because of its potential of setting a precedent. Most important, Peru marked a watershed in the relationship between banks and countries. For once, the banks tried to embark on a "stabilization program" à la International Monetary Fund in order to forestall default or rescheduling. The experiment failed decisively. Banks learned for certain what they had always suspected—they do not have the political leverage to dictate a country's economic policy. They realized once and for all that they need the IMF as a political front to restore financial order in wayward countries.

A coup within the army replaced one ruling general with another in August 1975. Copper prices roller-coasted from about fifty cents a pound to three times that, and then back down to fifty cents in the period 1971–75. The renewed drop in the price of Peru's main export widened the country's trade deficit, and the central bank lost half of its $1 billion in currency reserves covering the gap. The banks got jittery and began to resist Peruvian requests for money. They also cut back existing lines of credit. It was a pilot model of the situation for most developing countries in the recession of the early 1980s.

To preempt any Peruvian moves to reschedule the country's debt, or worse, to declare a unilateral moratorium, Citibank (again) organized a six-bank steering committee to negotiate new credits for the Andean country. The committee arranged a loan of $386 million, more than half of it from American banks, on the condition that Peru pursue an IMF-style policy of devaluation and deflation. The banks played a new part in this game of "house." They took the role of the Fund, and arranged to pay the credit out in two installments. The second installment was to be disbursed only after a review of economic measures satisfied the banks that Peru was keeping to its side of the bargain.

So far, so good. The first embarrassment came with Peru's announcement that it was buying $250 million worth of fighter-bombers from the Soviet Union. Weapons are a luxury good. Imported jet fighters are about as useful to an economy as French perfume and Scotch whisky. A big-ticket arms purchase, from the Russians, no less, hardly seemed in keeping with economic austerity, draconian import cuts, and reduced government spending.

The banks showed all the backbone of a paper tiger. Despite the arms purchase and despite the failure of Peru to meet any of the economic targets agreed upon, the banks pusillanimously handed over the second installment of the loan on schedule. So much for playing house.

As Peru's economy continued to deteriorate, though, the banks were deaf to any further requests for money. They pointed Peru in the direction of the IMF. Lima became like a "financial war zone." Two finance ministers and one central bank president resigned in the first eight months of 1977. There were riots and strikes. Twice an IMF team made the trip to Lima, only to leave again empty-handed. The third time Peru suggested a rendezvous, the normally mild-mannered managing director, Johannes Witteveen, snapped that the Peruvians could come see the IMF in Washington. They did, and got their IMF money in November 1977. The standby was suspended in March 1978 and renewed in September. By that time Peru was fully ripe for rescheduling. The Paris Club rescheduled $586 million of official debt and the banks, $800 million. Peru did finally cut government spending, and increased copper production, resumed fish meal exports after the return of its mysterious disappearing anchovies, and brought a pipeline on stream to earn more foreign exchange by exporting oil. By 1979 Peru had turned around its payments position and was talking about prepaying some of its rescheduled debts.

Peru did prepay some credits in April 1981, after the civilian government of President Fernando Belaúnde Terry took power. Belaúnde's premier and finance minister was an engaging *bon vivant,* Manuel Ulloa Elias, an old Wall Street hand. Ulloa was happy to win the confidence of his old New York cronies by retiring some rescheduled debts ahead of time. But Peru had accumulated the extra money because of buoyant mineral prices. When prices declined again in the recession, so did Peru's fortunes.

If the bankers had learned something from their previous experience with Peru, so had Peru. Before the going got really tough, Ulloa traded on his standing with New York to cadge $350 million out of a fifty-one-bank syndicate. In June 1982 Peru practiced what the Fund often preached. It went to the IMF of its own accord, before worried creditors pushed it. The country obtained a three-year $960-million standby credit. By its early action, Peru beat the rush. When the Mexican crisis dried up credit for all Latin-American countries, Peru was affected too. But it had all the levers in place that other countries had to install. It was a simple enough matter for the IMF to make clear that further disbursements in Peru's standby credit depended on the banks' giving Peru the $800 million or so that it was asking for 1983.

Meanwhile Ulloa resigned, as he had planned. A Latin-American finance minister often turns out to be the fall guy. Ulloa wanted to succeed Belaúnde in the 1985 presidential elections and so was eager to distance himself from the distasteful tasks of cutting food subsidies, restricting imports, and raising taxes. But Northern bankers had no reasons to worry. Ulloa's replacement as finance minister was one of their own. Carlos Rodriguez Pastor, who stepped right into the post, had made a career for himself at Wells Fargo, the San Francisco bank descended from the stagecoach line.

Peru's generals had not learned anything, though. Living in constant fear of an invasion from Chile, the Peruvian armed forces again provided a counterpoint for the weighty financial negotiations by announcing they would go ahead with a planned purchase of twenty-four Mirage jet fighters from France for $685 million. The fact that France was financing most of the purchase with a subsidized credit did little to console the bankers, who found Peru's debt, in the meantime swollen to $11.5 billion, already big enough. Still, Peru seemed a bit like old home week. Bankers looked back to the nerve-racking days of Peru's earlier problems with something approaching nostalgia. Life was relatively simple then, had one only known.

4

Turkey marked a watershed in sovereign loans because it called for an unprecedented cooperative effort by the banks. About 220 banks fell victim in 1978 to Prime Minister Suleyman Demirel's ill-conceived scheme to lure foreign exchange into Turkey through the convertible Turkish lira deposit. The idea was simple. Depositors, generally foreign banks, put dollars or marks or Swiss francs on deposit with a Turkish bank. This bank sold the foreign exchange to the central bank for lire, which it then lent to domestic customers. Domestic banks got liquidity and Turkey got foreign exchange. To make the deposits palatable, the Turkish banks offered interest at 1¾ points above going Euromarket rates and guaranteed the exchange rate. If that was not enough, the banks sweetened the deal with a front-end fee—that is, a one-time bonus payment to the depositor just for making the deposit.

The disadvantage became quickly apparent. The deposits had a maturity of twelve to eighteen months. The depositor could withdraw the funds or roll them over. But because the deposits in effect functioned as loans, the same rule applied to them as to loans. Unless the funds were invested in a project that earned the foreign exchange to pay them off, there was little assurance that the currency would be there when the loans fell due. The problem was that any major industrial project would take several years to start earning money, certainly more than eighteen months.

The system functioned well enough, not surprisingly, for a couple of years. But early in 1977, foreign banks noticed that foreign exchange was not readily available from the Turkish central bank. It began overdrawing its foreign accounts. Finally foreign exchange almost evaporated, and Demirel confessed at one point, "Turkey cannot spare seventy cents." Demirel was turned out of office at the end of the year when eleven parliamentary deputies defected from his coalition, and Bülent Ecevit became prime minister. Demirel later maintained that his rival had undermined the deposit scheme by alarming foreign bankers with statements that Turkey was bankrupt.

When bankers looked hard at the country's balance sheet, though, it seemed that Ecevit was right. Foreign exchange reserves had dwindled from $2.1 billion at the end of 1974 to $327 million in 1977. Foreign debts topped $10 billion. Half of that was due by the end of 1977, including $2.1 billion in the convertible lira deposits. One banker commented that the Turkish situation made Zaire look like peanuts. Peanuts are relative; Poland and Mexico later made Turkey look like peanuts.

Just establishing the amount of debt proved to be difficult. In the midst of its rescheduling efforts, Turkey signed on the troika of investment bank advisers originally engaged by Indonesia in 1975 to sort out the tangled debt of its national oil company, Pertamina. The financiers from Lazard Frères in Paris, S.G. Warburg in London, and Lehman Brothers Kuhn Loeb in New York generally find their first task is to make an accurate account of how much debt is owed. Incredible as it sounds, many sovereign borrowers do not have an overview of their total debt. In the case of Turkey, Ankara officials assured the impatient troika team that the government would provide them with a detailed list. After two more weeks' waiting, the experts asked if they could at least talk to the official responsible for compiling the list. They were led down a winding, badly lit corridor in the Finance Ministry to a tiny room hardly twenty feet square. Half the room was filled with stacks of paper. These were the eighth carbon copy of loan agreements. A hunched-over gentleman with thick glasses was painstakingly trying to decipher the scarcely legible numbers.

Tabulation of existing debt is the inescapable starting point of rescheduling it. In Costa Rica, for example, government officials were literally opening up drawers and discovering new loan agreements. The final reckoning almost by definition came out higher than any estimates. The lack of any certainty on the numbers continually unsettled bankers in the series of later reschedulings.

Because of the large number of banks involved in Turkey—220 foreign banks had deposits with twenty-three Turkish banks—the foreign banks formed a steering committee of seven to get things organized. Morgan Guaranty, Citibank, and Deutsche Bank led the way, along with Dresdner Bank, Chase Manhattan, Barclays, and Union Bank of Switzerland. These banks went on to play a dominant role in the major reschedulings of 1982–83. The group rejected the title "steering committee" but they functioned as one in leading the negotiations and coordinating the eventual restructuring. After months of difficult talks, the banks restructured the $2.1 billion in deposits plus $400 million in direct central bank loans. About forty of them joined in a new syndicated credit of $500 million for Turkey.

The marathon workout overwhelmed the banking world at the

time. The Turkish case, despite its eccentricities, was characteristic of later crises. A rapid, uncontrolled buildup of short-term debt in a last-ditch effort to make the great industrial leap forward characterized later debt crises as well. No one else bothered with the charade of convertible deposits, but as in the Turkish case, lenders remained ignorant of the accumulation of short-term debt. Also illustrative in Turkey was how the first whisper of trouble precipitated the crisis. Had Turkey been alert enough, it might have gotten a medium-term loan to pay off enough deposits to keep the others rolling over. Once the fragile confidence of the market was lost, though, Ankara had no alternative but to negotiate with the banks.

As with Zaire, the bankers made their agreement contingent on the economic stabilization program of the IMF, enforced by the Fund's three-tranche loan discipline. (The IMF makes loans in three installments; payment of the last two depends on the country's meeting certain economic targets.) Banks went Turkey one better by actually providing new money. The need of countries involved in rescheduling to obtain new money became a controversial part of the huge rescue packages for Mexico, Brazil, and Argentina.

With Zaire, Peru, and Turkey behind them, bankers were getting an intimation that international banking was not all fun and profit. *Institutional Investor,* which faithfully reflects the mood of the community it serves, ran a cover in June 1981 with the blurb, "Is international banking really such a good idea?" Generations of hard knocks had long since tempered corporate and personal loans. Criteria were fixed; loan applications came in triplicate. The learning curve on sovereign lending had just started to rise.

Bankers are not reflective people by nature. Subtle lessons are lost on them. Only the bottom line speaks. As Wriston said, what's so exciting about $40 million, especially when the money has not been lost for sure.

References to Turkey's strategic importance are so frequent that the claim seems banal. But it's true. Bridging Europe and Asia, bordering on Greece, Bulgaria, the Soviet Union, Iran, Iraq, and Syria, controlling the entry to the Black Sea and Russia's warm-water ports, Turkey is in a strategic situation that can hardly be exaggerated. The country's penchant for problems has earned it the familiar sobriquet "the sick man of Europe." Europe takes care of its own. As long ago as the early 1960s the West Europeans and their allies, through the Organization for Economic Cooperation and Development, formed a special aid consortium to sort out Turkey's external finances. This consortium was reconstituted in 1979. It provided nearly $1 billion in government aid to Turkey, and rescheduled the official debt. Shortly thereafter, the IMF came through with its SDR 250 million loan and stabilization program, which entailed a 44-percent devaluation of the Turkish lira. (SDR, or Special Drawing Rights, refers to the notional currency devised by the IMF for its accounts. It usually is worth slightly more than one U.S. dollar.)

Turkey hiccuped its way along. On September 12, 1980, as the number of political killings approached the level of civil war, the military removed Demirel from office. The generals proceeded to restore political and economic order. Financial czar Turgut Özal rescheduled commercial bank debt again in January 1981. Turkey managed to reduce inflation, 130 percent in March 1980, to 30 percent by May 1982. During 1982 the country syndicated some $300 million of loans in international markets in its first timid steps on the way back to creditworthiness. Turkey so successfully mastered its foreign exchange problem that by 1983 Finance Minister Adnan Basar Kafaoglu was complaining of a surfeit of foreign currency and a shortage of Turkish lire.

THE UMBRELLA
MYTH
CHAPTER FOUR

1

Commercial bankers had a lot to learn in developing countries, but their ignorance regarding the Communist bloc was even greater.

The East European line officer at one of the Big Four clearing banks in London, a garrulous fellow, was explaining the Breakfast Index to Quality of Life. After years of visiting East European capitals he had decided that there was a direct correlation between the quality of breakfast served up at the hard-currency hotel and the overall quality of life in the country. "The Hotel Metropole in East Berlin served the best breakfast," he concluded. "You can't even get a breakfast that good in London." He was well aware that the average East German citizen was not going to get bacon and eggs and orange juice and aromatic coffee every morning. But he reasoned that a country which can organize such a breakfast for hard-currency visitors can organize a reasonable quality of life for the everyday citizen too.

It seems a superficial way to make judgments about a country's economy, but Western bankers often felt they had little more to go on. Economic statistics required from even poverty-stricken developing countries simply were not forthcoming in Eastern Europe. As *The Wall Street Journal* acidly observed following Poland's debt crisis: "The banks asked Poland precious little about its economic health or how it expected to pay all the money back. Frugal middle-class Americans would have had to give more information to their friendly neighborhood banker to get a car loan than Poland gave to develop a country."

Such information as was given often was fiction. Interpreting Eastern bloc data was an arcane art in itself. Veteran Eastern Europe watchers Wharton Econometric Forecasting Associates observed scornfully once that even so reliable a group as the Economist Intelligence Unit drew completely distorted conclusions about Romania's trade balance by confusing the exchange rates in Romania's two-tier currency system. This comparison of apples to oranges led the EIU to report that Romania's trade deficit tripled from one year to the next.

For the banks, though, Eastern European lending was a willy-nilly headlong rush into a new market. In the slow-growth environment of the industrial countries after the first oil shock, the Eastern European countries represented for the banks vast new opportunities for lending, and for their industrial clients, new opportunities for selling. The thaw of détente broke the Cold War ice that had prevented an earlier move into the Eastern bloc.

From 1972 on, the annual hard-currency borrowing of the Comecon countries doubled. Their new loans reached a peak of $14 billion in 1975. The rate of new borrowing slackened off after that. North Korea's default in 1975 braked lending to Communist countries. The Soviet invasion of Afghanistan in 1979 and the sharp political reaction further dampened Eastern bloc loans, particularly from American banks. From 1979 to 1980, Comecon's portion of Euromarket borrowing was cut in half, falling to 3 percent of new loans in 1980 from 6 percent the previous year.

Buyers and sellers, lenders and borrowers were all so anxious to please in the early years that business was negotiated on eggshells. "Who would have asked Gomulka critical questions about a steel plant?" pleads a West German banker. He was referring to the intimidating Polish leader of the 1960s. It was Gomulka's successor, Edward Gierek, who actively encouraged Western banks and companies to help Poland make a dash for growth.

Poland's ambitious industrialization carried the seeds of its own

71

destruction, though. This was clear enough to hard-nosed economists not carried away by the hurly-burly of business. Richard Portes, an American and onetime Rhodes scholar who divides his time teaching between London and Paris, wrote in *Foreign Affairs* as early as July 1977: "Only a very large increase in the price of copper would offer any real hope that Poland might be able to meet its hard-currency debt repayment schedule at the end of the decade." He was right on target, although Soviet support postponed the actual default. Portes and another Poland expert, Paul Marer of Indiana University, spread their warnings among businessmen and bankers at special seminars organized by the U.S. Department of Commerce, but their predictions fell on deaf ears.

Poland was the worst case, but the problem plagued all Soviet satellites in Eastern Europe. They adopted the Soviet model of building up heavy industry rather than capitalizing on their own strengths. Often the technology they bought from the West was obsolete or unsuited to the Eastern European market. Poland overlooked a potential problem in remaining dependent on Western imports for much of the production in the turnkey factories bought from the West. This came back to haunt the country when it had no foreign exchange for those imports. The factories were idle, but the debt built up to buy them was still falling due.

Romania similarly miscalculated. It invested heavily in downstream petroleum operations because it had considerable oil reserves. By the time these operations came on stream, though, energy consumption had risen to the point that Romania had to import oil. The extra cost of world market prices had not been factored into the refineries and manufacturing facilities. They did not pay.

Yugoslavia's problem was different. The mistakes did not result from miscalculations by a central planning bureaucracy, but from the duplication and lack of coordination in a decentralized political and economic system. Each autonomous republic pursued its own policy of industrialization, sometimes building the same facilities. This duplication wasted expensive capital and reduced the value of the investments.

All of the Eastern bloc countries forgot about agriculture. Farming does not take care of itself, even when it is left in private hands.

Poland and Romania, both of which used to export food, woke up only with the debt shock and started to do something about increasing agricultural production.

Western credit magnified the planners' miscalculations. The economist credited with developing Hungary's mixed economy, Rezso Nyers, does not mince words: "The strategy of relying on Western credits without economic reform failed. Experience has shown that credits are not well used in a centralized economy because there is no efficient mechanism for allocating resources."

2

Poland marked a quantum leap in the debt crisis. The amount of debt at stake was much bigger at $24 billion than the amounts at risk in Peru, Zaire, or Turkey. The familiar supports were gone. No alliances, no hegemony, no International Monetary Fund were there to stand behind the bankers.

Poland punctured some favorite myths. Western businessmen had been known to say that they liked doing business with Eastern Europe because "they don't have a problem with strikes." Solidarity's strikes in the summer of 1980 not only created an economic crisis but challenged a whole social system. Poland's precarious sovereignty, threatened for months by a potential Soviet invasion, made debt negotiations especially delicate.

The Polish crisis buried the longstanding belief in a Soviet umbrella. Westerners implicitly believed that Moscow would not allow one of its satellites to damage the bloc's creditworthiness by defaulting or even delaying payments. Bankers believed that ultimately a loan to Poland or Romania or East Germany or Czechoslovakia was backed by the considerable resources of the Soviet Union. Once the Polish crisis broke, it was apparent to everyone that the short-term financial resources even of the Soviet Union were nowhere near equal to coping with the swollen payments requirements of Poland alone, let alone the entire bloc. In the past, the Soviet Union and its charges had been punctilious in all financial dealings with the West. Financial correctness was part of the credibility Moscow wanted to have vis-à-vis the West. What surprised Western bankers was the Kremlin's careful calculation that the banks' need for credibility would require action sooner than Moscow's.

The banks' exposure to Poland had reached a critical mass. Their main worry in Zaire and Peru was the setting of a bad precedent. As Wriston said, the numbers were not very exciting. The Polish numbers, though, quickened the pulse of most banks, especially those in Europe. In the case of Poland, the banks were for the first time clearly prisoners of their own commitment. Yves Laulan, an economist for the big French bank Société Générale and a member of the bank panel monitoring Poland's economic progress, observes that "the usage of the financial weapon is practically as dangerous for the lender of funds as for the borrower. Beyond a certain degree of indebtedness, the lender becomes the borrower's prisoner."

The boom was lowered on March 27, 1981, when Poland's chief borrowing officer, Jan Woloszyn, met with seventy representatives of the more than five hundred banks that had lent money to Poland. In the elegant ambiance of Plaisterers' Hall in London, the Polish banker, a veteran of fifty years in a career that started in the prewar Bank Polski, told the banks what they had feared: Poland was broke. The country had no foreign exchange to pay the interest or principal on either its official or commercial debt. That London meeting on a dreary March day marked a watershed for postwar banking. The tension and confusion of the following months was the acknowledgment that Eurobanking had lost its innocence.

The March meeting came on the heels of a smaller powwow in Frankfurt, when Woloszyn and other officials from Bank Handlowy z Warszawie, the state bank which handles foreign exchange for Poland, made a last-ditch effort to enlist support for a $1-billion jumbo loan. The bankers, who had been applying the brakes on Polish credit for nearly two years, balked. In fact, sensing the gravity of the situation, they went home from the Frankfurt meeting in January and began withdrawing short-term lines of credit to Warsaw. This hastened Woloszyn's hour of reckoning two months later in London.

During the whole preceding year Woloszyn had been losing ground with the bankers. His attempt to raise $500 million in a

Eurodollar syndication met with so much resistance that Poland finally had to settle for just $325 million, and a sizable portion of that came from the Comecon banks operating in the West. West German banks coughed up DM 1.2 billion in response to a Polish request for DM 1.5 billion. Helmut Schmidt's government in Bonn brought unprecedented pressure on the banks to make the loan. Even then, Bonn only guaranteed a third of the credit.

Striking out with the banks, Poland went to Western governments, asking $3 billion from the United States and another $5 billion from the others. The governments dithered but did come up with some food credits to ease the strain of the economic difficulties: $670 million of U.S. grain sales were financed with guarantees from the Commodity Credit Corporation, and the European Community sold $320 million worth of food at a discount, with finance from individual exporting countries. For its part, the Soviet Union did extend a small umbrella. Wharton reported foreign trade subsidies up to $3.2 billion in 1980, compared with $1.5 billion in 1979. Moscow's hard-currency loans totaled an estimated $1.5 billion in the twelve months to June 1981. By the end of 1979, Poland's debt service was already eating up more than 90 percent of its export revenues.

Professor Portes was by now calling attention to the obvious in a report published a month before Woloszyn met with the London bankers. "The short-run financial position in convertible currencies is desperate," he wrote.

The pseudo-project loan gambit had been played out as well. Banks made loans ostensibly for a particular project, although the money actually was used by the government as general revenue. When Chase Manhattan tried to segregate $525 million in loans it had made in 1975 and 1978 for a copper project from the rescheduling process, the other banks were quick to complain. Tagging the loan for a natural resources project, the other banks felt, was more to satisfy bank supervisors in New York than to produce copper in Poland. "There was only the shadow of a project loan left," was one comment. In 1979 a consortium of West German banks made a loan of DM 850 million to finance exploration of vanadium in Poland. No vanadium was found, but somehow the DM 850 million got spent.

The months following that March 1981 session brought a hectic series of meetings as commercial banks mounted their biggest rescheduling effort ever. Chase Manhattan coordinated the formation of a twenty-bank steering committee, which attempted to render its function blander with the title "multinational task force." Already at this initial stage there was friction as national groupings of banks sorted out pecking orders. The source of greatest tension soon emerged. The American banks, which had never been very strong in Poland or the rest of Eastern Europe and had slowed down sooner, wanted to take a hard line with Warsaw. No rescheduling, no new money, and no concessions until the Poles committed themselves to full economic disclosure and the Western monitoring that implied. The Europeans, especially the West Germans, had much more at stake both in terms of money committed and future business relationships. They pushed for conciliation.

The soft-guy approach prevailed at a meeting of the banks in mid-April in London. A subcommittee started work on rescheduling proposals, and a panel of bank economists was formed to consult with Polish officials on data and monitoring procedures. That same month, fifteen Western governments with credits or credit guarantees to Poland agreed in Paris to reschedule the approximately $2.6 billion in official credits falling due between May and December 1981. The next scene was at Dresdner Bank in Frankfurt. West Germany's second-largest bank had been the agent for most Polish syndications in that country and eventually had the ambivalent honor of coordinating the entire Polish rescheduling. On May 20 the full task force of banks looked at a draft proposal for rescheduling Poland's debt.

Although they could not agree at the time, the draft contained the main conditions that eventually won approval. The banks proposed to reschedule 95 percent of the $2.4 billion of debt due in the last nine months of 1981 over seven and a half years with a grace period of four years. Interest was to be set a 1¾ points above Libor, a spread double that of most of Poland's borrowings, but the borrower would not have to repay principal during the grace period.

The banks continued to argue about "conditionality." Despite their unfavorable experience in enforcing policies with sovereign borrowers like Peru and Zaire, the bankers felt obliged to attempt an IMF-style monitoring of their wayward client. A brash senior vice president of Bankers Trust, Frederick Schwartz, gained a brief notoriety when he put the hard-line case in harshest terms at a June meeting of the American bank caucus in New York. He was voted in as one of the U.S. representatives (the other, predictably, was from Citibank). Two weeks later, Schwartz electrified his European colleagues at a meeting in Paris with his announcement on behalf of the American banks that "we're not going to be pushed around."

Intensive lobbying over the next month avoided a complete break. At a full task force meeting in July in Zurich, the bankers found their way to an agreement. They set a deadline of December 10 for Warsaw to bring interest payments up to date and to sign the rescheduling agreement. Having finished their own haggling, the bankers then had to take on the Poles, who naturally sought some amelioration of the terms. The meetings moved eastward, with the grand finale coming in Vienna at the end of September. The participants shuttled between the *fin-de-siècle* offices of Creditanstalt-Bankverein, the big Austrian bank whose collapse in 1931 was a catalyst for the banking crisis of the Great Depression, and a nearby hotel. The banks tried to browbeat Woloszyn and his delegation into agreement. Frustrated by the continuing deadlock, the bankers dispatched a seven-member delegation on a chartered plane to Warsaw to meet with Finance Minister Marian Krzak and wring consent from him. "We said that if he didn't sign the memorandum that afternoon the banks would declare a default. There would be no more loans to Poland for twenty-five years. The consequences for the whole of East-West trade would be incalculable," one banker related. Krzak signed.

But Poland did not meet the December 10 deadline. The game of chicken between Warsaw, with Moscow in the wings, and the Western bankers went on. The final sticking point was $500 million still due to cover the 5 percent of the debt not rescheduled and the interest for 1981. The Poles still did not have any money and the bankers were in no mood to lend it to them. They felt that Moscow should be able to scrounge up that much hard currency to bail out Poland. A French effort to organize a $500-million loan from Western central banks through the Bank for International Settlements foundered on opposition from Bonn.

Poland finally signed its rescheduling accord with the banks on April 6, 1982, more than a year after Poland threw in the towel. After paying dribs and drabs on its bill, Warsaw paid over $290 million in March to clear the way for the agreement. European banks, which had to get their 1981 balance sheets approved, sighed in relief. Any further delay might have necessitated expensive write-offs.

The bankers then rolled up their sleeves to start work on rescheduling Poland's 1982 debt. Commercial bankers were not ready to give up what was fondly known as the short-leash approach. Appearances carry a lot of weight in the legalistic environment of Western finance. Bankers did not want to give the appearance that rescheduling was routine. Each exercise had to be seen as critical. The crisis of 1981 was not the crisis of 1982. It could well be, and was in fact, that one year's crisis leads to the next, but this could not be conceded ahead of time. In spite of the horrendous drain on management resources in each rescheduling, the banks wanted to take each year on its own merits.

Western governments, which had quickly rescheduled official Polish debt in 1981, sat out 1982. The NATO allies, led by the United States, decided in January 1982 that no further consultations on Polish debt would take place until martial law imposed at the end of 1981 was lifted, political prisoners were released, and the social dialogue initiated by Solidarity was resumed. Poland, for its part, maintained its willingness to talk about the debt. Meanwhile it suspended all payments of principal and interest on the debt. Every bankrupt country should hope for such punishment. Poland had neither to service nor to reschedule its official debt, estimated at $14 billion altogether. The Western allies consigned Polish debt to political limbo. Far from bringing pressure on the Polish regime, this arrangement relieved it of a good deal of financial strain. By early 1983, the European Community's ministerial council was looking the anomaly in the face and suggesting that Western countries should resume debt talks with Poland. Douglas Hurd, minister of state in Britain's Foreign Office, admitted that the situation was "slightly absurd."

The bankers could not allow themselves the luxury of punishing Poland in this way. When all is said and done, banks have to account more stringently for their depositors' funds than governments do for taxpayers' funds. Rescheduling was easier the second time around. Poland held out for a couple of additional concessions. Although the bankers still refused to reschedule interest, for appearances' sake, they found a formula that made Poland's interest payments all but a fiction. They agreed to "recycle" half of the $1.1 billion interest due in 1982 back to Poland in the form of a three-year revolving trade credit. Poland desperately needed import finance to get production going again. The bankers did not want to forego interest repayments, but also did not want to lend Poland fresh money. So Poland gave them the money long enough to book it as an interest payment and then the banks gave half of it right back. Moreover, the interest for 1982 was paid in three installments, in November and December of 1982, and in March 1983 (again, before the banks' books had to be balanced).

The neatest trick, though, was the postponement of the principal that was not repaid. Again for appearances, the banks refused to reschedule 100 percent of principal. They insisted that Poland retire at least 5 percent of the principal due in 1982. But they graciously postponed even that 5 percent until October and December of 1983!

The Poles bargained hard because their backs were up against the wall. The lack of foreign exchange to pay for imports had made a deep dent in living standards. Lack of imports created a bottleneck in production and exports. Finance Minister Krzak complained once before foreign journalists that Poland had plenty of hams to export but no cans to pack them in. Imports dropped 21 percent in 1981 and slid a precipitous 54 percent in the first half of 1982. The West German newsmagazine *Der Spiegel* described in grim detail what this meant for Poles. Shoe stores ran out of merchandise because no leather could be imported. A washing-machine factory was shut down because Poland could not import stainless steel. New washing machines became so rare that they were rationed out to large enterprises and raffled off to employees. A Gdansk shipyard with 14,000 workers, for example, got thirty-two washing machines to raffle off, along with two sewing machines and twenty-seven television sets. Factories continued to produce farm equipment like haulers and threshers, but the number taken out of service for lack of spare parts available only as imports far exceeded new production. Even primitive utensils like sickles and pitchforks could not be produced for lack of raw material imports. One clever Warsaw woman arrived in a farming village with a caseful of pitchforks, which she traded for sugar. She returned to the capital and made a killing selling sugar at black market prices. Corruption, thievery, and black market activity thrived in the shortage economy even more than usual in the Eastern bloc. Stealing on the job became almost obligatory: "If you don't swipe something, you hurt your family."

Small wonder that Polish officials began to make public statements that debt rescheduling could no longer come at the expense of declining standard of living. Bankers were annoyed to see that the 1983 budget passed by the Polish parliament, the Sejm, called for a net increase of $3 billion in hard-currency debt. Polish planners expected by some miracle to raise $800 million in new loans during 1983, and, most galling to the bankers, not to pay any of the estimated $2 billion in interest due for the year. More worrying, though, were suggestions in semiofficial publications that the only way out of Poland's debt impasse was a fifteen-to-twenty-year moratorium.

It was quickly becoming clear to all parties involved in the debt talks that it would take more than four years' grace for Poland to get back to where it could manage its debt. Even though Poland produced a trade surplus of $500 million in 1982 and aimed for $700 million in 1983, there was no way in the foreseeable future that it could earn the foreign exchange to pay off the rescheduled debt when 1985 and 1986 rolled around. European banks began to make large loan-loss provisions for the whole or partial debt forgiveness that more and more seemed inevitable in Poland's case.

The retirement of Jan Woloszyn in early 1983 did not encourage Western bankers. Though Woloszyn, who was seventy when he did step down as first vice president of Bank Handlowy, had been talking about retirement for years, the timing was not propitious. The president of the Warsaw bank, Stanislaw Kobak, who had been in the job only eight months, also resigned, apparently because Warsaw wanted to push a harder line in debt negotiations. His replacement was Kazimierz Glazewski, who at least was familiar with Western bankers after several years in Vienna at Centrobank, a joint venture between Bank Handlowy and several Western banks.

The moral ambivalence of banking could hardly have been more evident than in the Polish crisis. Public opinion muted bankers' resentment of the disruption resulting from Solidarity's bid for democratic freedoms in Poland, but there was resentment nonetheless. Generally, if they expressed it at all, the bankers couched their displeasure in disapproval of "excesses." Strikes and expressions of liberty were all well and good, but not in excess. "It's nice to have a year off," snarled one European banker, "but now they have to go back to work." A West German complained, "They don't want to work anymore. They seem to think that a Western living standard comes with democracy. We worked damned hard for that."

Many Poles undoubtedly felt that they had been working damned hard, too, and had precious little to show for it. A damning account of Soviet exploitation of the Polish economy published in *Commentary* underlines the basic injustice of the Polish economic system. The author, writing pseudonymously, recounts a Polish joke caricaturing the bitter reality: "Soviet scientists have developed a new animal by crossing a cow with a giraffe; it can graze in Poland while being milked in the Soviet Union." The Soviet Union had systematically creamed off the best of Polish production, including the Western technology and material purchased by Poland with Western credits. Only when the bills fell due, the Soviets suddenly found a use for Polish autonomy.

But bankers make a point of ignoring moral niceties. When General Wojciech Jaruzelski lowered the inevitable boom on the Polish summer, Citicorp vice chairman Thomas Theobald obliged with a sufficiently callous comment that was widely quoted: "Who knows which political system works? The only test we care about is: Can they pay their bills?" A bit more diplomatically, a Dresdner Bank executive said later, "One may well regret that business relations between the two ideologically divergent blocs are not shaped by economic considerations alone."

Once again, profit justifies the means. Felix Rohatyn, André Meyer's brilliant protégé at the New York investment bank Lazard

Frères, polished his reputation as a maverick with his unequivocal call for Western governments and banks to formally declare Poland in default. For Rohatyn, a card-carrying Democrat and no reactionary, the ideological lines were clearly drawn: "It is to the clear advantage of the West to put the burden of the Polish economy squarely on the Soviet Union. It is also to our advantage to emphasize the economic bankruptcy of Communism by declaring Poland a bankrupt," he wrote in the New York *Times*. He continued: "In our constant competitive struggle with the Soviet Union, capital can be as potent a weapon as intercontinental missiles. Why should the West supply the Soviet Union with such a weapon?" In testimony before Congress, Rohatyn's reasoning was persuasive. Loans to Poland were already bad. Declaring them in default, he argued, would not make them any worse. "Accounting fictions should not dictate our foreign policy," Rohatyn concluded with a flourish before the lawmakers. His opinion carried a good deal of weight because he had masterminded the Municipal Assistance Corporation that rescued New York from its fiscal crisis in 1975 (see Chapter Seven).

Seen from New York or Washington, the situation was doubtlessly simpler than it appeared in central Europe. For Germany, a nation split by the ideological conflict, the answers were not so easy, either politically or economically. That lifestyle West Germans have worked so "damned hard" for rests on foreign trade, which accounts for more than half of the West German gross national product. West Germany is the biggest exporter of capital goods in the world and Poland, practically a neighbor, was one of the biggest markets for capital goods. Steel, machinery, turbines were big-ticket items that provided a lot of West Germans with jobs and Bonn with a lot of taxes, not to mention the profits that went to West German banks for financing this trade.

David Kern is a diminutive Romanian who tracks Eastern European economies for National Westminster Bank in London, among other things. He observes that the United States kept missing the point in criticizing the Europeans for their participation in the Soviet Union's huge Yamal gas pipeline. "It's not the gas the West Europeans need," Kern emphasizes, "it's the trade." Indeed, if the United States had been successful in dissuading its NATO allies from going through with the project, the loss of turbine orders for the pipeline might have been the straw that broke AEG-Telefunken's back (see Chapter Eight).

West Germany accounted for more than one fifth of all Western exports to the Comecon countries, while the United States' share was less than one tenth. West Germany took nearly the same proportion of Eastern bloc exports. The United States bought less than 5 percent of Comecon sales to the West.

Economic considerations alone make East-West trade a more complex matter for West Germany, Austria, Switzerland, and even France. In addition, as the Federal Republic of Germany moved out of political adolescence in the 1980s, the country felt the need to identify its own priorities in relationships with the Soviet bloc.

It was Willy Brandt's Ostpolitik that reconciled West Germany in 1970 to the postwar division of Europe and earned the West German chancellor a Nobel Prize for peace. It paved the way for expanded trade and credit, and for Richard Nixon's 1972 visit to Moscow and the proclamation of détente. In the decade 1971–81, East-West trade grew sevenfold, from an annual $6 billion to $40 billion. In the same period the hard-currency debt of the Warsaw Pact countries grew tenfold, to $87 billion by the end of 1981.

Economic and financial relations between the East and West are doomed to ambivalence. The debate will never be resolved. The ameliorists will continue to argue that commercial relations are mutually beneficial, ease political strains, and improve the chances for peace or even increased liberty in the East. Hard-liners question the motivation of businessmen and bankers, and maintain that Communism must be allowed to collapse from its internal contradictions. Trade and credit seem destined to fluctuate according to who gets the upper hand in the debate.

3

The months of negotiation with Poland had a nightmarish quality for the banks. They were so preoccupied with the prospect of a major sovereign default and the dent in their earnings that they thought very little about the wider issues at stake. Rather, their reaction was at the gut level. Not only did they cut off all credit to Poland, but they began to scale down their engagements in other Eastern bloc countries. This caught Romania, for one, off balance. While bankers wrangled with Polish officials in Vienna in late September, Romanian trade minister Stefan Niza tried to explain to British exporters in London why Romania had not paid them for nine months. By late fall rumors were rife that Romania was missing loan installments and interest payments. Remaining credit lines were withdrawn, and Romania plunged into practical default.

Ceausescu's minions were not as gentlemanly as the Poles were about being broke. There was no guildhall meeting for bankers in London. The Romanians adamantly refused to admit there was a problem. Telex queries from worried bankers were ignored. Telephone conversations were cut off in midsentence. The none-too-savory reputation enjoyed by the Romanians in the market was reinforced. One cultured Viennese banker, enunciating gracefully in Oxford English, characterized the prolonged negotiations typical of Romanian deals this way: "It's not that they were such tough bargainers. They *were* terribly fatiguing, unpleasant . . . boring."

With $10 billion in hard-currency debt, Romania was a smaller problem than Poland, but the last thing bankers were ready for was a general default on Eastern bloc debt. The Comecon countries, including the Soviet Union and the consortium banks the bloc operated, had more than $80 billion due to the West. Add the nearly $20 billion owed by Yugoslavia, which was walking a precipice of its own, and the West was facing a whopping $100 billion of debt in Eastern Europe.

No time now to ask searching questions about Eastern bloc debt. Having committed massive sums of depositors' money on assumptions that turned out to be fragile and illusory, the banks scrambled desperately to avoid a debt meltdown of catastrophic proportions.

Romania finally sought rescheduling in March 1982. By that time the bankers had grown to accept the inevitability of rearranging Romania's debt. Once past the initial trauma, the bankers rose to the challenge; they had no choice. But, almost automatically, they redlined all of Eastern Europe.

The Romanian case typified a crisis that came to be routine in 1982. Bucharest's sharp run-up in short-term debt, estimated to

84

have been 40 to 50 percent of overall debt by the time rescheduling was asked for, foreshadowed similar moves by Mexico and other Latin-American borrowers. Short-term debt is more invisible than other kinds of bank debt because statistics cannot begin to keep up with three-month money, even if the information is reported.

When the International Monetary Fund agreed in June 1981 to give Romania a $1.4-billion credit over three years, the help backfired. Instead of seeing the accord as a mark of confidence, bankers concluded that Romania's situation was more serious than they realized if Bucharest had to borrow from the IMF. This two-edged sword of IMF aid is one of the main reasons countries are so coquettish about going to the IMF. Part of the reluctance is plain old pride: economic managers feel they have failed if a country has to submit to IMF discipline. But another main reason is the psychological impact IMF treatment has on the market. As with devaluations, recourse to the IMF becomes more likely the more often a government denies the intention.

Romania also innovated in the nascent art of rescheduling. When the country declared in March that it was unilaterally suspending all debt payments so that no creditor would be favored while rescheduling talks were going on, Romania introduced a concept that several Latin-American finance ministers found useful a few months later.

By summer 1982, things started falling in place. Romania persuaded the International Monetary Fund to restore its credit line, which had been suspended in November when the country stopped paying on its debt. Romania promised both the Fund and the banks to deliver more information on the economy, leading to an accord in principle with the banks for rescheduling about $2 billion. In July, Romania won agreement from fifteen Western countries to reschedule over six and a half years 80 percent of $480 million in official debt due in 1982. These terms were proposed to the banks as well. They accepted them and signed an agreement on December 7, 1982. In the meantime Romania fulfilled its pledge on the figures. The Wharton economists gave the statistics a seal of approval. The Western experts pronounced Romania's credit now better than Bulgaria's or East Germany's, although still lagging behind the rest of Comecon.

Ceausescu demonstrated what an iron fist can do. The trade account registered a $3-billion swing between 1981 and 1982, from a deficit of $1.5 billion to a surplus in that amount. This formidable accomplishment resulted partly from a rigorous counter-trade law that forced foreign trade partners to accept part of their payment, sometimes even all, in goods rather than currency. But the success was partly due as well to draconian restrictions, especially on food. (Ceausescu said that Romanians eat too much anyway.)

Staples like flour, cooking oil, and bread were rationed. So were milk and meat, but they usually were not available. There was a return to the queue mentality: Whenever you see a line, go stand in it, because they must be selling something good. Lines blocks long, like those that became commonplace in Poland, also came to Romania.

Such hardships remained local news. Ceausescu caused international waves with his announcement early in 1983 that emigrating Romanians would have to pay the state back for their education—in hard currency. The uproar that followed in the West did some injustice to a genuine problem experienced not only by Romania. Most Western press reports neglected to mention that education is practically free in most Eastern bloc countries. Doctors and professors are precisely the people most likely to leave the country. They live well in Romania, but they would live better abroad. The brain drain has long been a problem for developing countries. It was requiring the payment in hard currency that made the Romanian measure seem like a ransom, especially since there is no legal way for Romanians to acquire hard currency while living in the country. The amounts demanded, running to tens of thousands of dollars for professionals, also seemed very high. The United States said it would withdraw "most favored nation" trading status from Romania, which means Romanian exports to the States would be subject to higher tariffs. West Germany, concerned about emigration rights of the German-speaking population in Romania, refused to reschedule its bilateral debt with Romania. It was a classic vicious circle caused by debt. Romania's need for hard currency prompted the measure. The political retaliation impaired Romania's exports, making it more difficult to earn hard currency to pay off the debts. In the end, Ceausescu backed down. The heavy deposit was lifted, the United States renewed Romania's trade status, and Bonn resumed talks on the debt.

Romania had already taken the unilateral step of informing its Western creditors that it would also reschedule its 1983 debt. Earlier, the government had said that it would resume normal debt service by 1983, but creditors were hardly surprised by the new Romanian maneuver. They actually welcomed the forthrightness. By February the commercial banks had agreed to reschedule 70 percent, or $600 million, of Romania's medium-term debt, on the same terms as the 1981–82 rescheduling. By that time Western bankers, who had graver issues confronting them, felt that Romania was out of the woods as far as finances go. Western governments rescheduled 75 percent of slightly more than $200 million.

But a lower standard of living and the emigration restrictions reminded Romanians that Ceausescu, whose propagandists accord him titles like "leader of leaders" and "the premier thinker of the world," had made some miscalculations. Overindustrialization, particularly in the petroleum industry, at the expense of agriculture, had put the country on a wild-goose chase, financed by Western debt.

4

Once they realized there really was no Soviet umbrella, bankers took a new, hard look at other Eastern European debtors. Hungary's $8 billion gave it the highest per capita debt in the bloc. Hungary had long been a favorite among Western bankers. Its much touted shift to a partially market economy, with private business and property, made it the most liberal of Communist countries. More to the point for bankers doing business with Budapest, the Hungarian finance officials were top-notch professionals. Chief among them was Janos Fekete, the ebullient deputy president of the central bank. His competence, wit, and Western attitudes made him everyone's favorite Eastern European banker.

A Communist and a nationalist, Fekete was also a convinced central banker. He had been at the Hungarian National Bank since 1953 and was deeply committed to Hungary's spotless payments record. The country had no unsettled debt claims, despite the disruptions this century has brought. During the 1956 uprising in Hungary, Fekete made his way at considerable risk to Vienna. There he conducted the national bank's business from the offices of a subsidiary, so that Hungary did not miss an international payment even as the battle raged in Budapest.

Master salesman that he was, Fekete had his work cut out for him in the wake of Polish and Romanian troubles. In the first quarter of 1982, the Hungarian National Bank lost $1.1 billion in deposits. The hardest blow may have been the Soviet Union's withdrawal of its hard-currency deposits in Hungary. Among the ironies of the Polish crisis is that the Soviet deposits probably went to the Western banks as part of Poland's overdue payment on 1981 interest. It hardly seemed fair. Hungary had worked so hard for so many years to show that it was different from other Eastern European countries. Now that the crunch had come, Fekete & Co. were tarred with the same brush as Poland.

Sympathy is not always a tangible asset in international finance. But Fekete won some useful sympathy from Fritz Leutwiler, the independent-minded head of the Swiss National Bank. As president of the central bank, Leutwiler virtually determined Swiss economic policy. In Switzerland's cantonal system, that is tantamount to running the country, the important sector of national defense aside. The urbane and distinguished-looking central banker had also just acquired a new title—president of the Bank for International Settlements. The designation put Leutwiler at the head of the bank's board of governors, who are the European central bankers. Fekete lost no time getting to Zurich to ask Leutwiler for help. The Swiss, worried about the impact of a generalized credit boycott of Eastern Europe, persuaded his counterparts in the other central banks to fund a special bridging loan for Hungary. Budapest had already drawn down a standing $300-million line of credit at BIS. Leutwiler and his cronies raised another $210 million to tide Hungary over until it could get some money from the IMF. BIS "bridging loans" were later to become a standard feature in the rescue of bankrupt countries.

The previous November, Fekete, seeing which way the wind was blowing, had rushed to Washington with a membership application for the IMF. He seemed anxious to distinguish Hungary from other Comecon countries by joining the Western-dominated Fund. Although the Soviet Union and its satellites had flirted with membership in the Bretton Woods institutions after the war, since the early 1950s Moscow had effectively discouraged any affiliation. Yugoslavia and Romania had joined to demonstrate a measure of independence from Moscow. Poland, which had belonged briefly to the IMF after the war, followed on the heels of Hungary with its own IMF application just a week later.

Hungary pushed the BIS for an additional $300-million credit. The central bankers balked at first. With talk of further BIS money in the air, though, Fekete was able to enlist support among commercial banks for a $260-million loan that was finally signed in August 1982. Eventually the BIS, too, coughed up the new credit.

There were precedents for these bridging loans from the central bank of central banks. The Basel-based institution had loaned a whopping $5.3 billion to Britain during the sterling crisis of 1976. Smaller amounts went to Portugal after its revolution and to Turkey during the convertible lira deposit crisis. Reaching farther back, the BIS was simply reviving a tradition that accompanied its birth in 1930 (see Chapter Six).

Fekete soon demonstrated that his charm had not worn off. After the critical bank credit in August, the first to any Eastern European borrower since the Poland crisis, Hungary got its second loan from the BIS for $300 million. by December the IMF had authorized nearly $600 million in standby credits for its new 146th member. Moving along, Fekete persuaded Deutsche Bank, one of the giants of the Euromarket, to stake its prestige on a new $200-million bank loan for Hungary. After a slow start, Deutsche eventually enlisted fifteen other banks to join the syndication and the three-year loan was signed in April.

It was not all clear sailing. Hungary sought about $240 million in credits from the World Bank to finance grain storage facilities and industrial energy conservation. The U.S. administration tried to block the credits. The Hungarian loan requests in the spring of 1983 came just as the Reagan administration was pushing approval of the IMF quota increase through Congress, which might be annoyed at seeing new loans to Communist countries. The United States argued that Hungary's per capita income exceeded the $2,650 maximum to qualify for loans from the World Bank.

Meanwhile Hungary took some small steps to encourage further inflow of foreign exchange deposits, offering anonymity like Swiss bank accounts. Interest rates on foreign exchange accounts were pegged two to three percentage points higher than comparable rates in the West. Hungary reasoned that foreign exchange even at these rates was cheaper than the 1 1/4 points over Libor that the banks wanted.

It all adds up, and 1983 looked a lot better than 1982—the trade surplus seemed likely to reach $1 billion, enough by itself to meet debt payments during the year. The country had succeeded in getting new loans despite residual animosity to East European borrowers. Hungary seemed ready to continue its diversification away from the Soviet model of central planning. The country moved to set up a domestic bond market and planned for duty-free industrial zones for Western companies. The country's virtuoso performance even won accolades from the new Soviet leader Yuri Andropov. Two weeks after taking office, Andropov said that the Soviet Union could learn some important lessons from "fraternal countries."

5

Even more than Hungary, Yugoslavia was anxious not to be caught in the bad company of Poland and Romania. Yugoslavia does not belong to Comecon. It is a founding member of the nonaligned movement, and in fact is much less aligned than many other countries in this group. Yugoslavia is an anomalous country, a federation of six republics and two provinces which operates on a decentralized basis, like Canada. More than any other country, Yugoslavia exemplifies "Balkanization."

Yugoslavia had developed its own version of Marxist society. Based on worker management rather than central planning, the Yugoslav system is less efficient on paper but somehow seems to work better. Yugoslavia enjoys a reasonable freedom of expression and since 1963 the borders have been open. The country was miffed when Poland's problems spilled over to its credit relations with the West. A $400-million credit that Yugoslavia tried to mount while bankers were sorting out Poland's debt in 1981 languished. A renewed effort did not bear fruit until nearly a year later, in November 1982, when thirty U.S. and Japanese banks, led by Citibank, granted Yugoslavia a $200-million credit for the somewhat timid period of eighteen months. The New York branch of a Yugoslav bank had to chip in $15 million to bring the credit to a round number.

In a last-ditch effort to avoid rescheduling, Yugoslavia slapped on severe economic measures in October 1982. The government rationed gasoline and required a deposit for foreign travel. The deposit of $80 represented a half month's average wage. Because it was deposited for one year with no interest in a country running 30 percent inflation, it amounted to a tax. A week later, the government devalued the dinar by 20 percent. It also limited withdrawals from private hard-currency bank accounts to $250 a month.

Yugoslavia's foreign debt was nearly $20 billion. In addition, it seemed that the $8 billion in private hard-currency accounts had been spent. The money was still credited to the accounts, but withdrawal would have been impossible because the hard currency was no longer in the safe. This realization turned Yugoslavia's attempt to conserve foreign exchange on its head. The Yugoslavs who work in the rich Western European countries contribute significantly to the country's currency reserves by sending part of their earnings home. But worries about getting their hard-earned hard currency back, plus some annoying import duties and customs harassment at the border when they returned home for vacation, decided many of the migrant workers to keep their Western money in the West.

The government was no luckier with its own guests. Yugoslavia is a popular tourist spot with Europeans, particularly West Germans. But many tourists in 1982 found that they had to stand in long lines with the natives for their food purchases. Bookings for 1983 dropped off as word got around. Another major source of foreign exchange ran dry.

There were other problems. Yugoslavia's international airline, JAT, got so far behind in its fuel payments to Shell that the oil company threatened to seize JAT planes in foreign airports. The airline canceled flights to forty-two foreign destinations until the regional banks scraped together enough money to pay Shell.

Decentralization meant that neither debts nor repayments were coordinated. The country might well have the foreign exchange to meet its payments promptly, but it might not be in the bank that has to make the payment. Nonetheless, it was with some pride that the government announced early in 1983 that it had paid 96 percent of its principal and interest payments in 1982.

In the waning days of 1982, Yugoslavia met in Paris with fifteen Western governments about new aid to help it avoid rescheduling. Yugoslavia was a political hot potato. The NATO countries were keen to help because of the strategic importance of keeping the country out of the Soviet camp. But too heavy a NATO hand would also compromise Yugoslavia's independence and make the Russians more anxious to establish their hegemony. The United States initiated the government help, but asked someone else to take the lead. France and Britain likewise turned down the task. They asked Switzerland, a neutral firmly in the Western camp, to coordinate the rescue. Surprisingly, Switzerland, which normally goes its own way, accepted the role. Bern arranged the government relief, while Swiss Bank Corp., one of the three big Swiss banks, organized the commercial banks.

The week of January 17, 1983, was a whirlwind of activity. Commercial banks met Monday in Zurich, formed an advisory group, advised Yugoslavia to suspend all debt payments for ninety days, and got to work on plans to refinance the country's debt. In Bern on Tuesday and Wednesday, the governments firmed up plans for $1.3 billion in new aid, mostly in the form of export credits. On Friday the banks' steering committee met in London to discuss the rescheduling of $1 billion in debts falling due in 1983 plus a new loan for about the same amount. The week before, in Basel, the board of the Bank for International Settlements had revived Yugoslavia's four-month-old request for a $500-million loan. Typically gauche, the Yugoslavs had asked the BIS, which likes to make loans of three to six months, for a three-*year* loan. The timing had been bad too. The BIS had stuck its neck out for Hungary and Mexico and was feeling a bit exposed. In the new year, the move to help

Yugoslavia encouraged the BIS to look again. With more aid in view, the cautious central bankers were willing to consider a short-term bridge loan.

Yugoslavia in fact had several friends. A former U.S. ambassador to Belgrade, Lawrence Eagleburger, had meantime become the ranking civil servant in the State Department. The Secretary of State himself, George Shultz, a onetime Treasury secretary, was taking a great interest in the debt crisis anyway and devoted personal attention to Yugoslavia's case. He was worried, though, that new government money might find its way back into the banks' pockets. "We must avoid a situation where governments bail out the private banks," he telexed U.S. embassies in Western Europe. Even though Yugoslavia was pressing for cash, the United States and most other Western governments granted their aid in the form of export credit guarantees.

The IMF had gotten used to flexing its muscles in the Latin-American rescue packages (see next chapter). It pushed the banks to come to some decision about Yugoslavia. A Fund official chaired the Zurich meeting of bankers on January 17. The IMF set a deadline of February 28 for the banks to decide what they were going to do. Without a firm commitment of bank help, the IMF would not follow through with the $600 million in credits that formed its part of the rescue effort. That sum was actually the third tranche of a $1.8 billion facility agreed to two years before. The IMF was still smarting from criticism of its Romanian package and wanted to keep Yugoslavia on the tracks.

There were lots of problems. The BIS wanted Yugoslavia to put up its gold as collateral for $200 million of its loan. Yugoslavia grudgingly agreed, but had to go to the banks for a waiver of the negative pledge clause. This standard feature of Euromarket loan contracts requires that no subsequent loan get a better collateral than this one. Barbarous relic that it is, gold is still seen in the market as better collateral than anything else. The banks, for their part, insisted that the national bank or government guarantee any new loans. They were tired of the disorganization of decentralized finance. The World Bank was waiting in the wings with $250 million. Some World Bank money intended for Yugoslavia in 1982 was never disbursed because the local part of the funding was lacking for some projects. The Yugoslav package dragged on for months. The country just managed to keep its head above water, at great cost to its populace. The nation of coffee addicts, for instance, often had no coffee at all.

6

East Germany for a while seemed headed for trouble. Going into 1982 with eleven to twelve billion dollars of hard-currency debt, much of it short-term, the other Germany seemed a likely candidate for rescheduling. But iron discipline and perhaps some under-the-table aid from West Germany tided East Berlin over.

East Germany always gets some help from its Western counterpart. This ranges from the steady flow of gifts—household items, food, clothes—from West Germans to their relatives in the East, to regular payments by the Federal Republic to the Democratic Republic. These include annual payments for West Berlin's sewage disposal and postal service as well as the lion's share of infrastructure projects like the divided highway beween Hamburg and Berlin. Trade between the two Germanies is not considered foreign trade but intra-German trade. It does not involve foreign currency; officially the "marks" of the two countries are equal in value. East Germany thus benefits from European Community membership by the back door. The icing on the cake is a so-called swing credit of DM 600 million–800 million to finance intra-German trade on an interest-free basis. (The West German central bank picks up the tab for most of this interest-rate subsidy.) Bonn also pays what amounts to a ransom each year so that a number of East German citizens are allowed to emigrate to the West.

Bankers were mystified about how East Germany avoided a payment crunch. "It's the greatest banking puzzle of 1982," said one in London. Jan Vanous, chief Comecon watcher at Wharton, speculated that offshore subsidiaries of West German banks might be lending money to East Berlin, perhaps with Bonn's tacit approval. Some spoke of a "West German umbrella," which protected East Germany from the rescheduling difficulties of its Warsaw Pact allies. On the other hand, East Germany is a particularly close ally of

94

the Soviet Union. If there is a Soviet umbrella at all, it surely covers East Germany.

Czechoslovakia had been so conservative in its post-Dubček incarnation that it avoided running up a high debt to begin with. One of the Czech party ideologues, Vasil Bilak, once compared borrowing from the West to a pact with the devil. Prague had kept its borrowing to between three and four billion dollars. By the fall of 1982, bankers were even suggesting to Czechoslovakia that it should tap the Euromarket for a loan.

Bulgaria, with the relatively high debt for its size of $4 billion, had been a worry earlier. The Soviet Union gave it extra supplies of oil to re-export at a profit, enabling the country to show a trade surplus. Bulgaria is so close in spirit to the Russians that Western creditors see it as practically part of the Soviet Union.

The Soviet Union itself was pressed, but the country is too rich and powerful to run into serious difficulties. It can and does sell gold and oil, even when the market is soft, to pay its bills. In the first half of 1981 the Soviet Union drew down its Western deposits by $5 billion, it borrowed money discreetly on a one-off basis from Western banks, it delayed payments the maximum permissible time. Cash flow was clearly tight, but no one questioned the country's credit standing. The currency shortage problem persisted into 1983 and looked as if it might last until natural gas exports from the Yamal pipeline start earning money in 1985. But by then the Soviet Union may be out of oil to export. Financing grain purchases in the West is the main hard-currency drain for the Soviet Union, but there was no reason to suspect that Moscow would solve that perennial problem.

THE POYAIS SYNDROME

CHAPTER FIVE

1

Latin-American countries began borrowing and defaulting as soon as they gained independence in the 1820s. The first wave of bonds issued in London were the subject of a speculative mania. So enthusiastic was the London market that a Scottish adventurer who had fought under Simón Bolívar succeeded in floating a £200,000 bond for "the ridiculous and largely mythical Kingdom of Poyais," ostensibly a new country in Central America. Gregor MacGregor, the "prince of Poyais," made off with the proceeds of the issue and was never heard of again. Poyais never paid a coupon, but neither did La Gran Colombia, the very real country founded by Bolívar that later split up into Bolivia, Ecuador, and Colombia.

By 1827, all of the £20 million-plus Latin-American bonds floated in London were in default. Nor did the situation improve with repeated reschedulings, called conversions in the case of nineteenth-century bonds. "Between 1826 and 1850 the dividends paid upon the securities of Spanish-speaking countries were negligible, and the prospect of ultimate redemption grew more hopeless with each of the incessant conversion schemes which gave constant employment to many London financiers," wrote one historian. Decades later, some of the Latin American countries finally retired the principal of these early loans. But only after successive write-downs, decades of lost interest, and considerable losses by the original investors. "Perhaps the most important fact about international financial relations of Latin America prior to the First World War was the failure to keep financial commitments," observed a French expert.

The fledgling nations were in good company. The former colonial power, Spain, started the ball rolling with its default in 1823. Portugal, Austria, and Russia all left British investors in the lurch. (Britain was the only European country to emerge from the Napoleonic Wars with excess capital to invest abroad.) In North America the default of eleven states on their foreign bonds in the 1840s brought the United States into low repute. The refusal of the U.S. Congress to honor the state loans made the United States a pariah for European investors. Baron James de Rothschild made U.S. credit standing crystal clear to presidential envoy Duff Green: "You may tell your government that you have seen the man who is at the head of the finances of Europe, and that he has told you that they cannot borrow a dollar, not a dollar." Some bondholders stuck with their debtor, injected new capital, and eventually salvaged the situation in some states.

U.S. investors replaced their British counterparts in buying Latin-American bonds after World War I. They fared no better. By 1940 nearly four fifths of all Latin-American bonds floated in North America were in default. One of the more interesting disputes to emerge was when Mexico failed to fulfill a debt rescheduling worked out in 1922 by Thomas W. Lamont, a partner at J. P. Morgan & Co. and chairman of the International Committee of Bankers on Mexico. As Lamont was seeking to revise the accord in 1927, his partner at Morgan's, Dwight Whitney Morrow, was appointed ambassador to Mexico. Morrow quickly ascertained that "the real difficulty down here is that the government is insolvent and doesn't know it yet." Despite his Morgan background, Morrow argued against a separate agreement for the bondholders represented by the bankers' committee. He urged an overall program of settling creditors' claims against Mexico, similar to bankruptcy proceedings in a company. His model was the Egyptian settlement in the latter part of the nineteenth century, where creditors were grouped into classes and paid off proportionally according to class with the resources available.

"Lamont maintained that a nation could never be insolvent since it always had taxing power. Morrow countered that a nation could reach the point where despite the taxing power, it could not meet in full its obligations. He believed that Mexico had reached that juncture." This historian's description showed the debate of the 1920s to be timely in the 1980s. In the earlier case, Morrow blocked any separate agreement for years. His departure from Mexico and premature death left the field open to Lamont, who pressured the Mexican Government into a new debt accord. By that time, though, the onset of the Great Depression compelled Mexico once again to renege on its debt.

A peek into the history of Latin-American debt is not reassuring. It might remain true that countries do not go bankrupt, but they do default, repudiate and reschedule their debt to the point that many loans are worth only a fraction of their nominal value. Countries may not go bankrupt, but over the years many investors have gone bankrupt because of loans to such countries.

2

It was payments problems in Argentina in the 1880s that nearly bankrupted Barings. In the postwar era of this century, it was Argentina that convened the first meeting of the Paris Club in May 1956. The country required three subsequent reschedulings of official debt in Paris. Argentina enjoys vast natural resources, rich agriculture, and substantial accumulated wealth. Buenos Aires long enjoyed a European standard of living. The country suffers, though, from political instability.

Bankers had been edgy about Brazil for years. It was the Falklands war between Argentina and Britain, though, that first gave bankers intimations that a new wave of Latin-American defaults was upon them. Mexico beat Argentina to the punch and set off a chain reaction of credit retraction. The best efforts of Paul Volcker, Jacques de Larosière, and Walter Wriston could not prevent banks from retreating as much as possible. They stopped giving new credits, cut back credit lines, withdrew deposits. Within months of Mexico's moratorium, Argentina, Brazil, Ecuador, Chile, Bolivia, and Uruguay had sought IMF aid and a rescheduling of their bank debt. Venezuela tried to consolidate its short-term debt, before dallying with the idea of a full-fledged rescheduling.

Latin America became *the* financial crisis. Zaire, Peru, and Turkey were forgotten. Poland was just a bad memory, Romania an annoyance. Mexico, Brazil, and Argentina alone had at least $200 billion in debt. They bulked so large in the months to come that bankers referred to the "MBA problem" in shorthand.

Debt rescheduling took on even bigger dimensions. Mexico's proposal to the banks arrived on a telex 19 feet long. Transmission took one hour, so that it required several machines two and a half days to send the rescheduling proposal to the thirteen hundred-odd creditor banks. Argentina's proposal was 18 feet long. The programs came from the countries after they conferred with the IMF and the banks' steering committees set up for each country as it came on the block. As bankers somewhat numbly scurried around from meeting to meeting in the fall of 1982, they hardly anticipated that just weeks later they would hand over nearly $10 billion more to Mexico and Brazil, even though they had no idea how the earlier debts would ever be repaid. They did not have to grope toward the internal logic of the situation. De Larosière, backed by the American authorities, made it crystal clear to the banks that the only way to maintain any semblance of orderly debt management was for the banks to inject massive new money into these countries. Without the new loans, the last thin veil of contractual rectitude would be withdrawn and reveal sovereign bankruptcy in its ugly nakedness.

Debt service for the big Latin American countries had skyrocketed. Prompt payment of Argentina's principal and interest in 1982 would have required nearly twice as much foreign exchange as the country earned that year in exports. Mexico, Brazil, and Chile also needed more for debt service than they earned in exports. Their debt service ratio exceeded 100 percent, according to the figures compiled by *The Economist*. Venezuela, Colombia, and Peru were well above 50 percent. The traditional rule of thumb for a manageable debt service was 20 percent of export revenues. Whether that ever meant anything or not, the Latin-American borrowers were clearly in an impossible situation with their 1982 ratios. A report from the Inter-American Development Bank estimated that total debt for twenty Latin-American countries represented 202 percent of export revenues in 1982. Debt service for the group was 53 percent.

To resolve the crisis, government officials, IMF experts, and bankers were locked into a round of twelve-hour days, working weekends, and shuttling back and forth between New York and Washington and various Latin-American capitals. President Ronald Reagan's swing through the region in November 1982 stiffened the resolve of administration officials to support Latin-American rescue efforts. Not that the United States had to reflect too long about aiding its southern neighbors—U.S. business trades more than $70 billion annually with Latin American countries. U.S. banks had lent $65 billion to sovereign borrowers in the region, enough to raise the specter of a bank panic in the United States if these loans turned bad. American fears about Nicaragua and El Salvador also kept political considerations in the foreground. President Reagan reportedly intervened with bankers personally about keeping a lifeline to Brazil.

As far back as the turn of the century, President Theodore Roosevelt was worried about the Monroe Doctrine after German and English gunboats bombarded Venezuela to collect on debts. Roosevelt wanted the United States to police the Western Hemisphere. He sent U.S. tax collectors into the Dominican Republic in 1904 to collect customs revenues for European banks. Later, the United States landed Marines in the Dominican Republic to quell civil strife and keep the tax revenues flowing. Marines stormed Haiti in 1915 to secure the island's gold when the government failed to pay its debts.

U.S. relations with Mexico were always querulous. Mexico lost Texas and Southern California to the United States in the nineteenth century. U.S. troops occupied part of Mexico even in the twentieth century. The relationship prompted the famous sigh of Mexican leader Porfirio Díaz early in the century: "Poor Mexico! So far from God, so near to the United States."

After Mexico's payments collapse in 1982, the rescue moved inexorably forward. The rescue team brought Mexico under control just in time to turn its attention to Argentina. Brazil beat back the flames until after its mid-November elections, and the firemen rushed there from Argentina. Uruguay, Ecuador, Bolivia were casualties along the way.

The job of finance minister, a thankless task in the best of times, became a hot seat. Mexico kept Jesús Silva Herzog despite a change of government, but other debt managers found themselves out of a job, often enough just after coming back from talks with bankers. Finance Minister Luis Ugueto returned to Caracas in October after a swing through New York and London to talk about Venezuela's short-term debt and had to leave his cabinet post. Peru's debt manager, Roberto Danino, followed Premier Manuel Ulloa out of office in early 1983. After Chile, too, started on the rescheduling trail in early 1983, Finance Minister Rolf Luders lost his job just days after returning from a handholding session in London. The personnel changes further disrupted delicate negotiations. Bankers were a bit off balance seeing new faces across the conference table. They complained that they dealt with four Argentine finance ministers in 1982.

3

The Mexican team remained intact, which seemed to reassure the bankers. Perhaps it is reassuring to have people named Jesús and Angel running the show. But it was the same team that had borrowed and spent Mexico into its fix. The president-elect, Miguel de la Madrid Hurtado, had been secretary for budget and planning, the ministry responsible for that government overspending bankers saw as the root of all evil. Lame-duck presidents have their uses for everyone. Bankers decided that Silva Herzog, Gurría, and Madrid had performed as well as possible with somebody like López Portillo running around loose. The unspoken feeling was that it was better to have orthodox-thinking men who make mistakes than the Cambridge-trained left-wing economists who gained ascendancy in the waning days of López Portillo's government.

Silva Herzog, then undersecretary of finance, and Gurría, director of external credit, had planted the seeds of the 1982 crisis in the summer of 1981. Mexico failed to react quickly enough to the oil glut that was developing. The state-owned oil firm, Pemex, first cut its oil prices, then annulled the cut, throwing the market into confusion. Exports plummeted to one third of normal levels in July and August. Meanwhile two major jumbo loans were delayed in negotiations, and Mexico suddenly had a liquidity gap of ten to twenty billion dollars. The financing team went into the market for funds on whatever terms it could get, mostly short-term. Despite the evident problems, Mexico pumped the market for an extra four to five billion dollars. Bankers rushed to oversubscribe Mexican syndications.

Nicholas Asheshov, a veteran Latin-American correspondent, asked after this 1981 performance, "Did bankers really know what they were doing this year as they forked out $1 billion in new money every month for Mexico?" His answer was no. One Mexican banker scathingly observed that loan managers quibbled incessantly about an extra eighth of a point on interest or fees while ignoring the big question what the risk was. The banks sent salesmen to Mexico, not analysts. Promotions and bonuses resulted from deals and profits, not from mealymouthed excuses. The banks anted up $20 billion for Mexico in 1981 alone.

All of 1982 was difficult for Mexico. In February, the government devalued the peso for only the second time after more than twenty years at a fixed rate. In April, López Portillo clamped down an austerity program. The country's largest industrial conglomerate, Grupo Alfa, told its 130 foreign bankers that same month that it had to suspend principal payments on $2.3 billion of foreign debts. It was a harbinger of things to come. Silva Herzog began making his trips to Washington; bankers began to soft-pedal Mexican loans.

Momentum picked up. On Sunday August 1, the government doubled the price of corn, which had a like effect on the price of tortillas, which are made from corn and are a staple of the Mexican diet. On Friday August 6, Mexico created a two-tier foreign exchange rate. By freeing the peso from its peg to the dollar for most transactions, the move was in effect a massive devaluation. The preferential rate, for essential imports and debt payments, attempted to soften the blow.

102

The currency regime marked a radical departure for Mexico. The country had long prided itself on its free exchange policies, which allowed the U.S. dollar to circulate as a parallel currency in Mexico. But the devaluation was imperative. Without some preferential rate for imports or debts, the impact would have been incalculable. If foreign currency debts had been subject to the full devaluation, Mexican companies would have needed five times the number of pesos to repay the debt as they got with the original loan, not counting interest.

On August 12 Mexico drove another nail into its currency coffin. It froze $12 billion in U.S. dollar accounts held in Mexican banks. By the stroke of a pen, these dollars became pesos at a rate of seventy to the dollar. By the time the pesos could be withdrawn, they were worth half that in dollar terms, and a fifth of the value the dollars had when they were deposited. Silva Herzog made his phone call to McNamar and boarded the central bank's private plane to fly to Washington for the Mexican Weekend.

4

As the financial world recovered numbly from Mexico's debt shock, López Portillo prepared further jolts. The Mexican president had set up a secret commission to study bank nationalization. The commission conferred in Paris with French Socialists, who had nationalized the French banking system earlier in the year. López Portillo fell under the sway of government officials who had studied radical economics at Cambridge. Chief among them was Carlos Tello Macias, a onetime budget and planning minister who had studied under neo-Marxist economist Joan Robinson. Tello had resigned his portfolio in 1977 in the wake of a clash with the finance minister about increased government spending. He favored rapid industrialization and strong government intervention. He wanted to close the Mexican economy through protectionist trade barriers and exchange controls in order to free the country "from the tyranny of the international capital markets."

Another proponent of Cambridge policies was José Andres de Oteyza, López Portillo's minister for National Patrimony and Industrial Development. De Oteyza routinely pushed for nationalization of the banks at the annual cabinet meeting to review the president's state of the nation message. As the September 1 date of the speech approached in 1982, though, De Oteyza did not need to make his request. López Portillo stunned Mexico and the rest of the world with his surprise nationalization of the country's sixty banks. Agustin Legorreta, head of Banamex, one of the two big banks, literally fainted when he heard the president's speech. In the Mexican Congress, López Portillo received a standing ovation.

The president castigated the banks for "looting" the country. They abetted unpatriotic citizens who transferred billions of dollars out of Mexico, he charged. López Portillo said $22 billion of flight capital had left Mexico in the previous two to three years. He put Mexican deposits in the United States at $14 billion and real estate investments at $25 billion. The banks, he railed, had made it all possible. No more. Now the state owned the banks.

López Portillo handed over copies of the property registries from fourteen states in the United States to the Mexican Congress. An investigative panel sifted through millions of names to identify Mexican buyers of property. It was not a big surprise that many of the offenders were government officials who had enriched themselves through Mexico's traditional corruption.

The country's endemic corruption took on new significance in the light of the foreign exchange shortage. New reports emerged in Mexico. The mayor of Mexico City, it turned out, had bought a $2.5-million estate in Connecticut. The police chief in the resort town of Zihuantanejo had built a mansion with a park and private drive for $10 million. López Portillo himself followed the traditional route of retiring presidents. He built four mansions for his family on a hill outside the capital. Satirists quickly dubbed the location "Dog Hill," from López Portillo's 1981 statement that he would "defend the peso like a dog." Corruption accentuated the crass discrepancy in incomes in Mexican society. The rich in Mexico live better than the rich in the United States, as a contemporary joke illustrated. A Mexican dog comes up to a Polish dog, a Russian dog, and an American dog. He complains that he had to bark two hours before the maid would give him any meat. "What's meat?"

asks the Polish dog. "What's barking?" asks the Russian dog. "What's a maid?" asks the American dog.

Wild rumors of coups and assassinations preceded the president's September 1 speech. López Portillo ostentatiously breakfasted with the military chiefs of staff and regional commanders the day after the speech. Defense Minister General Felix Galvan declared his support of the bank nationalization. The government bused tens of thousands of workers and peasants to Mexico City's huge square, the Zócalo, two days later for a huge rally in support of the move. The bank nationalization was compared to the takeover of the oil industry in 1938. The unexpected measure distracted the public, and perhaps history, from the less savory legacies of the López Portillo regime.

The president also announced full exchange controls in his speech. Like the bank nationalization, the decision was taken by López Portillo alone. He presented both measures to his cabinet the evening before as a *fait accompli*. Under Mexico's political system, the president has virtually complete power to do as he likes. Silva Herzog offered to resign. Like most of the orthodox men in charge of Mexico's money, he had always opposed exchange controls. López Portillo rejected Silva Herzog's resignation because he was deemed too important for the success of negotiations with the banks and the IMF.

But the president happily accepted the resignation of central bank governor Miguel Mancera Aguayo, who just four months previously had published a brochure explaining why exchange controls could never work in Mexico. That brochure became a bestseller when controls were implemented, because it explained the various ways of evading controls. Carlos Tello took over the central bank. It was a lame-duck appointment from the beginning, but Tello lost no time in making his mark. President-elect Madrid also had not been consulted by López Portillo on the nationalization or foreign exchange controls. Following the ritual of presidential accession, he kept quiet in the long period between his July election and December inauguration. One of his first moves as president, though, was to reinstate Mancera as central bank governor.

Tello established a two-tier foreign exchange system completely controlled by the government. The scheme set two different rates for the dollar. The whole arrangement was largely theoretical, because the government still had no extra dollars to sell and no one was buying pesos. Tello also lowered interest rates, even though inflation was soaring to a 100 percent annual rate. Orthodox policy would have dictated interest rates keeping ahead of inflation. Tello was hardly a wild-eyed radical. His father had been foreign minister; his brother was deputy foreign minister under López Portillo. But Tello certainly saw things differently than the conservative Bank of Mexico or than the IMF.

López Portillo's surprise decisions annoyed Washington. Treasury Secretary Donald Regan said Washington was not consulted and not even informed of the plans. The IMF stewed. Its mission had returned from Mexico just before the speech, but had no intimation of what was in store. The IMF abjures exchange controls. Bankers at first welcomed the notion that the Mexican banks were now the responsibility of the government. That seemed more secure to them than a private enterprise, which might be allowed to go bankrupt. Once it sank in that López Portillo had pushed Mexican policy decidedly to the left, American bankers were less happy.

More significant for the rest of American business was the imposition of exchange controls. Practically every one of the Fortune 500 companies did some business with Mexico. Many of them had operating subsidiaries. The new currency regime limited repatriation of dividends to 15 percent of the Mexican subsidiary's net worth. This, too, was largely theoretical as long as no dollars were available to repatriate. When priorities for use of foreign exchange emerged, profit repatriation was not high on the list. Even in normal times the limit would constitute a major restriction. There was widespread hope in the United States as well as in Mexico that the new government would remove the exchange controls, but López Portillo had deflowered Mexico; once gone, innocence of controls could never be regained. Even if the government removed the controls, foreign investors could never be sure that some new expediency would not bring them back.

This left Silva Herzog with a lot of explaining to do when he got to Toronto in early September for the joint annual meeting of the International Monetary Fund and the World Bank. This annual event, held alternately in Washington and somewhere else in the world, has ballooned in the last few years into a full-fledged financial jamboree. Ostensibly the formal assembly of the finance ministers who make up the boards of the sister institutions, the meeting is a freewheeling bazaar. Bankers flock to the meeting as "observers," seeking to buttonhole finance ministers and offer them some loans. This year, the bankers rather pegged a couple of ministers with overdue payments to the wall while the others had to do the buttonholing if they wanted any bank finance. The whirling round of banquets and cocktail parties went off as usual, but Mexico had really rained on the annual outing.

Silva Herzog, ashen-faced much of the time, had to explain policies he'd had no voice in formulating, and make promises that neither he nor his interlocutors could be sure would be kept. The harried finance secretary blurted out to Mexican journalists that Mexico would not be paying any of the principal on its debt until 1984. Because the banks had only granted a ninety-day moratorium on August 20, this revelation was like a thunderclap to them. Regan reportedly gave a stern lecture to his Mexican counterpart. Silva Herzog issued a statement vague enough to be construed as backtracking, but which left the way open for further postponements. These invariably came. As the November 23 expiration of the first moratorium drew near, Mexico requested a new six-month rollover. And when that expired, it was extended another six months, and so on.

The bankers were also worried that Mexico's nationalization would mean including interbank lines in the rescheduling process. (These lines are the short-term liabilities, or debts, between banks.) About $6 billion was at stake in liabilities of Mexican banks to other banks outside the country. After some dithering, Silva Herzog issued a statement that they would not be included. However, he added, keeping them open was "crucial" to the success of the rescheduling. In other words, the banks would not have to reschedule them as long as they kept them open.

The whole thing gave rise to a gallows humor. As one banker said of the interbank lines, "One of the reasons we are not asking for the money back is we are afraid we would not get it if we asked for it. We don't want to upset the cart." That mentality was in line with the spontaneous decision of the banks to go along with Mex-

107

ico's moratorium in the first place. "We had the choice of saying 'yes' or of saying 'yes!' " is the way one banker put it.

In Mexico itself, the witticism made the rounds that Mexico had reached the edge of an abyss and was about to take a giant step forward.

Silva Herzog made it through the Toronto meeting. That he dropped out of sight for a couple of weeks upon his return home was due, it was said, to an appendicitis operation.

Everybody was on edge. When a fire broke out in Pemex headquarters and gutted the building, anxious London bankers telexed the oil company to make sure that loan records survived the fire intact. About one third of Mexico's $60-billion public sector debt was in the name of the oil company.

Saudi Arabia made discreet approaches to the Mexican government, offering concessional loans in exchange for Mexican adherence to OPEC pricing policy. The fourth-largest oil producer in the world, Mexico had preferred to go its own way rather than join OPEC. The Saudis evidently feared that the United States was ready to exploit the Mexican situation in order to undermine OPEC price levels. One report put the price of the special strategic reserve purchases at $24 per barrel, well below OPEC's official price of $34. Mexico quickly came to the conclusion that the United States was much bigger and much closer than Saudi Arabia, and refused the Saudis' offer. An unconfirmed report said the Saudis had offered $12 billion at an interest rate of six to eight percent.

Meanwhile, Monterrey businessmen grew restive. An industrial capital, Monterrey is closer to the U.S. border than to Mexico City. The business community there had been proud of its independence. After the bank nationalizations, they started agitating for a one-day shutdown of business throughout the country. The government quickly defused the action. Customs officials impounded 120 golf carts at the swank Monterrey golf club, discovering suddenly that they did not have proper import papers. Even more persuasive was the visit by government auditors to 320 prominent taxpayers in Monterrey.

Fly-by-night money changers sprang up all along the two-thousand-mile-long border between Mexico and the United States. The rate for the peso was much lower than Tello's seventy to the dollar for normal transactions. In this black-market trading, which was legal on the U.S. side of the border, the Mexican currency soon dropped to 150 to the dollar. The peso, which had been worth eight cents from 1954 to 1976, was now worth two thirds of a cent.

U.S. citizens who had deposited their retirement savings in dollar accounts in Mexican banks were hopping mad at having their dollars turned into devalued pesos. U.S. ambassador John Gavin cabled home that Washington had better do something about American losses in the Mexdollar accounts if it wanted to keep supporting Mexico. By one reckoning, $5 billion of the $12 billion frozen belonged to Americans. There were lawsuits in California and New York to have Mexican assets in the United States attached for eventual compensation on losses from the dollar grab.

The Commodity Credit Corporation had difficulty implementing its part of the U.S. rescue effort. The $1-billion line of credit guarantee in the original package could not proceed because banks balked at putting up the funds. The CCC normally guarantees "only" 98 percent of the credit. The banks insisted that the U.S. Government guarantee 100 percent. They literally did not want to lend one more penny to Mexico at their own risk. The only precedent for a total guarantee was Poland. The CCC agreed and also improved the interest rate guarantees to make the credit attractive. In December, First Chicago and an international consortium signed a $450-million loan under CCC guarantees, the largest loan ever made under its aegis.

In Mexico, rumors mirrored middle-class fears. One rumor had the government impounding safety deposit boxes. Another said that Washington had agreed to freeze bank accounts of Mexican citizens in U.S. banks. More concrete was the inability to keep up payments on U.S. mortgages. Middle-class Mexicans who had purchased condominiums on resort islands in the Gulf found their payments quintupled. They had to sell at a loss.

Tourists stayed away. The exchange rate mess was too confusing. The number of passengers going through Mexico City's airport dropped by half, to 20,000 a day. Eastern Airlines bookings to Mexico were off 58 percent. Air France halted its Concorde flight to Mexico for lack of passengers.

109

Everything seemed to turn on getting the new government installed. Bankers especially looked to the inauguration of Miguel de la Madrid Hurtado to restore some sanity and order to Mexican economic policy. It was a nightmarish *déjà vu*. The last months of Luis Echeverría's government in 1976 also brought two devaluations. At that time, the financial world looked forward with anticipation to the right-thinking president-elect, José López Portillo.

The López Portillo government carried on the negotiations for the IMF stabilization programs, although aides of President-elect de la Madrid kept their hand in. The main negotiating point was how much to reduce the deficit on Mexico's public sector spending. The IMF always bears down on government spending to restore internal financial equilibrium. Mexico's budget deficit in 1982 neared 17 percent of gross national product. Three percent is considered high in industrial nations, although many countries exceed that figure. The IMF wanted Mexico to cut its budget deficit to 6 percent. Cutting deficits usually means cutting spending. The other method, increasing tax revenues, is practically impossible in a recession. Cutting spending means reducing subsidies and services, and that means a palpable cut in living standards. In Mexico, where the state provides much of the employment, it results in a huge increase in unemployment. The round figure for unemployment was already 40 percent of the 20-million-strong work force. The Mexicans argued that reducing the deficit to 10 percent of GNP was as far as they could go without causing severe social stress, which is bureaucratese for riots in the streets.

Meanwhile unions agitated for a 50-percent wage increase. Workers struck Mexicana Airlines and the huge national university. But Mexico's Party of the Institutionalized Revolution (PRI) kept a firm grip on its union supporters. The union demands did not seem too serious. Rather, the union appeared to use the IMF as a foil. They knew the lending agency would never allow such a big wage increase, but they could ask and then blame their failure on the imperialist technocrats.

When the letter of intent with the IMF was finally signed in mid-November, it was vague. The letter is the first step in securing IMF credits. On the basis of the program set out in the letter, the IMF board can approve or reject the loan. Because there is consultation at each step, the board approval at the end of negotiations is pro forma. But the need for approval gives the IMF negotiators considerable bargaining leverage. The letter of intent specified that Mexico reduce its budget deficit to 8.5 percent of GNP in 1983, to 5.5 percent in 1984, and to 3.5 percent in 1985. There was vague talk of exchange controls being temporary and wage increases being reasonable, but no deadlines or limits were set. The left celebrated the agreement as a victory against the IMF. But the first measures of President de la Madrid's government indicated that the incoming officials and the IMF had an understanding.

López Portillo signed the agreement, although he would have preferred to avoid the political ignominy. Tello, too, had to sign, which had its own irony. One point in the dispute that had led to his resignation from the cabinet in 1977 was his opposition to kowtowing to the IMF. But in 1982, Mexico needed the money and had no time for political sensibilities. The IMF loan facility was worth $3.9 billion over three years—the second-biggest granted up to that time. (The biggest was $5.3 billion for India in 1981.) In addition, the agreement made available another half-billion dollars from the IMF's Compensatory Financing Facility. This special fund, set up in 1963, awards credits to offset losses of export revenues from circumstances beyond a country's control, primarily from a decline in commodity prices.

The IMF money was a lot, but that was not all. The BIS had released only one $600-million tranche of its $1.8-billion credit to Mexico. The rest was contingent on an accord with the IMF. The central banks disbursed a second tranche when signing was imminent, and the third tranche became available when Mexico finally signed. Likewise, any progress with the negotiations to reschedule the bank debt depended on reaching agreement with the IMF. It is this gatekeeper function that gives the IMF such immense power. Governments, central banks, and commercial banks use the IMF as a stick. The carrot only comes afterward.

De Larosière spelled it out. With the IMF money and $2 billion of other official aid, Mexico would still need $5 billion in the course of 1983 to make the stabilization plan work. The banks had to provide that. If all of them chipped in, that would be equal to about 7 percent of their existing exposure. If they rejected the 7-

111

percent solution, the IMF would not approve the credit, Mexico would stop paying interest on its debt as well as principal, and the banks could see what they would do.

After the initial shock, the banks realized that indeed they were the only ones with the kind of money Mexico needed. It was easier if an official body like the IMF took the leadership role in organizing bank participation. Bankers hailed the IMF action as a new stage in international cooperation. It was only later that everyone had second thoughts. The IMF had cracked the whip in a new direction. The banks, which had been happy to see the IMF bully developing countries, now found *themselves* bullied. A tiger previously exempted from the circus act suddenly found itself jumping through hoops with the other cats.

The November 16 meeting was a watershed. In telling the banks that they *had* to lend more money, and even setting the amount, De Larosière broke new ground. Banks had jealously guarded their freedom of making credit decisions from central banks, regulators, shareholders, and boards of directors. Making loans *is* banking. De Larosière's reasoning had a Cartesian logic characteristic of the French mindset, but it ran up against centuries of banking tradition summed up in principles like "Don't throw good money after bad" or "Don't lend money to someone who doesn't have it."

The campaign to muster support for the $5-billion Mexican loan turned into a two-month telethon. The thirteen commercial banks on the steering committee got on the telexes and phones and badgered, bullied, and barnstormed assent from the fourteen-hundred-odd creditor banks. William Rhodes, the Citibank senior executive who headed the Mexico committee, personally spent hours on the phone in gentle and not so gentle persuasion. Top officials at the Federal Reserve, the Bank of England, the Swiss National Bank, and the Bundesbank also got into the act. They put the moral authority of the central banks squarely behind the IMF action. Financial papers tabulated the "pledges" as they dribbled in. "Mexico loan gets backing of U.S. and U.K. bankers," trumpeted a *Financial Times* headline on December 16. "Most banks back loan to Mexico," echoed the *International Herald Tribune*.

De Larosière set a deadline of December 15. On December 14, Lloyds Bank invited the fifty-three British banks with loans out to

Mexico to a cozy little meeting at the Bank of England itself. The Old Lady of Threadneedle Street, which rears up its modest marble head in the heart of the City, is the stuff of legend. Sober, proper, pragmatic, it is easily the most prestigious of the big central banks. The banks it supervises do not always like the suggestions of the Bank, but they invariably respect them.

The Bank made its conference room available for the meeting. The Bank's deputy governor, Christopher McMahon, addressed the assembly and asked for cooperation. Whatever the Bank said about the unofficial character of the meeting, the commercial bankers got the message. Following the meeting, one bank at least clearly stated its motivation when telexing its pledge to the coordinator, Lloyds Bank: "We are only doing this because the Bank of England asked us to."

On December 23 the IMF executive board, like a bureaucratic Santa Claus, approved the Mexico loan. De la Madrid's newly installed government started meeting the terms of the IMF accord. The government lifted or loosened price controls on 4,700 items, keeping the price lid on only 300 basic goods. It announced the closure of 106 state companies and agencies. Wage increases were held to 25 percent, even though inflation was running at 100 percent. The exchange rate for normal transactions was set loose, which brought a devaluation of 53 percent, to 150 to the dollar. The preferential rate was reduced 47 percent, to 95.

5

Argentina was a special case from the beginning. The richest and most unstable country in South America pitched headlong into a war with Great Britain in the spring of 1982. The subsequent defeat stripped the military government of whatever legitimacy it had. Argentines literally took to the streets in a series of demonstrations to force the military to hold elections and give up power.

The war destroyed in a stroke the fragile economic structure painstakingly built up from the rubble of 1976, when the military deposed Isabella Perón. With an external debt about half of Mexico's at $40 billion, Argentina had a manageable if precarious position. The war, at a cost conservatively estimated to be $2 billion, drained financial reserves. It also disrupted trade, which hurt Argentina's external payments.

The hostilities extended to finance. Argentina suspended debt service payments on all credits from British banks. Britain froze Argentine deposits in its banks. Given London's preponderance in the Euromarket, fears arose that the dispute would affect all syndicated loans to Argentina. When Venezuela transferred $5 billion in deposits out of London, the potential financial repercussions of the war grew ominous. Fortunately, the hostilities were soon over.

José Maria Dagnino Pastore, the national economy minister in the new government installed after the war, wanted to refloat the Argentine economy by boosting exports and encouraging domestic consumption. But stimulative measures fueled inflation, and Pastore was forced out of office just two months after his appointment.

Pastore's ouster unsettled the financial world. It came just after Mexico's August 20 rendezvous in New York and just before the IMF confab in Toronto. Reynaldo Bignone, the retired army general who became president after the war, tapped Jorge Wehbe to take the finance job. Wehbe, sixty-two, had already held the post in 1962 and in 1972. Displaying Latin macho and economic pragmatism in equal measure, the new economy minister once remarked, "Men should fall in love with women and not with economic theories." Wehbe went off to Toronto with visions of Argentine autonomy dancing in his head, even though the country was more than $2 billion in arrears on its debt payments. The General Confederation of Labor, the main trade union group, warned pointedly that debt renegotiation should *not* include deflationary measures. This put Wehbe in the position of maintaining that he wanted old debts stretched out or rolled over and wanted new financing, but that that had nothing to do with the arrears, the sanctions against Britain, or the IMF. This position did not hold too long. The banks insisted that any arrangement on the existing debt, let alone new money, depended on an IMF program. Everybody insisted that Argentina and Britain regularize their financial relations before anybody could proceed.

U.S. Deputy Treasury Secretary McNamar, still riding high from the Mexican Weekend, offered to undertake an "elevator shuttle"

114

at the Toronto meeting. The U.S. delegation was on the sixth floor of the Sheraton Hotel, the British on the seventh, and Argentina, conveniently, on the fifth. McNamar's work as go-between helped. On September 13, the week after the Toronto meeting, Britain and Argentina lifted their financial sanctions.

There were still hurdles. Argentina had said something during the dispute about keeping its British debt payments in an escrow account. But Buenos Aires did not transfer the overdue payments, eventually tabulated at $440 million, right away. It began making current interest payments, but only after much to-ing and fro-ing did Argentina agree in November with the big four British clearing banks that the disputed principal payments be rolled over six months from their original due date and interest be paid immediately.

In the meantime, Argentina went ahead with its application for an IMF loan, its seventh since joining the organization in 1956. Political opposition to the IMF remained intense. The Peronist union suggested scurrilously that Argentina should simply hand over its foreign assets to the international creditors. Any leftover funds should be deposited with the central bank. Admiral Emilio Massera, a onetime junta member, recommended a purge in all banks and government agencies of anyone trained abroad in a creditor country. These people had served as "Trojan horses" in the past seven years, he claimed. The Peronist and Radical parties wanted to form a common front with Mexico and other Latin-American borrowers in talks with the banks.

The IMF mission got stuck again, as in Mexico, on the question of government budget deficits. Agreement came at the end of October. The IMF credits were to be $2.2 billion. The maturity was set at fifteen months because that was the deadline for restoring a civilian government to power, which would then have to settle with the IMF on its own terms. One stipulation of the agreement was that inflation had to be brought down to 160 percent; it was raging at an annual rate of 500 percent when the accord was signed.

Because of Argentina's hyperbolic economy, the IMF wanted monthly reports instead of the usual quarterly ones.

Once Argentina reached its arrangement with the British banks for its arrears, it jumped the BIS hoop. The Bank of England had been blocking an Argentine approach to the BIS. The British central bank now dropped its opposition but it still refused to participate in the loan. The central bankers trimmed Argentina's $750-million request to $500 million.

Wehbe and his cohorts did not do much better with the banks. Citibank again headed the eleven-bank steering committee, which also included the familiar Bank of America, Manufacturers Hanover, Morgan Guaranty, and Chase Manhattan as well as Crédit Lyonnais, Crédit Suisse, Lloyds Bank International, Royal Bank of Canada, Bank of Tokyo, and Hamburg-based Deutsch-Südamerikanische Bank, a subsidiary of Dresdner Bank. Argentina's efforts to get a billion or two dollars from them dragged on for months. The decision in late November to "nationalize" the $5.5-billion debt of Argentina's private sector did not help any. It amounted to a unilateral rescheduling of the debt, contracted a year and a half earlier by private enterprises with exchange rate guarantees from the Argentine government. Subsequent devaluations of the peso had made the dollar debt prohibitively expensive for the government as guarantor. It didn't have any extra dollars, and $3.2 billion of the debts were falling due in the next few months. So it decided to issue government bonds to the creditors of the private companies, who technically owed the money. The five-year bonds were to be redeemed in four installments beginning in 1986. Interest was set at 1 point over Libor. The only alternative open to creditors, short of declaring default, was to write off the debt.

Also, the government had $14 billion in currency swaps swimming around. These were rolled over for six months during the Falklands crisis and for three months in December. No surprise, they were then rolled over again in March. Argentina "asked," the banks assented.

The request to the banks formed into two loans—a "bridging" loan of $1.1 billion over fifteen months, and a medium-term credit of $1.5 billion over five years. In addition, the banks were supposed to reschedule $5.5 billion in medium-term debt. It is difficult to fathom what gap the commercial bank bridge loan was supposed to bridge. BIS bridging credits filled in until IMF money was available. In this case, the IMF credit was available simultaneously. The second and third tranches of the "bridging" credit were even dependent on fulfillment of IMF targets. The bridge in fact was a boomerang. It was simply money for Argentina to keep its interest current. The funds came right back to the banks. This kept the banks' loans good. Most of the financial rescues turned on this all-important need, but the self-interest of the banks in making their bridge loan was especially evident.

The negotiations turned out to be particularly onerous. The signing of the bridge loan came only on New Year's Eve, when an ill-tempered covey of bankers gathered in Citibank's conference room, worrying much more about their accountants' closing of the books for 1982 than Argentina's prospects for 1983.

Talks on the medium-term credit spun out until the summer. Argentina irritated the bankers with its careless attitude toward arrears. This was due as much to bureaucratic muddling as to lack of funds.

6

Brazil had a long love affair with the banks. The Brazilians sold them the superpower of the twenty-first century and the banks bought it. The fifth-largest country in the world in area, Brazil has little oil but other natural resources in plenty, tremendous agricultural potential, and a newly industrialized economy. Moreover, it had energy, vision, and discipline.

The banks were like bears in a honey pot. When the United Nations Commission on Transnational Corporations surveyed the activities of eighty-four major international banks, they found that Brazil ranked third, after the United States and the United Kingdom, in the number of units of these banks. Citibank reported in 1977 that it derived a full 20 percent of its profits from Brazil— more than from the United States!

Brazil was the classic example of a country's borrowing its way around the oil shock. The country had $12 billion debt at the end of 1973. Medium- and long-term debt at the end of 1982 was more than six times that. But Brazil borrowed to build. A decade previously, Brazil had depended on coffee exports to earn its way in the world. An untimely frost meant recession. In 1981, Brazil had earned more from exporting autos and auto parts than from its coffee sales abroad. Now it was recession in industrial countries that brought recession to Brazil.

Brazil enjoyed the title of the Third World's biggest debtor up until 1982. In the first wave of worry about developing-country debt in the late 1970s, the hypothetical question was always: What happens if Brazil . . . ? But Brazil never did. The economy seemed to be careering out of control in 1980, but super-Minister Antonio Delfim Netto, Brazil's beefy economic czar, switched gears from fast-track growth to slower-paced consolidation.

Delfim Netto came across as a supremely self-confident man. He was the chief architect of the Brazilian miracle, the period from 1967 to 1974 when Brazil averaged 10-percent-plus economic growth per year. A self-made man of Italian extraction, Delfim was always understood to have presidential ambitions. Consigned to political exile as Brazil's ambassador to Paris, the decidedly un-diplomatic Delfim negotiated a return ticket to Brasilia as Minister of Agriculture. After galvanizing Brazil's agricultural industry, he bulled his way into the planning ministry. Not so much a planner as a crisis manager, Delfim had his hands on the main economic levers from this key ministry.

His antidote for bankers' anxiety was higher spreads. Brazil borrowed at margins of 2 points or beyond. The country wanted to avoid the dangerous bunching-up of short-term debt, and paid more to get the maturities it wanted.

The Brazilian policy on spreads highlighted an anomaly of sovereign borrowing. Prestige rode on an eighth of a point in setting margins on syndicated loans. But that eighth was all but insignificant when added to a Libor that could swing from 12 to 20 to 16 percent at the market's whim. The difference between a 3/8 margin and 1/2 becomes the difference 123/8 and 121/2. Not much of a difference compared to the 123/8 the borrower pays in one six-month period and the 143/8 it pays the next. When dollar interest rates rose to such high levels in 1982, it hurt every borrower, whether the margin was 3/8 or 3/4 or 13/4.

Margins *do* make a difference, though, to the banks. One benefit Brazil hoped to gain from its high-margin policy was bank loyalty. The country needed large amounts of new finance each year. The important thing was to have the money available, even if that meant paying a premium.

Loyalty is a fleeting thing in finance. All that goodwill Brazil had paid so dearly for evaporated in a twinkling after the Falklands war and the Mexican moratorium. Brazil maintained loudly that it was different from Mexico or Argentina. It had not bunched up maturities or frittered loans away on consumption or fought a quixotic war. It did not depend on the price of a single commodity for its export earnings. Its companies were not bankrupt. Its currency was not grossly overvalued. Brazil was different. Citibank got the message, and Chase, and Morgan. Regional U.S. banks and continental European banks did not have the vested interests in Brazil that U.S. money-center banks had. Latin America had become a bad risk; they pulled out.

At first Brazil tried to bluster its way out of difficulties. Government officials claimed at the end of September that foreign funds had resumed their normal flow after a brief hiatus in the wake of Mexico's problems. But wishing did not make it so. Before very long, the marketplace worked its magic and Brazil was broke. The Brazilians were bitter and mad enough to spit. All the efforts to rebuild their image in the market, their care to stagger maturities, their willingness to pay higher margins did not save them from the same fate as Mexico and Argentina when the herd of international bankers stampeded in a mad panic out of Latin America. "I think we could sue Mexico in the courts for what they have done to us," remarked a Brazilian diplomat caustically.

Brazilian debt managers tried to keep a lid on their problem until after the November 15 elections for state governors and the federal congress, the first really open elections in Brazil under military rule and a dress rehearsal for presidential elections in 1985. Delfim and central bank governor Carlos Langoni made quiet approaches to the International Monetary Fund while denying that Brazil intended to take an IMF credit. Brazil made even quieter approaches to the Reagan administration. The ubiquitous McNamar conferred with Brazilian Finance Minister Ernano Galveas as the two of them attended October's ministerial conference of the General Agreement on Tariffs and Trade in Geneva. The two agreed for the U.S. Treasury to lend Brazil $1.23 billion from the same Exchange Sta-

119

bilization Fund tapped for the Mexico loan. The U.S. disbursed the money in November, but made the loan public only on the occasion of President Reagan's visit to Brazil on December 1.

Bankers did not know this. They were also kept in the dark about the state of Brazil's currency reserves. These were put at nearly $7 billion in August, but Brazilian newspapers said they had dwindled to just under $5 billion by the end of September. Delfim then adopted the clever tactic of not publishing reserve figures any more. This did not allay bankers' fears. One problem with Brazil's reserves was that they were not always liquid. One of the most poignant ironies of the whole debt crisis was the fact that Brazil was one of Poland's biggest creditors. Poland owed Brazil $1.5 billion. Brazil sorely needed the cash, but Poland had no more money for Brazil than it did for anyone else. Brazil also had loans out to Mexico, but it gladly took oil from cash-poor Mexico. Poland had no oil, but did offer some of its plentiful coal. In an ultimate gesture of goodwill, Poland also offered balmy Brazil a state-of-the-art icebreaker from its Baltic shipyards.

Brazil had always been keen to promote trade with other big developing nations. Now it made a special effort to put the trade on barter basis. Besides Mexico, Iraq and Nigeria, also major suppliers of oil to Brazil, were short of cash and willing to take grain or weapons from Brazil in payment for oil. Barter cut both ways, though. Brazil set an ambitious target in its trade account for 1983. After a measly $50-million surplus in 1982, Delfim's planners aimed at $6 billion. Barter diverted exports that could have been sold for cash. Taking oil in payment locked Brazil into certain deliveries that might hamper its flexibility in restricting imports.

Debt renegotiation became a campaign issue. Debt service was consuming 86 percent of Brazil's export revenue in 1982. Celso Furtado, a pre-military government planning minister who enjoyed considerable prestige, urged Brazil to form a common front with other Latin-American debtors in winning more favorable terms. Delfim took another tack. He announced with great fanfare that Brazil would tailor its economic objectives in 1983 to fit the funds that bankers were ready to lend. After consultation, the Brasilia planners figured that bankers would lend $10.6 billion in 1983, down sharply from $17 billion in 1982. In the past, Delfim noted, sovereign borrowers had set their growth objectives and then sought the finance. Brazil's innovation was to plan economic targets in line with available finance.

But this was more shadowboxing. At the end of November, Brazil announced it would indeed go to the IMF for money and the attached strings. In December, amid reports that the United States had decided "at the highest political level" to support Latin-American countries in their financial difficulties, President Reagan came to Brazil and announced the Treasury loan. The depth of U.S. commitment was still a matter for some skepticism. Reagan, whose sense of geography is weaker than his ideology, unwittingly toasted the good citizens of Bolivia in Brasilia. (He apologized by saying he would be in Bolivia the next day, although his actual destination was Bogotá, Colombia.) Also, Reagan announced a relaxation of U.S. quotas on sugar imports as if it were a boon to Brazil. U.S. analysts quickly pointed out that increased U.S. imports of sugar would benefit Brazil's Caribbean competitors, who paid no customs, at the expense of Brazil, which did pay duties. "The locale of the announcement was a source of some amusement in the sugar industry," chortled one analyst.

Believer in market forces that he is, Reagan nonetheless felt it incumbent to publicly urge in São Paulo that financing for developing countries be assured. The U.S. government pushed hard behind the scenes to whip up commercial bank support for Brazil. The Treasury never denied reports that the Administration guaranteed or even provided the funds for a $600-million bridge loan to Brazil from six big U.S. banks in November. The names of the participating banks by now are familiar: Citibank, Chase Manhattan, Bank of America, Bankers Trust, Manufacturers Hanover, and Morgan Guaranty. Officially, Treasury "encouraged" the banks. The $1.23-billion line from the Treasury was paid back in part, but renewed as necessary in tranches of $200 million and $300 million. It was necessary on several occasions before Brazil made it out of 1982.

Brazil's resentment at this parlous state of affairs found expression in a telex the government sent to bank creditors early in December. The language was high-handed, even arrogant, setting a rendezvous in New York for December 20 to discuss Brazil's financing plan for 1983. The situation worsened. By mid-December

121

there were shudders in the New York money market when the news spread that Banco do Brasil, state-owned and the country's biggest, needed an emergency injection of funds from New York banks to meets its end-of-the-day currency obligations. Banco do Brasil's cashbox was empty and the New York branch needed $300 million in overnight money to meet its commitments. The problem arose repeatedly in the following days. The whole question of interbank lines became critical in Brazil's rescue plan.

Langoni and Galveas met with 125 bankers at the Plaza Hotel on December 20. They proposed a four-point program: a jumbo credit of $4.4 billion in new money (about 7 percent of the banks' $59-billion exposure), a rollover of $4 billion on an eight-year basis in medium-term credits falling due in 1983, a restoration of trade credit facilities to the level of $8.8 billion, and a restoration of interbank lines to their June 30 levels. The last point proved the most difficult. Brazil finally settled for a return to $7.5 billion, about 85 percent of June 30 levels. Interbank lines had sunk to $5.5 billion.

The Brazilian proposal prompted a discussion of interbank lines. Many criticized the "abuse" of these credits. The purpose of interbank lines, reasoned the critics, is to keep excess liquidity employed. Banks who have more money than they can use lend it to banks who need more money than they have. Brazilian banks, which are active in financing trade, needed a lot, and Brazil came to count on having this foreign exchange available as "working capital." But the whole point of short-term lines is their short term. They can disappear overnight, and did. Brazil insisted that it did no good to safeguard its medium-term credits unless these short-term credits also were assured. But linking short-term lines to medium-term credits defeated the purpose of having short-term lines. They, too, became medium-term commitments.

The argument was ontological. It was tantamount to the medieval debates about how many angels could fit on the head of a pin, but bankers took this debate as seriously as scholastic theologians did theirs. Money is money, and someone who needs it is not picky about where it comes from. There was a good deal of hypocrisy in the criticism. Many countries, including industrialized countries, routinely relied on interbank lines to cover shortfalls in external payments. France was a prime example. Its big state-owned banks always carried big currency liabilities.

The interbank debate got so prickly that Brazil, in cahoots with its bank steering committee and the IMF, embarked on an unprecedented program of blackmail to bring recalcitrant banks into line. Many banks, particularly in Europe, had responded to peer pressure to reschedule medium-term loans. But they felt, reasonably enough, that interbank loans were their own business. Brazil decided to rip the veil of confidentiality off of interbank dealings. When interbank pledges were still lagging by February, Brazil and its big bankers took to publishing the lines country by country, bank by bank. There was no rest for the wicked. The printout showed June 30 lines, rescue plan targets, and the difference, plus or minus, in current lines. West German and French banks emerged as particularly remiss. The computers at Bankers Trust crunched numbers overtime to produce the tabulation of 500 banks each week beginning February 2.

Jacques de Larosière passed the first batch out to a stupefied group of central bank chiefs, urging them to get on the phone to their commercial banks. Citibank vice president William Rhodes burned the wires with threats, cajoling, and begging to muster U.S. regional banks. Pink-faced, the Europeans fell into line, except for Italian, Swiss and Spanish banks.

This high-level extortion produced a sharp reaction. Fritz Leutwiler, the governor of the Swiss National Bank and president of BIS, warned in London about central bank pressure on commercial banks in this matter. By depriving commercial banks of their freedom of action, the central banks took over a good deal of the responsibility for these credits and for Brazil's creditworthiness.

In the first panic, the question seemed academic. If Brazil defaulted, the central banks were on the spot anyway as lenders of last resort to keep banks from collapsing. Better to avoid the default, central bankers reasoned, by pressuring the banks now to keep the money flowing. Later, the normal post-panic reasoning set in. What was so scary after all? Bad business for central banks to get mixed up in credit decisions. Leutwiler may have had reservations all the way along. But he put up the BIS rescue loans and made public statements about cooperation. Much of the backtracking afterward was designed to transfer the responsibility back to the commercial banks.

Treasury Secretary Regan took Brazil's problems to his meeting with the other Group of Five finance ministers in Kronberg, West Germany, December 9. Afterward, Brazil made its pilgrimage to Basel for a $1.2-billion BIS loan. The United States put up $500 million; fifteen other countries provided the rest. Brazil might still be different, but it was tying up what had become a standard rescue package. De Larosière attended the Plaza Hotel meeting with the bankers and explained the IMF program. He wielded his big stick a bit more softly, because by now the bankers understood well enough their self-interest.

The IMF program itself was surprisingly easy on living standards in Brazil, partly because the government had anticipated the normal IMF prescriptions and imposed austerity on its own. Horst Struckmeyer, the IMF official who headed the mission to Brazil, went on national television to explain the program in fluent Portuguese. The IMF seal on a slow-growth policy prompted the leading business magazine, *Exame,* to headline a "Farewell to Megalomania."

There was room still for a little megalomania. The IMF package totaled $6 billion, the biggest ever. Brazil qualified for a $4.9 billion stand-by credit in three tranches, and two tranches from the Compensatory Financing Facility worth $1.1 billion. The main IMF requirement was to cut overall government spending by 2 percent in real terms. State-owned agencies and companies were to cut investment 20 percent in real terms (ending their megalomania at least). The plan targeted a budget deficit of 3.5 percent in 1983, after 6 percent in 1982.

The bankers mulled over Brazil's plan during the Christmas holidays. To focus their minds, Delfim and crew played one more card before calling it a year. Just before New Year's, Brazil sent out telexes notifying its creditors that it would not pay over any installments on principal in the first two months of 1983. By March 1, Brazil expected to have a rescheduling agreement for the year and did not want some creditors to have gotten money when others would not be receiving any. The Romanian gambit recast as the Sambatorium (see Notes). Langoni asserted that the action was taken in consultation with the bank steering committee and was not a moratorium, all appearances to the contrary notwithstanding. It was an "operational procedure." He went so far as to promise that the due payments would be kept safe for the banks and would be paid over on March 1 if there was no rescheduling agreement. But then, he added ominously, they would have to find some other way to rearrange Brazil's 1983 finances. The implied threat was "Your money or your money." Play the game your way with contracts and agreements, or . . . play it another way.

Langoni, a thirty-eight-year-old native of Rio de Janeiro, was the point man for most of Brazil's debt rescue. He traipsed to Washington for the talks with Regan, Volcker, and De Larosière, and to New York, London, Frankfurt for conferences with commercial and central bankers. Brazil numbered 1,400 commercial banks and twenty-nine central banks among its creditors.

As with some earlier cases, the first problem the banks had was tabulating their exposure to Brazil. Was the loan from a West German bank through its Luxembourg subsidiary to the Brazilian subsidiary of a German multinational a Brazilian risk? Some cases were even tougher. Suppose the Düsseldorf or Munich headquarters of the multinational had deposited funds with the Luxembourg bank subsidiary in the same amount as the "loan" above. Suppose further that the "interest" on this loan paid by the Brazilian subsidiary to the Luxembourg bank is passed on to the German headquarters of the subsidiary, minus a small commission for the bank. In fact, the interest payment represents the repatriation of profits, disguised in such a way as to evade Brazilian taxes. Well, should the Luxembourg bank, or its West German parent, count that loan as part of its exposure for the 7-percent solution? Hard questions like these kept the banks busy until February 25, the Friday before Langoni's March 1 date. Deadlines, it seems, do work.

In New York, 169 banks agreed to lend Brazil $4.4 billion over eight years and to roll over the $4 billion in 1983 principal repayments for the same maturity. The interbank lines were up to $7.1 billion, still short of the target, but the banks had overshot on trade credits, anteing up $10 billion instead of the requested $8.8 billion. The next Monday, February 28, the IMF board, seeing the bank package in place, approved its credits to Brazil.

There was a lot of grumbling by bankers about how "unfriendly" the Brazilians were. There was no end to their tricks. For instance, Brazil made its $590-million order for nine Airbuses, the medium-range airliner made by a European consortium, dependent on a further $280-million Eurocredit, ostensibly for the purchase of airport navigation equipment. The demand hit Europeans where it hurt in Airbus's perpetual struggle to steal a march on Boeing.

The Brazilians overreached themselves, though, when they took the fight into the central bank camp. They tried, in their iconoclastic fervor, to *postpone* repayment of a BIS loan. It may be all well and good for overly impetuous commercial banks to eat a little crow and reschedule their imprudent loans, but to suggest that the Bank for International Settlements, the central bankers' central bank, should reschedule was a penetration into the Holy of Holies. The central bankers did give Brazil two weeks to come to its senses, delaying the first repayment to March 15 from March 1. But then a chastened Brazil dutifully reimbursed $400 million of its BIS loan.

Three months later the same problem arose. This time the IMF held up the second installment of its credit because the agency was not satisfied that Brazil was keeping the targets set in its letter of intent to the Fund. Brazil argued that the BIS bridge had to extend a little farther, because it was supposed to be paid back with the IMF money. The central bankers wisely decided to grant Brazil a month's grace on the $450-million payment due at the end of May. The IMF was flexing its muscles by delaying Brazil's money. But BIS President Leutwiler was not worried about the IMF coming through with the funds, so that the BIS could get its money back. There was "no chance" that the IMF would actually suspend the Brazilian credit, the Swiss told an inquiring journalist at the BIS's annual press gathering in mid-June. Had he spoken to De Larosière about the matter? "You better believe it," snapped Leutwiler in idiomatic English.

Meanwhile it became clear that Brazil would need another $2 billion or so in 1983, due partly to the continuing failure to maintain interbank lines at the desired level. Fed chairman Volcker met with officers of six big New York banks (the usual crowd) to discuss the matter. The message seemed to be that the Treasury and the Fed had given all they were going to give and any solution was up to the banks. Talk of a moratorium wafted through the air. The crisis, it seemed, was not quite over.

Delfim was very worried about his trade surplus. January's trade produced a timid $55-million surplus. So Delfim gave a great yank on the devaluation lever, cutting the cruzeiro's value by 23 percent. It was the first maxi-devaluation since 1980, and it sent private Brazilian enterprises into shock. They had been encouraged by the Brazilian Government to borrow abroad; suddenly their debts were 30 percent higher (there are always two sides to a devaluation coin, depending whether you start from the devalued currency's base or the other's). Two weeks later, the government came up with some aid to alleviate their losses. The devaluation achieved its goal, though. In March Brazil reported a $514-million surplus, just the right amount to rack up $6 billion for the year.

7

The falling dominoes finally toppled Venezuela. A founding member of OPEC, Venezuela had been riding the crest of its oil exports even before the 1973 oil shock. The debt shock jolted it back to reality. Venezuela managed its debt sloppily. Nowhere was the confusion in figures greater. For a while, the public external debt was given out at $18 billion, a different order of things from that in the MBA countries. It later emerged that the debt was probably double this figure.

Before anyone could get jumpy about oil-rich Venezuela in the wake of Mexico's moratorium, Caracas took the unusual step in September of consolidating the foreign currency holdings of its state agencies as central bank reserves. The central bank also revalued its gold holdings from $42 an ounce to $300 an ounce. The two measures lifted Venezuela's official reserves from $6.1 billion at the end of August to $17.4 billion. Caracas made the point that its foreign currency assets practically offset its foreign currency debt.

The oil price lurched downward, OPEC imposed production quotas, and Venezuela's revenues fell off target. Finance Minister Luis Ugueto woke up to the fact that nearly half of Venezuela's

127

borrowings were short-term, due within a year. He proposed conversion of about $9 billion short-term debt into medium-term loans, on a voluntary basis. To underline the volitional character of his proposal, Ugueto set generous margins for the new loans, 1 to 15/8 points above Libor, for maturities ranging from two to seven years. While Ugueto was launching this modest proposal, the comptroller-general, Mañuel Rafael Rivero, let the cat out of the bag with his estimate of public debt at $35 billion.

Bankers put Venezuela on a back burner. Their hands were full. Ugueto resigned at the end of November. Venezuela had always been sloppy about making payments on time. In the nervous New Year, this mattered. The Hong Kong branch of Nordic Bank Ltd., a London consortium bank owned by several Scandinavian banks, got a New York court to attach some assets of the Venezuelan development agency in New York. The agency, Corporation Venezolano Fomento (CVF to its friends and creditors), missed a $2.6 million payment to Nordic on a credit it had guaranteed for a Venezuelan hotel developer. Other banks quickly joined in the suit. Could this be the disaster scenario in the making? Venezuela's new finance minister, Arturo Sosa, stepped in and said the government would make good on $81 million in CVF debt arrears. The agency had also missed a $15-million payment on a syndicated loan in its own name.

The government had to put out other fires. The huge trade union bank, Banco de los Trabajadores, had fetched up in November with an inexplicable $200-million gap in its books. A government commission took over operation of the bank. Eventually the government felt compelled to liquidate the bank and take over its external liabilities. Three state-owned banks also caused difficulties in the market, requiring government action.

The worst was yet to come. Venezuelan reserves had dropped from $20 billion at the end of 1981 to the $6 billion in August. After September's cosmetic application, the newly constituted reserves continued to seep away. Capital flight, always a steady stream out of Venezuela, swelled to torrential proportions. An estimated $6 billion flowed out of the country in the six months following the September reserve measures. By mid-February currency was leaving the country at the rate of $150 million a day. Sosa

128

broke off a trip through Europe rekindling interest in the $9-billion refinancing. On February 20 Venezuela shut down its foreign exchange markets for the first time in nearly twenty years. They remained closed for a week while Sosa debated with central bank president Leopoldo Díaz Bruzual. The latter wanted a straight devaluation on the order of 40 to 45 percent. The government opted instead for a split rate, to soften the impact of devaluation. The old rate, 4.3 bolivars to the dollar, was kept for debt repayments and essential imports. A new fixed rate of six to the dollar applied to other normal imports. A free rate applied to luxury imports and foreign travel. The free rate came to 7.4 bolivars when the market reopened.

Venezuela hemmed and hawed its way through the remainder of 1983, not wanting to negotiate seriously before the elections at the end of the year.

LENDERS OF LAST RESORT
CHAPTER SIX

———∞———

1

A coterie of white men from rich countries run world finance. That is a statement of fact, neither sinister nor provocative. The word "coterie" comes from the feudal practice of assigning a fief to a group of peasants. The fief in this instance is the world's money. The group of peasants are the central bankers and international monetary officials. Western governments play the role of the feudal lord. Even the modern meaning of coterie, "a social circle," can stretch to cover the clubby gatherings of financial officials.

These men think alike. Their views are orthodox—the same as those of the men running the commercial banks, the investment banks, and many of the big corporations. They believe in money. They believe that man should be free to earn, to save, and to invest his money. Self-interest motivates the marketplace, which magically allocates resources in the most efficient manner. Wealth is created. The rich get richer, but so do the poor, which does not exclude their getting relatively poorer.

This like-minded group of people is bound by an ideology as strong as any other. One French commentator referred to the "bankers' international," modeled after the Communist International. The International Monetary Fund is the world secretariat for this "International." It fronts for the big governments and big banks who control the world's money.

None of this is necessarily sinister. Rhetoric can stack the cards one way or the other. The fact remains that an inbred, homogeneous cabal controls the world's money. The debt crisis in 1982–83 demonstrated that their grip on money was much stronger than the oil cartel's hold on petroleum reserves. They came out on top, at least for the time being.

These men move in their careers through various functions. They know each other well. This is not at all bad. It allows for certain individuals to develop a wide expertise and immense personal authority. In times of crisis, the long and close association enables these men to act quickly.

In fact, the group that dealt with the debt crisis was forged in the currency crisis at the beginning of the 1970s. George Shultz, who later became Reagan's secretary of state, was secretary of the Treasury. His undersecretary was Paul Volcker, who subsequently became president of the powerful New York Fed and then chairman of the Federal Reserve Board. Helmut Schmidt was West German finance minister, and later, of course chancellor. His state secretary was Karl Otto Pöhl, who went on to become president of the West German central bank, the Bundesbank. The French finance minister was the future president, Valéry Giscard d'Estaing. These men formed the Library Club after an early meeting in the White House library to deal with the collapse of the postwar currency system in 1971.

The chumminess of international finance prompts formation of a number of clubs and groups. The most important of these in coping with the debt crisis is the Group of Ten, or G-10 in shorthand. That is the grouping of the ten member countries in the IMF who command a majority by virtue of the agency's weighted vote—the United States, Britain, France, West Germany, Japan, Italy, Canada, Netherlands, Belgium, and Sweden. Switzerland, which is not a member of the IMF, was long associated with the G-10 and formally joined in 1983, making it the Group of Eleven. The first five make up a subgroup, the Group of Five, G-5, which is actually the locus of decisionmaking. One could almost speak of a Group of One (G-1?), the United States. So heavy is the preponderance of the United States in the world economy and the dollar in world finance that no decision can be taken by the G-5, the G-10, or the Interim Committee (see below) or the whole 146-nation IMF without the consent of Washington.

The oligarchic tendencies of the United States were acknowledged by Fritz Leutwiler, the longtime president of the Swiss National Bank. Leutwiler has a reputation among journalists for indiscretion. He and the Swiss National Bank represent Switzerland in the Group of Ten. In a typically frank interview with *Fortune,* Leutwiler commented that the United States seemed to prefer consultations on the Group of Five level. "For some years now," he said at the beginning of 1983, "all that has been done at the meetings of the Group of Ten is to elect a new chairman and adjourn."

Donald Regan stirred up a diplomatic hornet's nest when he suggested that the seven economic summit countries meet after the OECD ministerial meeting in May 1983 to discuss linkages between trade and finance. France objected, claiming that such a meeting "institutionalized" the economic summits. The French boycott was embarrassing because the meeting was held in Paris. Regan did refer in Paris several times to the "Group of Seven." Seven seemed a much more manageable number than the unruly twenty-four industrialized countries grouped in the OECD (not to be confused, of course, with the Group of Twenty-four—see below).

When the system of fixed-rate foreign exchange rates collapsed in the early 1970s, the IMF formed a Committee of Twenty to deal with the problem, consisting of the G-10 and ten poorer countries. With the oil shock, this group was institutionalized as the Interim Committee, becoming the policymaking body of the IMF in between annual meetings. Technically it is an advisory group to the Board of Governors, which are the finance ministers of member countries. Because the committee did not deal very effectively either with the currency problems that called it into being or the recycling problems of the petrodollar era, one member, New Zealand Prime Minister Robert Muldoon, has witheringly observed that "the response of the committee to the new problem [oil prices] was to change its name."

A general rule of thumb with these groups is that as the numbers get higher the influence lessens. Moving along, there is the Group of Twenty-four, a steering committee composed of developing countries in the IMF as counterweight to the G-10. But it has neither the political nor financial weight of the G-10 within the IMF or anywhere else. Third World countries in the interim committee form a Group of Nine, which by now has eleven members.

The Group of Thirty has no direct connection to the IMF, although it is chaired by H. Johannes Witteveen, the IMF managing director preceding Jacques de Larosière. It is a private group which provides more ammunition to those fond of the Rockefeller "conspiracy" theory. It is in fact funded by the Rockefeller Foundation as a successor to the Bellagio Group, a Ford Foundation project in the 1960s and 1970s. The new group, inevitably known as G-30, brings together active and retired bankers, central bankers, and public officials to confer on financial matters and publish reports. Its influence derives from the considerable personal authority of its members, but in the end its direct effect on events is nil.

Separate from all this is the Group of Seventy-seven, the LDC clique in the United Nations which now numbers more than 120. The Group of Seventy-seven is a political group formed in connection with the United Nations Conference on Trade and Development. It gave birth in 1972 to the Group of Twenty-four to deal with questions on monetary affairs and debt relief.

In addition to the groups, there were the debt rescheduling clubs, so called to emphasize the noninstitutional nature of their deliberations. The London Club, the Hague Club, and, by far the most prominent, the Paris Club consisted of representatives of industrialized country governments who met with debtor nations to grant some relief on the "official"—that is, government-to-government—debt. The Paris Club handled most of the cases. There was no clubhouse—the group met in a conference center—and, technically speaking, no secretariat, although the French Treasury performed this function.

The Paris Club first met in 1956 to reschedule Argentina's official debt, and continued through the years under a succession of French officials. The chairman at the outbreak of the 1982–83 credit crisis was a likable civil servant, Michel Camdessus, who described himself as "impassioned" on the subject of developing-country debt. But Camdessus was the first to realize that this new debt crisis was completely out of the range of the Paris Club. The problem was not official debt, but the commercial bank debt. It was the bank steering committees, not the government clubs, who ran the show in these reschedulings. The Paris Club continued throughout the crisis to process those small, mostly African nations, who had no bank debt but who got caught up in the backwash of the credit crisis and needed to reschedule their official debt.

The BIS itself is often called a central bankers' club. The Bank holds monthly meetings in Basel that often are quite convivial. The central bank governors who attend these meetings wear two hats. The Europeans are members of the policymaking BIS board, who with the addition of North American and Japanese representatives become a G-10 forum. Switzerland, which is big in the BIS, did not formally belong to the G-10 because the Swiss have never joined the postwar international organizations—the IMF, the World Bank, or even the UN.

The BIS also sponsors a group known formally as the Basel Committee on Banking Supervision and Regulatory Practices. It is commonly known as the Cooke Committee, and brings together bank regulators from the G-10 countries plus Switzerland and Luxembourg under the chairmanship of the Bank of England's Peter Cooke.

Central banks have never been so prominent as in the past few years. Or rather, central bankers. A French magazine profiled the governors of the leading central banks under the heading "The New Money Masters." Paul Volcker, Gordon Richardson, Karl Otto Pöhl, Fritz Leutwiler became media personalities. They gave speeches, granted interviews, moved markets with their observations about the financial weather. They are the headliners at bankers' conferences. Theirs are the hands on the faucets of money and credit. They can flood the world with that wonderful elixir, or turn the faucet off and make the world choke.

Who are these men and who gave them that power? Not a generation ago, they moved in the obscurity proper to arcane technicians who fine-tune the credit machine. Faceless, they moved noiselessly about their task. In fact, they cultivated anonymity, shied away from the press, reveled in their quiet influence. They were men of numbers, not men of policy. Bookkeepers, they were not large-minded in their outlook. In the extreme, they were the nonentities described by economist John Kenneth Galbraith as "men who could not reliably be trusted to balance their own checkbooks." For the most part, they were what onetime Crédit Lyonnais chief Claude Pierre-Brossolette termed a "big zero."

There is less than meets the eye behind the silver hair and navy-blue pin-striped suits of central bank governors. What has changed in recent years is their environment. The one-two punch of collapsing Bretton Woods system and oil-price shock has placed new demands on these same men. The dam crumbled under the weight of the flood, disrupting the quiet life of the village in the valley. Sandbaggers that they are, the central bankers have been swept along with the flood, white hair and all.

Central banks like to appear rocklike in their stability. Sober, conservative men staff them. They cultivate the appearance of competence and power. But central banks make mistakes. The most prestigious of them, the Bank of England, badly muffed the secondary banking crisis in the early 1970s, and had to launch a lifeboat for several fringe banks. The West German Bundesbank angered the whole banking world with its precipitous closure of Bankhaus Herstatt in 1974, which rocked the financial system at the time and betrayed a remarkable lack of savoir-faire in the bank's governor, Karl Klasen, and the other directors. Further back in history, the U.S. Federal Reserve is widely held to be partly responsible for the Great Depression because it kept money tight when the country was gasping for liquidity.

Finance ministers, too, have enjoyed a new vogue in times of financial stress. Time was, not so long ago, that most Americans would have been hard put to tell the difference between the secretary of the Treasury and the other person who signs dollar bills, the Treasurer of the United States, a largely nominal position. The Treasury secretary, like finance ministers in other big Western democracies, has traditionally been a key figure in the arcane world of government budgets. The new fragility of state finance has heightened the importance of that traditional role. Meantime, the sequence of disturbances in international finance has thrust finance ministers into new prominence.

The past several years, in fact, have brought a shift in the locus of international relations. High diplomacy—complete with foreign ministers, ambassadors and the United Nations—has kept its importance, but receded from public attention as financial problems put the spotlight on a different stage. Finance ministers, central bankers, and the IMF now are seen on the front pages of newspapers rubbing shoulders with their eminent colleagues from high diplomacy. Monetary crises and conferences are media events. Central bankers, grouped in the Bank for International Settlements, and finance ministers, who make up the board of the International Monetary Fund, were on the spot when the debt crisis broke.

Nothing demonstrates the muddle of the world's financial system better than the fact that neither international lender of last resort was meant to be that. The two candidates for the role of monetary savior, the IMF and the BIS, were given modest objectives when they were founded. The IMF was supposed to coordinate postwar economic policy. That boiled down to smoothing out adjustments in a system of fixed exchange rates. When that system collapsed once and for all in 1973, the IMF was theoretically out of a job. The BIS had even more limited goals. It was established in 1930 to help European governments collect war reparations from Germany. The Hoover moratorium and Hitler's repudiation of reparations deprived the BIS of its *raison d'être*.

Bureaucracies are amazingly resilient when their existence is at stake. Both institutions bided their time, waiting and watching. The BIS grew into the central banks' central bank. The IMF staked out balance of payments adjustment in the wake of the oil shock. When the debt crisis of 1982–83 broke, both bureaucracies offered well-oiled multilateral machines for injecting large sums of money and even larger amounts of confidence into a shaky financial system.

2

The Bretton Woods conference in July 1944 set up the system of fixed exchange rates that regulated the postwar monetary system. It also established two international organizations to fulfill special functions. The International Monetary Fund was to maintain equilibrium in international payments and trade. It was to serve as a forum of discussion and cooperation to prevent the vicious spiral of faltering payments and collapsing trade that ushered in the world-wide depression in the 1930s. The International Bank for Reconstruction and Development, which came to be known as the World Bank, was to finance recovery from the war and provide long-term funding for economic development.

John Maynard Keynes, easily the most influential economist in the twentieth century, was one of the architects of the Bretton Woods institutions. He was not completely happy with the result. A witty man, he pointed out that the two should swap names. The Fund functioned more like a bank, clearing payments surpluses to cover deficits. The Bank was in reality a development fund, drawing its funds from capital subscriptions and long-term bond issues.

The World Bank had a high profile in the altruistic postwar generation. Decolonialization and development were popular. The IMF remained unknown in the United States. The organization could prompt virulent denunciations and even riots just by sending an expert "mission" to a developing country, but it was a nonentity in the rich countries. One former British executive director of the Fund got so tired of explaining his job at Washington cocktail parties that he began telling people he was with the World Bank. That they had heard of.

It seemed the most natural thing in the world. There it was, a potent, funded international organization responsible for maintaining order in the world monetary system. A lender of last resort made to order. The International Monetary Fund had the money and the mechanics for shuttling around the huge sums needed to rescue Mexico, Brazil, and Argentina. It had the men and the expertise to make sure the money helped get countries back on the straight and narrow of fiscal responsibility. It had the political weight and authority of 146 nations. It had the confidence of the world's bankers.

It seemed so natural for the IMF to leap into the breach of Third World insolvency that the startling originality of the move was overlooked. A scant half-dozen years before Mexico's moratorium, the IMF would not have had the means or the will to function as a lender of last resort. Only in 1974 did the Fund decide to extend its credits beyond a twelve-month period. Only in 1981 did it lift the amount of potential credit to 450 percent of quotas. Without this extra maturity and extra amount, the IMF loans would have appeared woefully inadequate to turn the tide of confidence. Even with these resources, only De Larosière's bold move to blackmail the banks into new credits made the loans work.

Up until the debt crisis of 1982–83, the IMF had a relatively modest role. It tided countries like Great Britian and Italy over oil-price-induced payments deficits in the mid-seventies. It chided some industrial countries for running up big budget deficits or devaluing their currency in order to increase exports. It made small loans to small countries whose problems were scarcely noticeable to the world at large. The banks noticed that it was easier to get these small countries to behave properly when the IMF took the heat. They kept that in mind as the situation got hotter and debt problems got bigger—Zaire, Peru, Turkey, Poland (they wished Poland were in the IMF).

The IMF is not a development institution. When the Fund went out on a limb and made its biggest loan ever to India in 1981, a chary U.S. administration slapped the agency's wrists. India had hardly exhausted other sources of credit. New Delhi took cheap money for dubious purposes—much was made of a subsequent purchase of jet fighters from France. The IMF reasoned that major shifts in economic factors, like the huge increase in energy prices, led to structural problems in economies that affected a country's balance of payments. Adjusting to these structural problems required more time than simply bringing payments into equilibrium. Also, this adjustment would be easier if the country started before the problem was acute. In short, the IMF poised itself to be a lender of *first* resort for medium-term structural adjustment. India's position was not acute, but the Indian loan was a model of the IMF's conception of its post-oil-shock role.

Critics said the IMF was just desperate to find a new job. In theory, the absence of fixed exchange rates meant that payments imbalances would sort themselves out quickly enough. Devaluations became shadowy, since major currencies were not really pegged to anything anymore, and minor currencies do not really count. The free-market Reagan administration did not see any need for a lender of first resort, certainly not in the form of an international bureaucracy.

Then came the debt crisis. In the summer of 1982, U.S. officials still played down the idea of an increase in the IMF's quotas. Quotas determined the amount of money members put into the agency. These were reviewed every five years and generally were increased. The eighth quota review was due in 1983 and talk had already started in 1982. The United States felt that the IMF had enough money to continue making small loans to small countries. If any big industrial countries ran into trouble, they could turn to the General Arrangements to Borrow, a 1962 agreement among the G-10 countries to pool as much as $7 billion for any G-10 country that needed it. It was the formation of the GAB, in fact, that established the G-10.

By the time the 1982 IMF annual meeting took place in Toronto on September 6 to 9, the atmosphere was different. Debt shock prompted calls for urgent new increases in IMF resources. At a stroke, the Fund seemed an indispensable lender of *last* resort.

Central banks are usually lenders of last resort. They still have money when everyone else has run out. They have it because they print it; they have, in that sense, an unlimited supply. The classic function of a lender of last resort is to feed money to banks when there is a run. The idea is not to transfer piles of money or an unlimited amount of credit, but, by making those resources available, to stymie the lack of confidence that leads to a run.

The IMF was a lender of last resort only in a derivative sense. For one thing, it was making loans not to banks who were running out of money, but to countries which had run out of money but still owed some to banks. In the end, it amounts to the same thing. The IMF kept the banks from going broke by injecting liquidity into the system. The banks would not have gone broke without the new liquidity, but a default by major borrowers would have created big accounting problems. Uncertainty alone could have started a run on the banks, either by the banks themselves, or at the good old-fashioned teller's window. The IMF loans were key in quelling any incipient panic. In that sense, at least, the IMF functioned as a lender of last resort.

But the Fund had one big problem in playing that role. It cannot print money; it does not have an unlimited supply of money or credit. It is a creature of its members. The IMF's credibility as a lender of last resort depended on its having adequate resources.

As the debt shock sent out its ripples, and country after country made its application to the Fund for money, it became apparent that resources which had seemed adequate in the summer of 1982 were no longer so. The Fund had lendable resources of about $26 billion in October 1982. The large loan commitments to Mexico, Brazil, and Argentina and a slew of sizable loans to other members reduced that sum to nearly $10 billion by early 1983.

By the annual meeting in Toronto, the United States had already softened its position. The Mexican Weekend had awakened Treasury officials to the magnitude of the problem. The U.S. delegation in Toronto conceded the need for a quota increase, but urged a small one. In addition, the U.S. Under Secretary of the Treasury, Beryl Sprinkel, suggested an emergency fund to cope with urgent problems like Mexico. Other countries, including those in Europe, were suspicious of the U.S. proposal. They feared the United States would try to get out of the quota increase.

The deliberations at Toronto were inconclusive. Succeeding weeks brought a deterioration in the debt situation. More countries needed help, bankers became more nervous, and scare talk made its way to the front page. Growing anxiety galvanized the big countries into action. Sprinkel met with the other G-5 "deputies," the number two or number three officials from the finance ministries and central banks, in November in Washington.

The firefighting fund proposed by the United States was institutionalized as an expansion of the existing General Arrangements to Borrow. The United States came closer to the European position of a 50-percent increase in quotas from its original insistence on a 25-percent maximum increase. The G-5 ministers convened at the Schloss Hotel Friedrichshof in Kronberg, near Frankfurt. The ornate hotel, the former palace of Kaiser Friedrich III's widow, is a frequent venue for distinguished gatherings. On a rainy December day, the Group of Five tried to iron out the differences. One delicate point in increasing quotas was to enlarge the quotas of Japan and West Germany to reflect the increase in their economic weight.

The United States, citing always congressional resistance to "foreign aid" programs, fought a rearguard action. The Administration seemed to brandish Congress in the same way Third World politicians sometimes waved the IMF—the stick driving them to do what they wanted to do anyway. But time was running out. Each new rescue package drained IMF funds and weakened its credibility. On January 18 the Group of Ten ministers met in the conference center on Avenue Kléber in Paris—the same building used for Paris Club meetings—to approve the GAB expansion and discuss once again the quota increase. The G-10 was directly responsible for the GAB. The ministers decided to increase the facility to $19 billion from $7 billion. Even more significant was the decision to make these funds available to any IMF member when, as in Mexico's case, a major disruption of world finance seemed imminent. Before, the GAB was open only to the G-10 countries themselves. The widened access effectively added $19 billion to the Fund's resources in bailing out developing countries.

The decision on quota increases at the IMF itself belonged to the twenty-two-member Interim Committee. Their meeting, originally scheduled for the end of April, was moved up to February 10 to 11 in Washington. De Larosière hosted a dinner for the group at the F Street Club. Treasury Secretary Regan held out until midnight, maintaining that the maximum increase in quotas should be 40 percent. The compromise was 47.5 percent, which translated into $32 billion, bringing the new total in quota subscriptions to $99 billion. The GAB and quota increases together added a full $50 billion to IMF resources. The amount of lendable funds was somewhat less because part of the quota increases would come in the form of national currencies. Only convertible currencies are useful for loans, though. De Larosière told a press conference following the Interim Committee meeting that the measures practically doubled the agency's lending resources.

Regan and his Treasury minions still talked a lot about the difficulty of getting congressional approval for the combined $8.4 billion the United States needed for its share of the increases. But the $2.6 billion for the U.S. share of the GAB increase was like a line of credit. It would have to be provided only when drawn. The $5.8 billion for the quota increase was not a budget expenditure, but an asset transfer. The government carries its credit with the IMF on the books as an asset. Still, as Regan pointed out in numerous appearances on Capitol Hill, the government had to borrow the money to transfer to the IMF. Augmenting the federal government's borrowing requirement, it was like an addition to the federal deficit. The IMF quota increase became a political pawn. Congress tied its eventual approval of the increase to tighter controls on the international activities of American banks. As Congress delayed its approval, the IMF itself, ironically, had to go to the BIS for a bridging loan. But the European central banks, exasperated with U.S. delays, dug in their heels and refused any loan until Congress approved the quota increase.

It turned out that congressmen had no difficulty in following the money's path from the IMF to the debtor countries to the banks. They readily saw that the IMF was functioning as a lender of last resort. The charge flung by Representative Fernand St. Germain and Senator William Proxmire and others was that the IMF was "bailing out" the banks. No amount of ingenuity by Federal Reserve Board Chairman Paul Volcker and other government witnesses about how IMF packages "bail in" the banks by forcing them to go along could change the fact that IMF liquidity enabled debtor countries to pay interest so that banks could avoid write-offs.

The IMF urged its members to hurry with approval of the quota increases so that they could go into effect by the end of 1983. The previous quota increase, approved in 1978, was not effective until 1980. The Group of Thirty, worried about this time lag, urged the IMF to borrow the money in the capital market. Otmar Emminger, the former head of the Bundesbank, chaired a G-30 study group which strongly urged this action on the IMF. The market had been practically salivating for IMF bonds since the agency began expanding its lending facilities in the mid-1970s. But the Fund had preferred to go directly to its members for supplementary funds. This fit in better with its status as a cooperative association. The G-30 proposal was not warmly received. IMF officials feared that commercial banks would be all too happy to buy up IMF bonds and excuse themselves from making further loans to developing countries, so that the IMF would become the chief intermediary for recycling.

The Brandt Commission also weighed in with a recommendation

for the Fund to borrow in capital markets. The independent panel chaired by Willy Brandt, the onetime chancellor of West Germany and Nobel Peace Prize laureate, had published a long report on North-South relations in 1980. The group was formed in 1977 at the suggestion of Robert S. McNamara, the former U.S. defense secretary who became the longtime president of the World Bank. The 1982 debt crisis prompted the group to reconvene. The commission met in December in Ottawa to approve a new report. This time the recommendations were not so sweeping, but instead were very concrete. The panel singled out finance as the most critical issue in North-South relations. At the top of its list for remedial measures was the doubling of quotas in the IMF, a new allocation of Special Drawing Rights (SDRs), increased borrowing from members' central banks and surplus countries, and borrowing from the capital market.

The Fund was willing to go again to one member that had funded it before. Saudi Arabia had agreed in 1981 to lend the IMF 4 billion SDRs each year for two years, with an option to extend another 4 billion the third year. There were a number of pilgrimages to Riyadh on behalf of the IMF as the agency scurried to replenish its resources. French Finance Minister Jacques Delors made an often-postponed trip to Saudi Arabia in December. He talked about bilateral matters, including a loan to France, but also about further support for the IMF. Delors was chairman of the Group of Ten. In January Sir Geoffrey Howe, Britain's Chancellor of the Exchequer, a suitably quaint title for England's finance minister, went to Riyadh in his capacity as chairman of the Interim Committee. Following the January 18 Paris meeting, where it was announced that Saudi Arabia would probably contribute to the expanded GAB as well, Bank of Italy deputy governor Lamberto Dini journeyed to the Saudi capital to fix the details. Dini, a well-traveled monetary expert, was chairman of the G-10 deputies.

The headquarters of the International Monetary Fund on H Street in Washington is not exactly palatial, but it is certainly handsome. A covered atrium in the middle of the thirteen-story structure makes a decisive impact on a visitor coming in the front entrance. The terrace restaurant on the ground floor of the atrium matches a Roman piazza in elegance. The menu is refined, with a pronounced French flavor and a Continental penchant for meals that go well with wine. In fact, the IMF cultivates an ambiance that welcomes premiers and finance ministers in the style to which they are accustomed. The building, with its elegance and attention to detail, contrasts with the generally functional design of the U.S. Government buildings in Washington. The IMF is cosmopolitan, a plush version of the United Nations.

The lord of this manor during the debt crisis was managing director Jacques de Larosière. A fastidious, well-groomed man, De Larosière wears metal-rimmed glasses. He dresses like the well-paid bureaucrat he is. He can and does turn on an effective Gallic charm for visitors to his spacious office. The general consensus among his colleagues at the IMF and earlier acquaintances from his days as director of the French Treasury seems to be that "he is not a nice man." He may be the most effective director the IMF has ever had.

The IMF prefers to style itself a "catalyst," rather than a lender of last resort. The IMF-approved stabilization program has often been compared to a Good Housekeeping seal of approval. As with any good brand-name product, you know what you're getting. The IMF's $30 billion or $60 billion of lendable resources hardly makes a dent in Mexico's $80-billion debt, let alone the half-trillion dollars of developing-country debt or the $2 trillion of Euromarket bank liabilities. But because other sources of funding depend on the IMF program, the lending agency mobilizes much vaster resources. Governments in the Paris Club or in bilateral debt reschedulings or rescues, central banks alone or through the BIS, and commercial banks always peg debt relief or new loans to a critical debtor to adoption of an IMF program. Even as a catalyst, though, the Fund needed ample resources. De Larosière spoke repeatedly of the "critical mass" of funds the IMF needed to back up its programs.

The true lenders of last resort remain the central banks, and ultimately the political authority behind them. The U.S. dollar remains the preponderant currency in the Euromarket and in international transactions. Only one central bank in the world can create dollars. It became clear to world monetary officials in the course of the debt crisis that the Federal Reserve is ultimately *the* lender of last resort. If the international monetary system starts to dry up, only dollars will keep it alive. And the only source of dollars is the Fed. Johannes Witteveen, a genial Dutchman who headed the IMF during the main recycling period of the 1970s, understands this point well. Witteveen keeps his hand in as an adviser to Amsterdam-Rotterdam Bank and head of the Group of Thirty. In October 1982 Witteveen reminded an audience in New York's Hotel Pierre: "The needed liquidity in case of crisis will for the largest part consist of dollars. . . . In the end, in a serious crisis, the problem may in this way converge on the Federal Reserve, the only central bank system able to create the necessary dollar liquidity."

The IMF, the BIS, the G-10 are all simply institutionalized ways of coordinating the Fed's relations to other central banks. As long as this coordination functions, the only uncertainty that remains is whether even the Fed can "lend" enough dollars in the last resort to stop a genuine, full-fledged worldwide financial panic. The Fed can manufacture an infinite number of dollars, but at some point even the belief in the dollar will snap. Then there is no lender of last resort. The world goes bust.

3

The other natural candidate for international lender of last resort was the Bank for International Settlements. The BIS is an anomaly, a very rich anomaly. It was established in 1930 to clear German war reparations. Belgian, French, British, German, and Italian central banks, together with a group of private American banks led by J. P. Morgan, founded the bank in Rome. Hardly a year was out before the central banks' central bank had to cope with the collapse of the Austrian bank Creditanstalt, which set off a wave of bank failures across the world and, in the opinion of many historians, turned a bad recession into the Great Depression. Ten thousand banks failed in the United States, and Franklin Roosevelt had to declare a bank holiday.

The 1932 annual report of the BIS had a surprisingly contemporary ring. "In rapid succession, the Bank for International Settlements was called upon to grant emergency credits to the National Bank of Hungary, the National Bank of Austria, the Reichsbank, the Bank of Yugoslavia and a temporary advance to the Bank of Danzig." Fifty years later, Hungary and Yugoslavia were again in line, and Mexico or Brazil could substitute for Germany. (Danzig, a free German city at the time, is now Gdansk, where the independent Polish union Solidarity was born.)

The BIS loans did not stop a financial disaster in 1931 and were not instrumental in preventing a crisis in 1982. The loans were "bridging" loans of a few months' duration. They were made for the most part against gold collateral or with guarantees from Western governments. They were not really made by the BIS. The funds came from the major central banks, who constitute the board of directors of the Basel bank. The bank itself was simply a conduit. The central bankers responded quickly in the Mexican case because they were asked to. Their responses got less quick as the cases multiplied and they got cold feet.

The BIS is a Swiss bank. Basel, a distinctive Rhine city where French, Swiss, and German borders meet, is also famous for its zoo and its pre-Lenten carnival. The eighteen-story building raised in 1977 to house the BIS has earned the name "Tower of Basel." Its design has been compared to that of a nuclear reactor.

The BIS seems in some respects to be a men's club for the bureaucrats who run central banks. Their fate it is to have the responsibility for billions and trillions of dollars, but to earn relatively modest salaries and to forswear aggrandizement or corruption. Paul Volcker talks routinely in billions when he discusses money, but as chairman of the Federal Reserve Board he earned $60,000 a year, lived in a small flat in Washington, and commuted home to his family in New York each weekend. Other central bankers are better paid, but hardly well-heeled by private-sector standards. Karl Klasen, the Bundesbank president who closed Herstatt in 1974, complained of his huge salary cut when he moved from the top management position at Deutsche Bank to take the Bundesbank post. But the Bundesbank president had a higher salary than the chancellor.

For these poor rich men, the BIS is a perk. They gather practically every month to discuss weighty matters like interest rates, exchange policy, and, for a good part of the fall and winter 1982–83, international debt. Much of the Basel tower remains empty most of the year. Each of the dozen directors has a huge office, with space for a secretary. The bank maintains a plush sports center outside the city. The central bankers dine sumptuously in converted chateaus in the area. A French writer, sensitive to the culinary overtones, speculated, "Who knows whether gold won't finally make its reentry into the international monetary system between the *turbot sauce hollandaise* and the *chevreuil aux myrtilles.*"

Such clubbiness does fashion an old-boy network. The central bankers put together their $1.85-billion loan for Mexico on the phone over the weekend. The fact is that in the crunch the only effective lender of last resort is the national central banks. The BIS is simply a convenient place to catch them all together. It is an effective coordinator and the perfect instrument for handling the mechanics of international lending. Like the IMF, the BIS is a shield that depoliticizes the involvement of individual central banks. The United States kept out of the BIS loans to Hungary. Britain avoided the Argentine loan. Such nuances are easily clouded over when talking about a "BIS loan."

Bundesbank President Pöhl told a Basel audience once that their city was like a "second home" to central bankers. "The chances for discretion are greater," he added in cryptic praise.

The BIS is a *private* club. There are no press conferences at the monthly meetings. The devoted press corps that covers central banking waits in lobbies and bars to buttonhole a participant. The rare press communiqué consists of a single mimeographed sheet—no printed letterhead, no fancy graphics—with a lapidary sentence or two: "27th January 1983—The Bank for International Settlements, Basle, announces the conclusion of an agreement with the Banco Central de la Republica Argentina under which the BIS is providing a bridging loan to the Banco Central of U.S. $500 million. In making this loan the BIS is backed by a group of its member central banks and by the U.S. monetary authorities." Short on details.

To render its doings even more opaque, and to indulge a pronounced idiosyncratic streak, the BIS balances its books in Swiss gold francs. This nominal currency, a holdover from prewar days, is worth $1.94, valuing gold at $208 an ounce. The BIS balance sheet at the end of fiscal 1982 (March 31) was 19 billion of these gold

147

francs, or about $37 billion. Practically all of this consisted of deposits from central banks which the BIS invested short-term in the Euromarket. The Bank is actually a private bank, although central banks hold a majority of the shares.

The $4.55-billion spate of loans—$1.85 billion to Mexico, $1.2 billion to Brazil, and $500 million each to Hungary, Argentina, and Yugoslavia—in the 1982–83 debt crisis marked an unusually vigorous involvement of the Basel bank. It was not completely unprecedented, though. In the preceding decade the BIS had given bridging loans to Portugal, Turkey, Belgium, and Sweden, and a whopping $3 billion to Britain in 1977.

By the time Yugoslavia came along with its request for $500 million over three years, if not sooner, the central banks felt overtaxed and their sense of urgency waned. Leutwiler told a cozy group of forty prime ministers and cabinet members gathered in the mountain resort of Davos, Switzerland, for the annual European Management Forum that the BIS was "tired" of providing bridging loans.

4

The World Bank is no such thing. It is not a bank, but a development agency. It makes loans for long-term economic projects. Developed countries' governments subscribe the capital, and private investors in the industrial countries buy World Bank bonds. The proceeds from bond issues are the funds lent to developing countries for specific projects. The official title of the World Bank is the International Bank for Reconstruction and Development. The name is unwieldy but more accurate. Pedants prefer to call the Bank the IBRD as a concession to acronymania.

When Harry Dexter White originally proposed an international bank for consideration at Bretton Woods, he had ambitious plans for a genuine central bank that would hold reserves and issue money. What emerged was much more modest. In its first phase, right after the war, the World Bank made loans, for reconstruction, to European countries. When the Marshall Plan came along, the Bank turned to Latin America. As countries and regions develop, partly through the Bank's efforts, they are "graduated" into the commercial market, and the Bank turns its attention to the next poorest class. After Latin America came Asia. Africa seems the likely focus for the 1980s.

After decades of a higher profile than its more arcane sister institution, the IMF, the World Bank felt upstaged in the debt crisis. If it was true, as everyone was saying, that it was a liquidity crisis, then the Fund was obviously the proper organization. But World Bank president A. W. Clausen, the former head of the world's largest commercial bank, Bank of America, made the point whenever he could that the World Bank had its role too. "Since the Third World debt problem will not finally be resolved without a recovery of Third World development, the Bank's support for development—although its effects are not as immediate—is just as urgent and vital to the solution of the problem as is the Fund's support for adjustment," he said in early 1983 to an audience at Harvard.

Clausen came to the World Bank abuzz with ideas of how to get commercial banks more involved with the lending agency's work. He had pioneered co-financing between private banks and the World Bank while still at Bank of America. It emerged in the course of the crisis that one of the great dangers was commercial banks' withdrawing from developing-country credit. Clausen saw a ready-made opening for the Bank. By getting banks in on World Bank loans, Clausen felt he could calm the private banks. Everyone agreed that the amount of financing necessary for continued development in the Third World had to come from the commercial banks in the end.

Co-financing, such as it was, consisted of banks' making loans on the same project as the World Bank. The Bank never financed a project completely; some local financing was always necessary. Commercial banks began taking over larger chunks of project loans. But the credits were not directly linked, only parallel. In January 1983 the World Bank announced a pilot program in direct co-financing. In addition to direct loans for a project, the Bank was going to participate in a commercial consortium. There were three versions. In one, the World Bank would join a commercial bank syndication to extend loan maturities. The commercial banks sign on for their normal seven, eight, or ten years, and the World Bank will add one or two years by waiting until the end for its repayments.

A second version is for the Bank to step into a loan if market interest rates go above the fixed rate granted to the borrower. The borrower would continue to make payments in the same amount, but amortization would not be completed on time because a greater portion of the payment would go for the higher interest. The Bank would step in at the expiration of the original loan and finance the remaining principal payments. In short, the Bank takes the sting out of interest-rate risk. Both borrower and lender can keep to planned schedules, with the Bank filling in any gap. This would alleviate the effects of sustained high interest rates like those preceding the 1982 crisis. Third, the World Bank gives a guarantee for later-maturing portions of a loan, again to encourage longer maturities.

In all three cases, the commercial banks continue to benefit from the Bank's careful vetting of promising projects, as in traditional co-financing. But the banks also benefit from the World Bank's moral authority as lender. The Bank always boasts it has never had a default, because no developing-country borrower would dare alienate the most potent development agency. The idea is that no loan involving the World Bank itself would be rescheduled, let alone repudiated. Another benefit is the extension of maturities. Much of the liquidity crisis in 1982 was due to "bunching" of maturities—a lot of debts falling due in a short space of time.

The World Bank allotted only $500 million for its pilot program, which was to last a year or two. A month after launching this experiment, the Bank announced a "special action program." Mainly this meant accelerating disbursements of funds for credits already approved and for increasing the Bank's portion of the project finance. Many loans in the pipeline were held up in the wake of the debt crisis because there was not enough complementary financing. The speedup was to cost $2 billion extra in two years. Altogether, the two measures were worth $2.5 billion—a drop in the bucket in view of the Third World's financing problems. The Bank hoped that its catalytic role would multiply the good effect of its measures. It obviously intended, too, to keep some momentum in developing-country loans with a push from its announcements.

The World Bank's other contribution was to step up its "structural adjustments loans." This innovation dated to 1980. The World Bank departed from its normal practice of making loans for specific projects like granaries and roads to make a medium-term balance-of-payments loan—the type of unsecured loan that got the commercial banks into trouble.

In all, the World Bank's effect as a lender of last resort remained marginal. Any positive effect from its efforts was offset by the difficulties in funding its soft-loan affiliate, the International Development Agency. The United States, courtesy of David Stockman, stretched out its new contribution to IDA over four years instead of the planned three. This reduced its 1982 contribution to $700 million from $1.1 billion. Terms of the agency's loans to very poor developing countries were so "soft"—i.e., easy—that they amounted to a giveaway. Maturities were fifty years with no interest. Repayments started after ten years and there was a service charge of 3/4 percent a year. Clausen's scramble to get the sixth round of contributions finished and to start people thinking about the seventh mostly added to the gloom about Third World loans.

The World Bank did function as a beacon of sorts nonetheless. Its conservative lending policies—loans outstanding cannot exceed subscribed capital—and its carefully maintained triple-A credit rating earned it a lot of goodwill. It was living proof that Third World lending could work. The World Bank even turned a nice profit, $598 million in fiscal 1982. Only professed ideologues like *The Wall Street Journal* remained skeptical. "How many of its borrowers," asks a *Journal* editorialist of the Bank, "could maintain their perfect repayment records if they had to earn their way instead of getting fresh infusions of capitalist money whenever they began to experience some difficulty."

The editorial touched on a sore point. The IMF, BIS, and World Bank may function as surrogate lenders of last resort in the international banking system. But their loans operate on a system similar to the last in, first out (LIFO) system in accounting. These international organizations may be the last to lend, but they are the first to get paid back. This caused more than a little annoyance to commercial bankers when De Larosière or various central bankers would jawbone them into providing new loans and rescheduling old ones.

151

Sovereign borrowers dare not defy the international organizations in such a way.

When Brazil timidly suggested it might postpone its repayment on the BIS bridging loan—after all, postponement was the order of the day—the Basel Bank threw up its conservative hands in horror and granted only a two-week respite for wayward Brazil to repent and repay. The World Bank's proud boast that it has never had a default or a rescheduling is due to a self-indulgence permissible only to a government-backed organization. Commercial bankers had to listen to lectures about solidarity, but the World Bank assigned itself a privileged position. The Bank simply declared by fiat that its loans would be repaid on time or else there would be no more loans. It is a holier-than-thou hypocrisy that got under the skin of reflective commercial bankers. They dared not complain out loud, though. When commercial banks were pressed to supplement Brazil's rescue package with more new loans, there was some muted grumbling that perhaps the World Bank, too, could wait a few weeks for its money.

Both Bretton Woods institutions figured prominently in any plan to solve the debt crisis. De Larosière seemed to relish his new role as world credit coordinator. He counseled commercial banks to put up a total $20 billion in new credits to developing countries in 1983. This represented an increase of 7 to 8 percent over 1982, compared with the 20 percent annual rate of increase in the foregoing decade. This, the Fund had calculated, was the amount needed from the banks to cover the Third World's minimum financing needs during the year. The whole world became a rescue program. Mario Henrique Simonsen, a former Brazilian finance minister who had always been sympathetic to the Fund's orthodox policies, even recommended that the Fund formally take charge of all Third World lending, setting guidelines for commercial bank loans to each country. The more elaborate schemes to convert bank loans into long-term bonds (see Chapter Eleven) invariably drafted the Fund or the World Bank into service.

Gordon Richardson was not so sure. The Bank of England governor had presciently warned about the banking herd's stampeding out of certain countries in a speech in Bonn in December 1981. In February 1983, just before taking his peerage into retirement, Lord

Richardson issued another warning in his valedictory to the Overseas Bankers Club in London. Lenders of last resort have no business in everyday affairs. "In looking ahead to more normal conditions, it is also, I think, plain that neither banks nor central banks should come to consider it part of the ordinary working of the market for the authorities to play as direct a role as has recently been necessary in the search for solutions to the current debt difficulties. Nor, I think, should it be the natural order of things that the programs of the International Monetary Fund be made strictly conditional on firm commitments by banks to provide specific amounts of new money."

"AND WHO'S GOING TO BAIL OUT THE U.S.?"

CHAPTER SEVEN

———∞———

1

The debt crisis of 1982–83 was not confined to the Third World. The liquidity problems of huge developing-country borrowers, loudly discussed by bankers and bureaucrats, seemed the most dramatic. They probably were, too, in terms of short-term risk. But debt problems in the industrial countries mushroomed as well. More nebulous, less urgent, these problems were more serious in the long run.

Industrial countries seemed to have lost control of their spending and were forced to borrow massively to pay their bills. Developing countries contracted debt to "develop." Developed countries contracted debt to maintain their standard of living. Both borrowed more than they could ever pay back.

At the same time the backbone of industrialized society, the large multinational corporations, became more fragile. Large and well-established companies came to the brink of bankruptcy, prompting extensive rescue efforts. These extreme cases, though, reflected increasing corporate reliance on debt, which itself taxed the whole financial system of the industrialized countries.

And all of this—the Third World debt, the national debts of industrialized countries, the corporate insolvencies—weighed so heavily on the banking system that it threatened to crumble.

Debt played a big role in toppling the government of Helmut Schmidt, the most popular chancellor West Germany ever had. Debt disrupted the enthusiastic plans that François Mitterrand's Socialist Party had for rejuvenating the French economy. Debt justified draconian budget measures and partial suspension of democratic processes in fat countries like Belgium and the Netherlands. Less dramatically, perhaps, debt brought down at least one Italian government in 1982.

These countries do not need to have the same problem as a Brazil or Mexico. What counts for developing countries is the external account, denominated in the real money of convertible currencies. West Germany and France, and to a certain extent other European countries, issue convertible currencies. At first, their debt problem came in the form of deficits on government spending. The governments spent more than they collected in taxes. But when they spend a lot more, the problem spills over into the external account, and becomes a currency problem for these countries in the same way it did for Brazil or Mexico.

Far and away the most serious problem was in the United States. The country that issues the dollar has a peculiar debt problem. It has an unlimited supply of the ultimate convertible currency. The regular increases in the national debt ceiling, set at $1.389 trillion at the end of May 1983, seem like a formality. A national debt of this proportion seems a fiction, a bookkeeping necessity that has no impact in the real world. But it does, and the Reagan administration adopted a fiscal policy that promised to add mind-boggling sums to unreal numbers. It was financial overkill, a megadebt as difficult to think about as the unthinkable dimensions of nuclear arms.

President Reagan, who came into office promising to balance the budget in 1984, ended up projecting a budget deficit of $210 billion for fiscal 1983, three and a half times the deficit of $60 billion racked up in the last year of the Carter administration and eight times bigger than the highest deficit passed by big spender Lyndon Baines Johnson. Wall Street guru Henry Kaufman warned repeatedly about the crowding-out effect on interest rates. Not only would the rapacious borrowing needs of the U.S. Treasury in the coming year reduce the amount of saving available for other borrowers, thus keeping interest rates high, but the *expectation* of the future borrowing would dampen investment plans right this minute. The whirring confusion of big numbers gave the whole discussion an aura of unreality. The message was clear, though: big deficits mean high interest rates mean weak recovery.

Perhaps the best way to indicate the dimensions of the U.S. debt problem is to point out that 12 percent of the $850 billion budget for fiscal 1984 was earmarked for interest payments on the national debt. That represented two fifths of the amount allotted for military spending. It also represented more than $100 billion. The interest payments on the U.S. national debt for one year came to more than the accumulated external debt of either Mexico or Brazil!

The debt instruments of the U.S. Treasury are almost by definition the least risky investment there is. The same is true, for West German investors, of the bonds and bills issued by the West German government, for the British of gilts, as government bonds are known there, and so on for other countries. A default or repudiation is difficult to countenance, and what else short of revolution could make the government unable to honor its obligations? Governments after all do not go broke. Especially not the governments of rich, sophisticated industrial countries. The guarantee for a sovereign borrower is its taxing power. If it needs more revenues, a government raises taxes. The ultimate security is the wealth-generating capital held by the government.

It is practically inconceivable that the federal government of the United States, or the central government of the United Kingdom, or West Germany, or France would go broke. It was at one time practically inconceivable that a big, rich city like New York, the very financial capital of the world, could go broke. But it did.

2

The effective default of New York City in 1975 gave the world of government debt a new perspective. The biggest city in the Western industrial countries, the cultural and financial capital of the biggest Western power and for much of the rest of the world, New York stood for success, money, power. The spectacle of the home of the world's largest capital market choking for lack of funds was a windfall in symbolism for Marxist commentators at home and abroad chronicling the crisis of capitalism.

New York Mayor Abraham Beame asked plaintively at the time, "Would the French disown Paris? Or the British allow London to become insolvent? Would the Soviets abandon Moscow?" It was weak rhetoric, ignoring the obvious differences in political and social structure, but the statement conveyed some of the underlying irony and pathos of the great city's bankruptcy. A Democratic city should *not* go bust during a Republican administration. East Coast Democrats should not have to beg at the door of Middle Western Republicans. New York willy-nilly went bankrupt under an unfavorable political constellation.

Once New York's immediate crisis was over, the most significant legacy of the incident was its exposure of the vulnerability of governments. Garnished as it was with a powerful tax base—$100 billion in business turnover, $80 billion in property, 8 million residents—New York nonetheless went broke by consistently spending beyond its income. All theories of taxing power notwithstanding, the city simply could not recoup an accumulated debt of $13.6 billion and it could not persuade financial markets to increase the debt. Nor could it suddenly make do with just its income. It was President Gerald Ford who drew out the implications of New York's collapse. With uncharacteristic insight, he concluded a speech to the National Press Club justifying his denial of aid to New York with the following observation: "If we go on spending more than we have, providing more benefits and more services than we can pay for, then a day of reckoning will come to Washington and the whole country just as it has to New York City. And so, let me conclude with one question of my own: When that day of reckoning comes, who will bail out the United States of America?" The question seems rhetorical perhaps, but New York's collapse demonstrated that even the unthinkable can come to pass.

By the time the credit markets for New York dried up in March 1975, the city needed to borrow half a billion dollars a month to keep going. City accountants juggled figures, fudged estimates, cre-

157

ated dubious financing agencies to keep creditors and legislators at bay. But by the spring of 1975, nobody would buy New York City's notes, and the bankers stopped bidding for the underwriting mandate. In a ghoulish precedent for the sovereign debt crises of 1982, the big New York banks formed a steering committee of senior executives to deliberate how to rescue New York from outright default. Citibank, Chase Manhattan, Morgan Guaranty, and most other big banks in New York—already pressed to the wall by losses on their real estate investment trusts and corporate bankruptcies like W. T. Grant—could ill afford to write off the $1.2 billion of New York paper they held for their own account.

The problem went beyond New York. Altogether, estimated the Securities Industry Association, twenty-nine U.S. banks held New York securities worth more than 50 percent of capital funds. Nine banks faced insolvency in the event of a New York default, and eighteen would be severely damaged.

Felix Rohatyn, a partner at Lazard Frères & Co. whose chief claim to fame was his role in creating the conglomerate International Telephone and Telegraph, got involved in the rescue effort that would make him a national celebrity. Rohatyn suggested to New York Governor Hugh Carey that a Municipal Assistance Corporation be formed to issue bonds for the city's finances and take responsibility for its fiscal administration. The state legislature created "Big MAC" in June and authorized it to borrow up to $3 billion on behalf of New York. Sale of the first billion met high resistance, and the banks had to buy half the amount themselves. Prices fell so much in secondary trading that further public issues of MAC bonds were excluded.

In August the state itself, with some grudging support from the banks, subscribed a further $1 billion. In November the state, which had taken control of the city's finances by means of the Emergency Financial Control Board, declared a forced moratorium on $1.6 billion of the city's short-term notes. Holders were offered the alternative of swapping the notes for MAC bonds. The drastic step gave the Ford administration an opportunity to soften its no-aid-without-default stance. A forced moratorium was near enough to default that Washington authorized $2.3 billion in loans over three years to help New York "adjust." The city's pension funds also had to ante up for MAC bonds, selling off other holdings at a loss to buy the MAC paper.

The state officials and businessmen on the Emergency Financial Control Board pared back city services even from the minimal level they had reached in the course of the crisis. Layoffs and budget cuts reduced levels of all services, from police and fire protection through schools and subways to garbage collection. In addition to a total of 40,000 city jobs that were lost, the constriction of the public sector cost thousands more jobs in the private sector. Rohatyn predicted at the time of the rescue that New York City would undergo "the most brutal kind of financial and fiscal exercise any community in the country will ever have to face."

New Yorkers suffered not only the costs and inconveniences of the rescue, but found themselves politically disenfranchised. Elected city officials had little say in directing the city's affairs. The state, businessmen, and bankers determined the course of the city's budget. Staten Island Borough President Robert Connors drew a telling analogy when he said that Mayor Beame had "all the power of the mayor of Paris during the occupation." The ultimate vulnerability in the case of financial crisis seemed to be more political than financial. The banks, which had earned and continued to earn substantial profits handling the city's debt, emerged relatively unscathed. What suffered extensive and partially irreparable damage was the freedom of New York's residents to determine their own priorities. It is true that political malfeasance was at the root of New York's financial problems—a Democratic machine had been too willing to buy social peace with money it did not have. But the question arising from New York's crisis, and subsequent cases of government liquidity crises, is to what extent democratic processes are expendable to reestablish financial equilibrium.

3

The decade after the first oil shock was hard on industrial countries. Except for the United States, and eventually Britain, most industrial countries do not produce their own oil. The higher price of oil ate up a higher proportion of export earnings. The almost continual state of recession in the wake of the oil shock slowed economic growth and trade worldwide. Inflation reduced the value of money. The normal consequence of all this would be a decline in the standard of living, resulting from a reduction in disposable income. But many industrial countries tried to avoid such a decline by borrowing. They reasoned that the problem was temporary and they could afford some indebtedness until things returned to normal. The advertising executive suddenly out of a job will borrow to keep up the payments on his East Side co-op, confident that a new job will come along soon so that he can go on living in the style to which he is accustomed.

First, the government runs a budget deficit. This results from the combined effects of higher unemployment benefits and lower tax revenues in a recession. Also, many governments try to fight unemployment directly by enlarging the government and hiring more people. For the generation of policymakers schooled in Keynesian economics, a budget deficit is the classic response to a recession or sluggish growth. The government stops the spiral of contraction by running up a high debt.

Each shortfall in the annual budget is covered—financed—by borrowing. The government can tap national savings through the domestic credit and capital markets. If the deficit is too big for the size of the domestic market, the government can borrow abroad, from the Euromarket or from huge capital markets in New York, London, Frankfurt, or Tokyo. A succession of big deficits can lead to a huge accumulation of debt. Before long, debt service becomes a big budget item in its own right.

A country also experiences another kind of deficit. It is the type that the big developing-country debtors ran into—a deficit on the current account of its international payments. This comprises merchandise trade, services, and various kinds of transfers like pension payments, migrant worker remittances, and tourism. It is essentially the accounting for all exchange of goods and services with the outside world. It balances when a country sells as many goods and services to the outside world as it buys. If the country buys more than it sells—imports more than exports—the current account is in deficit. In the end, though, all bills have to be paid. A country has to cover its shortfall in foreign currency. To do that, it can spend the reserves of foreign currency it has accumulated. Or it can attract foreign companies to invest in the country. Or it can borrow. Most countries borrow to finance at least part of their current account deficit.

The current account balance includes the trade balance. The current account is essentially a wider definition of a trade balance. The second component is sometimes referred to as "invisible" trade, to distinguish it from tangible goods and services. A country like West Germany, the world's largest exporter, runs up huge trade surpluses because it exports far more than it imports. But that surplus is partially offset by the large sums German tourists spend abroad (they spend more in absolute terms than any other nationality) and by the funds migrant workers send home, both of which constitute invisible trade. France, on the other hand, imports far more than it exports, but recoups some of the foreign exchange through the large number of tourists that visit the country each year.

A country can have two deficits to finance—a domestic one in the budget, and an external one on the current account. Borrowing abroad can kill two birds with one stone. A government can raise the money it needs to pay its bills, and at the same time get more foreign exchange to cover the current account deficit. The two deficits are clearly distinct. Foreign exchange to finance a current account deficit can come into the country any way. A private company or bank can borrow. Eventually the foreign currency winds up in the central bank because it is used to purchase the domestic currency. In a developing country, even a large one like Mexico, the government so dominates the economy that it carries on both functions simultaneously and almost exclusively. Also, a developing country usually has very little domestic savings to finance the government deficit, so that most government borrowing is abroad. An industrial country has a much more sophisticated economy. The lines are not so clear-cut. In the end, it comes down to the same thing. The government can accumulate a huge national debt through a series of budget deficits. It can also run up a huge foreign debt by borrowing to cover its budget deficit and, if necessary, the country's current account deficit.

New York is not a foreign country, but it is as big as some European countries in population and economy. The city's financial

161

problems illuminate the problems of sovereign borrowers in general. Because New York is not "sovereign" it does not issue its own money (although some of the city's tax anticipation notes had as much backing as confederate dollars—they were only worth the paper they were printed on). Sovereign countries can print money to cover their budget deficits, but this leads to bigger problems when inflation gets out of hand. Sovereign countries face the same basic constraints as New York did. This is especially evident in small countries.

Denmark has a smaller population than New York City, 5.1 million compared to the city's 8 million, and a smaller gross domestic product, or income, $66 billion (1980) compared to about 8120 billion. By 1982, Denmark had compiled a total debt of 229 billion Danish krone, or about $26 billion. More than half of that, about $15 billion, was foreign debt. The government's spending deficit was running about 12 percent of gross domestic product. This compares to the 3 to 4 percent the International Monetary Fund aims at for its developing-country clients in their stabilization programs.

Denmark is an old, rich country, but it lived beyond its means from the time of the oil shock. In the mid-1970s the Danish government had hardly any debt. The 1982 figure accumulated over seven years of spending more than was earned. The deficits were largely attributed to the social policies of the Social Democratic premier, Anker Jorgensen. Voters install Social Democrats because of these policies. In 1982 Danish voters decided it was time to get the debt under control and elected a center-right coalition. The new government froze wages, prices, and dividends, suspended indexing of wages for two years, and targeted a reduction in the budget deficit as a proportion of gross domestic product. But the measures were not too severe; the deficit was only trimmed from 13 percent in 1982 to a planned 12 percent in 1983 (compared to Mexico's IMF-mandated cut from 16 percent to 8.5 percent).

In December the Standard & Poor's credit-rating service put Denmark on its "Credit Watch," usually a prelude to cutting the rating. In January, S&P cut Denmark's rating from triple-A to double-A-plus, the first time a Western European country had borne any rating other than triple-A. The governor of the Danish central bank, Erik Hoffmeyer, an outspoken critic of the country's

162

reliance on foreign borrowing, got more acerbic toward the end of 1982. The central banker complained that journalists reduced the debt problem to the simple question of whether Denmark could get another loan. The answer is always "yes," he said. "This is like the drunkard who asks if one more drink will kill him," added Hoffmeyer.

There was talk of Denmark going to the IMF. There were whispers of default. But Denmark made a beeline for the market early in January 1983. It had diagnosed the psychology of the market properly. Bankers had redlined Eastern Europe and Latin America. Asia was taking it easy. A Western European country seemed like manna to starving international lenders. As a concession to its indebtedness, Denmark accepted somewhat higher margins for its interest charge. The original $1-billion credit was raised to $1.3 billion.

Across the Strait, Sweden put Olof Palme's Social Democrats into power once again. But the leftist government immediately devalued the Swedish kroner massively, by 16 percent. The move, which marked a sizable drop in Swedish standard of living but made Swedish exports cheaper abroad, stunned the rest of Europe, particularly Sweden's Scandinavian neighbors. The Swedish economy, twice as big as Denmark's, dominates Scandinavia. Sweden is a member of the Group of Ten, but broke the club rules with a competitive devaluation. The International Monetary Fund remembered its original function to monitor exchange rates and rushed to Stockholm with a catalog of twenty-seven questions on the devaluation. The Palme government announced a budget of the "third way," neither deflationary nor expansive but a bit of both. The budget, which froze prices and raised wealth and value-added taxes, tilted decidedly toward deflation.

Sweden's foreign debt of $14 billion, the same as Denmark's in an economy twice the size, was not yet worrisome. But the planned 90-billion-krone budget deficit, $12 billion, still represented about 8 percent of GDP (gross domestic product—a slightly different measure than GNP). The government did cut some subsidies to weak industries like steel. In foraging for savings, the Social Democratic government prevailed upon King Carl Gustaf to forego his

"Guadeloupe pension." The payment, which came to 300,000 krone, or $40,000 a year, dated back to the Napoleonic wars, when French Field Marshal Jean-Baptiste Bernadotte was made King of Sweden and turned against his former fellow officer, Napoleon. After Waterloo, England won possession of Guadeloupe, a tiny French island in the Carribean. The generous conqueror awarded the island to Bernadotte, now called King Carl XIV. Later, the forces of diplomacy moved England to give Guadeloupe back to the French (who are the proud possessors to this day). Rather than play Indian-giver, though, England saw to it that King Carl received an indemnity of 24 million French francs. But Sweden even then had foreign debts to pay. The parliament impounded the francs, but at the insistence of the king, who claimed that Guadeloupe had been a personal gift and not for the kingdom, the parliament granted a pension to the royal family in perpetuity. Perpetuity came to an end in 1983. So the Guadeloupe pension, which arose from debts in the early nineteenth century, fell victim to deficits in the late twentieth.

Political debate throughout northern Europe focused on deficits and debts. These countries, heir to the Social Democratic tradition, had built up generous social benefits during the years of postwar growth. The recession made many of these benefits too expensive. In Belgium, Wilfried Martens, a conservative, formed his fifth government to take a firm stand on Belgium's deficits. Government spending topped three fifths of gross domestic product, and the deficit was 16 percent of GDP. The nation of 10 million had borrowed $15 billion abroad. To avoid the political wrangling normally entailed in a country divided by two languages and a plethora of parties, Martens had parliament authorize his government to bypass normal legislative procedures to impose deflationary measures. The ploy was effective, but hardly reassuring in the matter of democratic principles.

Neighboring Netherlands also voted in a hard-line conservative government to cut budget deficits. The country's large reserves of natural gas shielded it from the worst financial effects of the oil shock. But the consequent failure to adapt industrial plant and consumption habits in line with new energy costs came to be known as "the Dutch disease." The gas formed a protective bubble, but the bubble would burst the day the gas ran out, leaving Holland dangerously exposed. The Netherlands avoided excessive foreign debt, thanks in part to a good-sized capital market of its own, but government deficits had grown to nearly 12 percent of GDP.

The Irish Republic reached a per capita foreign indebtedness higher than that of Mexico or Poland. In the national campaign in late 1982, Garret FitzGerald's Fine Gael party and Charles Haughey's Fianna Fail tried to outdo each other in belt-tightening proposals. The lot fell to FitzGerald, who came out with the standard tax boosts and spending cuts. Ireland followed the Scandinavian lead of getting into the market early. Its $300-million "jumbo" was more suited to the size of its economy, which is about one fourth of Denmark's. Overall foreign debt topped $7 billion at the end of 1982.

The enforced shift across the board to fiscal conservatism gave rise to a lot of comment with moralistic connotations. Small countries were "coming to their senses" after years of "profligate" spending. The fact is, of course, that all these countries were pursuing their own political priorities through democratic means. They could afford to do this for a while. Eventually, though, the dependence of their economies on the outside world meant that external finance played an increasing role in determining their political priorities. Financial propriety did not confine its dictates to tiny countries alone. The most economically powerful countries in the non-Communist world, the seven countries who met annually for an economic summit, each felt the contraint of debt.

4

Italian public finances defy logic to the point that press commentators usually use words like "levitation" or "tightrope walking" to describe them. Italy, after all, was the country that nearly ran out of money in 1976. That was the "liquidity crisis" that inspired Paul Erdman's glib but prescient bestseller, *The Crash of '79*. Italy levitated, turned around its payment accounts, and paid back the emergency loans ahead of time.

This time the Italians raised the alarm themselves. Even Italian governments always fall for a reason, and Italy's forty-second postwar government collapsed in late 1982 when the two ministers responsible for economic policy disagreed violently about controlling Italy's budget deficits. Treasury Minister Beniamino Andreatta, a roly-poly Christian Democrat with a sharp tongue, wanted to cut spending dramatically. Finance Minister Rino Formica, a Socialist, wanted cuts but no drama. The government fell, and Amintore Fanfani's new government presented a budget that imposed such hardships as requiring individuals to pay part of the price of medicine, instead of the national health insurance fully reimbursing them as before, or docking paychecks for the first day of sick leave to dampen rampant absenteeism. The drama came when government and employers began talking about an end to the *scala mobile,* Italy's lyrically named wage indexation. Hundreds of thousands of workers took to the streets throughout the country in riots and protests.

The 1982 budget deficit hit 71 trillion lire, or $48 billion, about 40 percent higher than the targeted 50 trillion, or $34 billion. Without Fanfani's measures, the 1983 budget seemed headed for $70 billion, a deficit that would be high for the United States, which has an economy six times the size of Italy's. In January of 1983, the domestic capital market got so tired of Italian Treasury bills that the Italian Government had to open an 8-trillion-lire line of credit with the central bank, worth $5.5 billion. The central bank credit had no peacetime precedent. Worst of all, because the Banca d'Italia had all its lire invested in those Treasury bills that nobody wanted to buy, new or used, its only source of funds was the printing press.

The Italian central bank likes to think of itself as an island of integrity in the sea of Italy's public sector corruption. Carlo Ciampi, the governor, is a pleasant, quiet person who struggles manfully to fill a job tailored for bigger figures like Paolo Baffi and Guido Carli, his immediate predecessors. Ciampi warned in November that the country's foreign debt had topped $50 billion *net,* which put Italy near the likes of Brazil and Mexico. Italy has a more

166

developed economy than the two Latin-American countries, but no oil or other natural resources. Italy, pleasant as it is, seems to have much more past than future in public finance.

It was in neighboring France that the Mexico comparison inspired a debate that could be termed passionate even in a country devoted to passionate debate. The mushrooming of France's foreign debt in 1982 gave opposition conservatives the political whipping-boy they had been hoping for. François Mitterrand's government was hapless in its economic policy. Eager, after twenty-three years in the wilderness, to effect a *changement* in French society, the Socialists came to power in 1981 and raised minimum wages, lowered retirement age, boosted social benefits. They loosened the exceptionally tight purse strings that outgoing Prime Minister Raymond Barre had held, hoping to spur economic growth. Unfortunately, France wanted to go up while the world's economic merry-go-round was on a downswing. The country did register growth while its European neighbors stagnated or declined, but such disparity among trading partners inevitably lifted France's trade deficit. The weak trade balance led to strong financial pressure against the French franc. Added to the market's aversion to Socialism, this pressure led to three devaluations in the first twenty-one months of Mitterrand's term.

Partly to finance the trade deficit and partly to defend the franc, France borrowed whatever and whenever it could. A *Le Monde* columnist with the *nom de plume* Christopher Hughes started needling the government in a weekly report on the Euromarket. *Le Monde* dropped the bombshell in November 1982 that French foreign debt had grown by $20 billion that year to more than $45 billion. The newspaper gleaned its information from the prospectus demanded by the U.S. Securities and Exchange Commission for a French agency's bond issue. Reading the fine print, *Le Monde* discovered that France was understating its indebtedness in francs by converting its foreign currency liabilities at a rate of 5.75 francs to the dollar, instead of the 6.80 rate then current. Also, the paper felt that the foreign borrowing of big French companies, most of which were owned by the government following Mitterrand's nationalization measures, should be included in the total even if they did not carry an official state guarantee.

Finance Minister Jacques Delors hotly denied the $45-billion figure, but declined to disclose the real one. He pointed out, rightly, that no big industrial countries disclose the amount of their foreign debt. The issue became a political football in the campaign preceding municipal elections in March 1983. Barre and former President Valéry Giscard d'Estaing took to the hustings with claims that France had borrowed as much as $25 billion in 1982, putting it ahead of Canada as the biggest borrower in the world. Delors, lifting the veil of secrecy, said France had borrowed only $8.8 billion. The Organization for Economic Cooperation and Development, the industrial countries' club based in Paris, weighed in with a median $14.5 billion.

The issue became thoroughly obfuscated. *Le Monde*'s redoubtable Christopher Hughes wrote that in addition to publicized credits and bonds, France had raised billions in very private placements in Japan and West Germany. Delors argued that France's claims on other countries offset all but about $7 billion of its external indebtedness. But his assertions met with further skepticism, for one thing because most of those claims were on the very developing countries whose debt problems had alerted everyone to the issue in the first place.

Laurent Fabius, a youthful protégé of Mitterrand's who served a stint as Budget Minister before moving on to bigger things, had kept France's budget deficit more or less to 3 percent of gross domestic product—better than that of most other industrialized countries. France's precarious external payments allowed the country no further room for expanding that deficit if it was to retain any credibility at all in international financial markets.

The country's borrowing needs required that it keep that credibility. In October, France mounted a 160-bank syndicate to raise a $4 billion jumbo Eurocredit to bolster reserves depleted in market intervention to support the franc. There was a lot of murmuring that the French Treasury pressured foreign banks with operations in France to go along with the loan. *The Wall Street Journal* published a cable from the U.S. ambassador in France, Evan Galbraith, himself a former Eurobanker, averring that this was the case. Some significance was attached to the absence of Swiss banks in the syndicate. They have no branches in France, an effective way to prevent

French tax inspectors from getting their hands on sensitive client records; also, it turned out, an effective way to avoid government pressure to join jumbo credits.

More embarrassing was the fight over three standard loan clauses: the *pari passu,* which obliged the borrower not to give a better security on other loans than on this one; the negative pledge, which specifically prohibits gold or other central bank reserves from being used as security in other loans unless this loan also benefits from it; and the cross-default clause, which allows the creditors to declare this loan in default if the borrower defaults on any other loan. France had not had these clauses in a 1974 credit, which was before they became standard, and now felt it below her sovereign dignity to make such commitments. They impugned, somehow, France's honor as a debtor. But the banks had plenty of reason in hand by October for impugning everyone's sovereign dignity, so France finally conceded.

France had given to understand that it would draw down only a third of the $4 billion in the first six months of the credit. By mid-January, it had taken down the whole amount, although Delors said he had not spent it yet. In December, Delors went to Riyadh to negotiate a loan from Saudi Arabia. The exact amount was never disclosed, but it fell somewhere between $2 billion and $4 billion. Still, as speculative attacks against the franc increased prior to the municipal elections, there was open talk that France would have to follow the well-beaten path to the International Monetary Fund. Instead, Delors announced his intention to get a loan from the European Community. By the time he did this in May, he had a battery of new arguments to convince his EC colleagues that France needed and deserved their support. At the end of March, Delors, a waxy-complexioned, sober man marked with a missionary sincerity, had administered a shock treatment to the French. He imposed a program of austerity that included higher tax rates, a "forced loan" for higher income brackets, a special charge to cover the social security deficit, and added taxes on tobacco and alcohol. The stinger was a new restriction on foreign currency for private travel, a measure resembling those taken by the likes of Yugoslavia and Brazil but hardly suitable for the once-great and ever-proud country of Napoleon and DeGaulle.

Until the March program, the government's determination to redress its payments deficit seemed more like a comic opera than the high tragedy promised in this program. In late 1982, the government sought to limit imports of Japanese videocassette recorders by requiring them to go through customs in Poitiers, a historic town far away from any ports, railroads, major highways, or buyers of videocassette recorders. That seemed like a lark compared to a limit of $300 per person per year in foreign exchange.

Once again, hapless France was out of sync. Just as everyone else was ready to start expanding their economies again, Mitterrand and Delors were fiercely deflating. The half of the electorate that romped in the streets the night of May 10, 1981, celebrating Mitterrand's victory, felt they had neither fish nor fowl, neither a conservative government that at least kept business happy nor a Socialist government that offered a true alternative to the restrictive policies of the preceding Prime Minister, Raymond Barre. In May 1983, protests by mostly right-wing students evidenced the tension very close to the surface of French society.

Delors got his loan. The EC granted a credit of 4 billion European Currency Units, called ECUs, which was worth $3.7 billion at the time. The credit came from the Community's "oil facility," a grab-bag category since all European countries except Britain import oil. France got two thirds of the 6-billion ECU authority, which miffed other deficit-ridden nations like Italy. Also, because the EC had to borrow the funds to provide the credit, the French credit forced the Community to double its planned 1983 borrowing to $8.3 billion. "Better you than me" was clearly France's attitude.

5

By the time the Reagan administration careered into its third fiscal year, there was no question anymore of balancing the budget. In fact, it seemed that the deficit had turned into a mad bull elephant, raging out of control. U.S. budget years begin on October 1. Fiscal 1983 began October 1, 1982, and not long after that estimates of budget deficits for the current and coming years went completely out of whack. The final tally for fiscal 1982 came out at a record $110.7 billion, more than double the $45 billion originally projected and nearly double the previous year's $58 billion. The Ford administration had set the previous record at $66.4 billion in 1976.

The target for fiscal 1983 was set at $115 billion, but everyone from the Congressional Budget Office to Henry Kaufman saw the deficit as topping $150 billion. Early in the calendar year 1983, the Administration itself revised its projection. All of a sudden, the fiscal 1983 budget deficit was put at $208 billion. As recently as 1971, the federal government's *total spending* was only as high as that ($210 billion). Not only did the projection give a new dimension to deficit spending, but doubling the original projections marked a new tack in the numbers game played by Reagan's budgeteers. Rather than playing down the deficit, the Administration began shocking the public with numbers bigger than ever before imagined.

David Stockman, the youthful director of the Office of Management and Budget, earned some notoriety in December 1981 when some frank statements of his about Reaganomics found their way into an article in *Atlantic Monthly.* Among other things, Stockman, whose stock in trade was mastery of the federal budget's intricacies, confessed, "None of us really understands what's going on with all these numbers." That storm blew over, but Stockman did not change his ways. Billions of dollars came and went in the budget director's fluid conception of government inflow and outflow. Treasury Secretary Regan opened one early press session on the budget by explaining that 8:30 A.M. had been chosen as the time "to keep Dave from changing those numbers anymore."

Always clever, Stockman adopted a "Montessori" method to get his point across to the President and his advisers. He drew up a multiple-choice decision paper for Reagan to decide which project expenditures to cut back in order to reduce the overall budget by $26 billion. The President had only to tick off the choice. The amount of cuts seems large by itself, but when the Office of Management and Budget can double its projected deficit for the current year from $115 billion to $208 billion without blinking an eye, $26 billion becomes relatively small. Nor does it seem the most thoughtful way to make policy, even from a strictly budgetary point of view, let alone the question of political priorities. A brutally frank report from Alice M. Rivlin's Congressional Budget Office remarked that "marginal tinkering" à la Stockman's decision quiz could hardly make an impact. The CBO's call for "broad strategies" was an understatement.

A chorus of protest from the financial establishment in early 1983 was the response to Stockman's budgeting. Volcker warned that high deficits meant high interest rates, which threatened an economic recovery that was at long last in full swing. The Conference Board, an influential business research group, called deficits in excess of 5 percent of gross domestic product a "time bomb." The National Governors Association pushed for cutbacks in planned military spending and in social security. Testimony before the House Banking Committee evidenced fears that high federal deficits would cut short the recovery in housing by 1984. The Business Council, made up of top corporate executives, said the fragile recovery would collapse unless deficits were brought under control.

Much of this was self-serving posturing. There was open speculation on Wall Street that the Administration was understating the economic recovery in its budget projections so that for once the end result would be better than the forecast. Bankers were keen to cast the deficit as the villain of the piece in the Case of Excessively High Interest Rates, so that the finger of suspicion would not point at them.

Nonetheless that mad bull elephant haunted financial markets like a specter. Government planners foresaw a $300 billion deficit by 1988 unless some action was taken. Martin Feldstein, who came to show some spunk as Reagan's chairman of the Council of Economic Advisers, warned, "The magnitude of the projected possible deficits is far greater than anything that we have known. The harm that such deficits could do is therefore also beyond our previous experience." Regan angered Reagan by privately suggesting tax increases to lift revenues. This was anathema under supply-side doctrine, which taught that tax cuts free funds for investment, which is necessary for renewed economic growth. The Treasury secretary became exasperated with the public focus on money supply to interpret economic policy, especially as the debate about renewing

Volcker's appointment as Federal Reserve chairman gained steam. "The greatest threat to our economic recovery now is the fiscal deficit of the federal government," Regan said in May. "We can have seventeen Paul Volckers in charge of the money supply, but if we continue to have $200 billion to $250 billion deficits next year and beyond, we are not going to get interest rates down."

Donald T. Regan looks the personification of Wall Street. The white hair, tailored gray suits, and monogrammed shirts scarcely conceal a rough-and-tumble trader. He walks, talks, and acts with the self-confidence born of success. Regan became a top executive of Merrill Lynch in the 1950s and helped build it up into America's premier securities group in terms of volume and market. He officially became chief executive in 1971. He set his sights on a cabinet job and got it—later than he planned, but nevertheless.

Regan felt that his years at the helm of Merrill Lynch more than qualified him for the job of Treasury secretary. He sprinkled his public declarations with the expression "after thirty-five years on Wall Street, I certainly know" or understand or realize whatever about international finance. He took umbrage once at a press conference in early 1983 because a columnist had written that Regan had "just discovered" the relationship between trade and finance. "Just discovered," the Treasury Secretary repeated witheringly. "After thirty-five years on Wall Street, I think I understand the relationship between trade and finance."

Knowing and understanding did not come across as Regan's strong suits. Rather, he projected the image of a man of action, a chief executive officer, a decisionmaker. He angrily countered the widespread impression that Federal Reserve Board chairman Paul Volcker or Deputy Treasury Secretary Tim McNamar had been the prime movers in the Mexican rescue package or subsequent crisis management. "Who was working with Paul Volcker all during those international negotiations last year? It was Treasury. Tim McNamar was doing it; he and Volcker were reporting to me. Every single thing they did they got my permission to do. I played the role of the C.E.O., which I'm accustomed to."

Regan irritated European finance ministers, particularly the French, with his high-handed denigration of a report commissioned at the Versailles summit on the effectiveness of foreign exchange intervention. Regan had no second thoughts. "I may be the only finance minister who's ever headed a currency-trading department," he could say, after thirty-five years on Wall Street.

In the debate on the mushrooming U.S. deficit, IMF managing director Jacques de Larosière echoed calls from various foreign monetary officials with his condemnation of budget deficits in general. "A durable recovery will involve rising demands for credit by the private sector and these can only be met if governments reduce their own demands on the pool of available savings." He proceeded to get more particular: "In a number of countries, policies to bring down budget deficits should be set in place as a matter of urgency so that the prospective deficits do not cast their shadow forward in the form of high real interest rates that would hinder the process of recovery. A solution to the budgetary problems of the United States is, in this regard, of very great importance." In the rarefied world of bureaucratic discourse, that amounts to an urgent plea.

Stockman's numbers might have been only diverting, a fiscal *Star Wars*, but for their effect on markets. The main importance of deficits projected for the end of the decade was their impact on investors, traders, and speculators as the long-awaited recovery got underway. Too many hopes were pinned on the recovery to play games with numbers.

More than that, the preoccupation with numbers turned the budgeting process on its head. John Kenneth Galbraith, crusty confessed liberal that he is, underlined the importance of deficits beyond their financial impact. "The problem of the deficit lies deeper than in the fact that more money is spent than received. It lies in the constraints and contradictions that this imposes on other economic policy." Galbraith refuses to let politicians weasel out of their responsibility with pleas of "structural deficits." "All administrations, of whatever political color, must be held firmly responsible for what happens in their own time. Otherwise, one day, some imaginative economist will attribute his failures to the erroneous economic framework established by Alexander Hamilton." (Hamilton was the first Secretary of the Treasury in the newly founded United States, two centuries ago.)

Another unreal number began to take on significance. The national debt always had an unearthly quality about it. It appeared more an abstract bookkeeping position rather than an actual fact. When the national debt crossed the trillion-dollar mark, its ethereal quality increased. Billions are already mind-boggling but at least they are commonly talked about. Trillions are unreal. But the national debt does reach down into the mortal sphere to scoop up interest due. The fiscal 1984 budget earmarked a full 12 percent of federal spending for interest on the national debt. The yawning deficits forecast for the rest of the 1980s guaranteed that debt service would take bigger and bigger shares of overall spending. At the rates projected, the national debt seemed likely to cross the $2-trillion mark as early as fiscal 1986.

The Administration tried various tricks. President Reagan agreed to a "contingency tax increase" if deficits had not fallen below $100 billion per year again by fiscal 1986. The budget team proposed a "limited freeze" on some nonmilitary items to cut projected deficits (more "marginal tinkering"). Reagan himself wanted to stay the course on supply-side economics even though massive defections among his economic advisers had reduced supply-siders to a minority sect. But Reagan stubbornly held out against reducing the planned increases in military spending or in reversing his tax cuts.

Also, for political reasons hardly particular to supply-side economics, Reagan wanted to keep his hands off the Social Security system. Peter G. Peterson, an investment banker and onetime Treasury official, pointed out that the trillion-dollar national debt paled next to the $6 trillion in unfunded Social Security liabilities. Unfunded simply means there's no money saved up to meet those liabilities. Equally unfunded were the pensions for federal employees and the military, amounting to another $1 trillion. Social Security and similar programs in other industrial countries were headed for collapse for demographic reasons alone. In principle, a tax on the active work force pays pensions to retired workers. When the generation of the postwar baby boom retired, though, the tax would become an unconscionable burden on the Pill generation. Benefits and the number of pensioners would be much higher, while the number of active workers would be proportionally smaller. Dates in the twenty-first century seem as remote as numbers in the trillions, even in the early 1980s but Social Security demanded measures to keep uncontrollable trends from getting established.

The United States has the biggest foreign debt of any country, but nobody ever talks about it. The dollar is the world's main reserve currency and main trading currency. Foreign central banks are willing to hold on to dollars as the ultimate foreign exchange. Even though they keep other convertible currencies—the Deutsche mark, pound sterling, French franc—the dollar is by far the most important money they keep in reserve. They do not stack dollar bills in a basement vault. They buy Treasury bills and deposit them with the Federal Reserve. Foreign central banks buy a certain portion of the billions of dollars in notes, bills, and bonds the U.S. Treasury issues to finance the deficit. They hold a sizable portion of that trillion-dollar national debt. At the end of 1982, the amount of Treasury obligations held by foreigners on deposit with the Federal Reserve was $140 billion. That is the minimum amount making up the foreign debt of the United States.

European nations sometimes resent that the United States does not share their need to borrow, but can simply print the world's reserve currency. But managing a reserve currency has problems of its own. The dramatic fall of the dollar in the latter half of the 1970s resulted from a saturation of the market with dollars. The world simply did not want any more, just as, in August 1982, the world did not want any more Mexican debt.

TOO BIG FOR BANKRUPTCY
CHAPTER EIGHT

∞

1

It was perhaps the biggest shock of all. Countries may not go out of business, but companies do. More of them went out of business in 1982 in most industrial countries than in any other year since the war. Among the thousands of bankruptcies, the insolvency of several huge firms pushed the banks up against the wall. Some companies are too big to go bust. They have too many employees, they owe too much money to too many banks who are too important to the economy.

Chrysler set the tone for big corporate bankruptcies. "Chrysler was really the first multibillion-dollar workout," commented one banker. "At the first Chrysler meetings, people had trouble saying the word 'billion.'" They got used to it. Another huge Midwestern firm, International Harvester, teetered on the brink. Across the Canadian border, Massey-Ferguson barely kept its head above water. Dome Petroleum ran up more debt than Zaire and had as little money. The creaky heavy industry in the Northeast began to talk of the recession's "Rust Bowl" like the Depression's "Dust Bowl." Felix Rohatyn, the Lazard Frères partner who had masterminded Big MAC and advised Chrysler on its rescue plan, led the call for resuscitating the Reconstruction Finance Corporation, Roosevelt's entity for injecting equity finance into ailing companies.

As in the Depression, the phenomenon was worldwide. The miracle was over in West Germany. A stunned nation watched one household name after another succumb to its debt. In February 1982, Pelikan, one of the world's biggest makers of office supplies, went bust. In May, Bauknecht, a leading European supplier of white goods, started its short road to bankruptcy. In August, AEG-Telefunken, a veritable symbol for German quality for nearly a century, petitioned the court for a debt settlement. Later that same month, Wienerwald, West Germany's fast food franchise, filed for reorganization. West Germany's noninterventionist government did give guarantees for AEG, but otherwise left debts and bankruptcies to the banks.

France took sterner measures. President François Mitterrand, a bit of a *naïf* in financial matters, shocked French businessmen and his own finance minister with an offhand remark about a debt moratorium for strapped French companies. This was eventually soft-pedaled into a subsidized rescheduling of loans which had fixed rates exceeding 12 percent.

In Britain, the Bank of England began borrowing long to lend short, turning upside down the conventional banker's task. The Bank issued gilt-edged securities in excess of the government's needs to purchase commercial bills from hard-pressed British industry. The British central bank was traditionally more activist in corporate finance. Its legendary Depression governor, Montagu Norman, played a pivotal role in restructuring British industry during the 1930s and the Old Lady of Threadneedle Street seemed poised to lend a strong arm in the industrial convulsions of the 1980s.

The reverse energy crisis, the precipitous drop in oil prices, threw whole industrial sectors into disarray. The shipping industry, which had caused much anxiety in the mid-1970s, once again seemed vulnerable. The exposure of world banks to completed or partially built tankers or bulk carriers was put at $35 billion. The oil glut and oil price fall caught lots of optimists in the American Southwest off guard. U.S. banks had at least $35 billion in loans out to energy corporations when the crunch came, compared to $43 billion they had lent to oil-producing developing countries.

Sovereign debt was nebulous and rescheduling was part of a regulatory limbo. There was nothing ambiguous about corporate bankruptcy or nonperforming loans. Banks had to charge write-offs or bad-debt provisions against earnings, without any ifs, ands, buts, or maybes. What was new, though, as in the case of sovereign debt, was the scope of the problem. Firms with billions of dollars of bank debt held their bankers hostage in the same way sovereign countries do. Big companies not only have big payrolls, but they buy many products from smaller companies. A big-company failure inevitably entails several small failures. The loss in employment and production makes the matter a concern for government. This is the rationale behind government-backed rescues like Chrysler and AEG even in laissez-faire countries like the United States and West Germany, and the almost constant state intervention in more centralized countries like France, Italy, and, until the Thatcher regime, Britain.

Companies are the most visible victims of debt shock, just as they are the most visible economic "factor." Governments are shadowy, insubstantial, and far away. Most people do not see social security benefits or food subsidies—automobiles, washing machines, tractors, combines, and oil wells are everyday acquaintances. Banks, even, seem to be more puff than substance. A manufacturing plant for a big company puts out a stream of very substantial products. It employs thousands of people. It is very easy to identify with a company. Every American feels as if Chrysler is a personal acquaintance, a known quantity. Every German knows what AEG-Telefunken is all about. No one living in the American Midwest can remain unacquainted with International Harvester.

Postindustrial society notwithstanding, industry is still the engine of the economy. Unemployment is another aggregate to the macroeconomist. He sees the cause in the drop in production index, the contraction of the money supply, or the decline in exports. For normal people, unemployment results from a company's laying off workers, or even closing its doors. Macroeconomists are so preoccupied with their "aggregates" and microeconomists concern themselves solely with the internal economics of a firm. The discipline of economics largely ignores the important interaction between manufacturing companies and the economy. *The Economist*

179

underlines this anomaly with a feeling that borders on personal resentment: "International analytical heavyweights like the OECD, the IMF and the BIS regularly pontificate on the world's economy and its economies. Yet to hear them you might think companies were about as important as a nation's stock of chickens. The OECD's most recent 89-page report on the American economy (in July 1982) devoted just four paragraphs (a page and a half) to America's corporate sector. In contrast it writes ad nauseam about the minutiae of fiscal and monetary policy."

Even without an adequate overview of proper analysis, the debt problems of companies added to the atmosphere of crisis in the summer of '82. That large, successful companies prove vulnerable, too, was unsettling. International Harvester is just one company; there are, after all, 499 other companies in the Fortune 500 and the large majority of them continue to make profits to pay off their creditors and shareholders. The psychological impact of one big company's failure, especially an industry leader, is much greater than the continued normal performance of all the others.

More tangible is the size of the problem. International Harvester with its $4.2 billion in debt, or Dome Petroleum with $6 billion, had a potential financial impact that is significant, especially because of the cumulative effect of debt problems. The same score of banks who lent out half their equity to Brazil or Mexico are the ones who pumped up the big multinationals. Moratoriums and rescheduling may erode the value of a Third World loan, but sovereign lending, short of an outright debt repudiation, has no risk as great as that trip to the bankruptcy court. Even short of a bankruptcy court, loans to companies in difficulty are more likely to be classified and require provisions. Bank regulators have much clearer ideas about provisions for ailing companies than for sovereign countries.

2

International Harvester mounted "the largest voluntary restructuring effort in the history of corporate America," Elmer Johnson, the company's general counsel, told a federal court in Houston in November 1982. That is why, the good lawyer continued, the Chicago-based multinational was pleading guilty to charges of bribery in a $10-million kickback scheme with the Mexican national oil company, Pemex. The case actually involved a San Diego subsidiary, Solar Turbines, that Harvester had sold off the previous year in its long-running campaign to avoid bankruptcy. Harvester maintained that officials of the parent company knew nothing of the corruption. The court let Harvester off easy, with a fine for $10,000, plus the typically disproportionate legal fees of $40,000. It was a sum that Harvester could still manage, barely.

The company, a world leader in agricultural equipment and heavy-duty trucks, racked up the largest quarterly loss in American corporate history in its fourth quarter ending on October 31, 1982. The loss of $1.01 billion actually exceeded its fourth quarter sales of $979 million. The loss for the fiscal year was $1.6 billion altogether, and would have given the company a negative net worth but for that modest "voluntary restructuring" program launched in October.

The company was so strapped for cash that it inspired one former employee living in retirement to send in a check for $1,000. He reasoned that if 1,000 former employees did likewise, Harvester would have another badly needed $1 million. The company sent back the check because it could not give the pensioner stock in return unless it sent him a prospectus.

Harvester competitor John Deere & Co., downstate in Moline, was not so generous. Deere won a $28-million damages award in a patent infringement suit. Harvester did not have that kind of cash, so Deere put a lien on some Illinois facilities. It just so happened that these plants were part of the construction machinery subsidiary that Harvester was trying to sell to Dresser Industries, again to raise cash.

Harvester had its share of problems. Chairman Louis Menk, who had been parachuted in May to rescue the hard-pressed company, told shareholders at a special meeting the end of October, "We are essentially broke." The company had convened the shareholders to approve issue of new stock as part of a complex debt-restructuring plan. Harvester had obtained refinancing of its $4.2 billion debt, including $1.9 billion for its financing subsidiary, but had to go to lenders, dealers, suppliers, and stockholders once again in the fall of 1982 for further measures. Harvester asked lenders to cancel three dollars of debt for every one dollar of "concessions" it won from suppliers and dealers up to a total of $350 million in debt. The company also asked bondholders to exchange old debentures for new ones at half the face value, but with a higher rate of interest and with warrants for the purchase of common stock. The complex conversion of debt to equity, if all convertible shares and warrants were exercised, would give 52 percent of the company's equity to new shareholders, including 32 percent to the banks. Shareholders nonetheless accepted this dilution rather than provoke a bankruptcy.

Harvester's ambitious rescue got underway slowly. The company's manufacturing and credit subsidiaries in Australia were put into receivership, which did not improve the psychology of the rescue effort. The record-breaking quarterly loss also dampened spirits. All 193 lenders approved the restructuring, the first requirement. Some banks held back. Harvester enlisted political spokesmen, including Senator Charles Percy in Illinois and Arthur Burns, the former Federal Reserve chairman who was ambassador to West Germany, to jawbone laggards. Shareholders gathered in Chicago's Art Institute auditorium to hear the grim details and to approve the equity issues. Harvester's top executives were at pains to stress that even full compliance in the rescue could not guarantee that the company would avoid collapse. Journalists, who were curious about the details of this potential collapse, were confined to the balcony. The executives exited by a side door to avoid any unwanted questions.

The financial restructuring paralleled a complete revamping of the manufacturing side. Harvester, if it survived, was to shrink from an $8-billion company to one with annual sales of $4 billion–$5 billion. The work force was to decline to 36,000 from 93,000. The number of manufacturing plants was to fall to eighteen from forty-five; the company would have only five plants abroad, compared to twenty-two in the summer of '82. The company sold what it could where it could. Solar Turbines, a profit-maker despite its ethical missteps, went to Caterpillar. Dresser finally got the construction machinery operation, but paid $83 million instead of the $100 million expected. Top executives of a French subsidiary,

Yumbo, bought out that company, but Harvester was saddled with the liabilities.

It was a humiliating process. Bankruptcy usually is. The longtime chief executive officer, Archie McCardell, found out just how humiliating before his ouster in May 1982. Creditors require chief executives of bankrupt companies to grovel. McCardell felt obliged to take calls from European bankers in the middle of the night. A banker commented, "Once he would have had thirteen secretaries to monitor his calls for him. Suddenly he couldn't risk not taking calls from some tiny bank out in Wyoming or somewhere, because that's the guy who could cause problems for him if he didn't." The ultimate humiliation, of course, was his forced departure from the company.

3

Dome Petroleum came into its own following the second oil shock. With prices above $30 a barrel, Dome Pete (its nickname in financial circles) stood a chance of realizing its long-term dream of getting oil out of the Beaufort Sea in the Arctic. John P. Gallagher, known as Smilin' Jack for his grin, had set his sights on an Arctic find since he helped launch the company in 1950. By 1980 Dome was still drilling for oil in the Arctic, but Canada's National Energy Program prompted Dome to do its part to bring the nation's energy wealth under Canadian control. The company's president, William E. Richards, an acquisition fanatic anyway, embarked on the biggest acquisition of all, the asset-rich Hudson's Bay Oil & Gas Co., which was controlled by Conoco of the United States. Richards's strategy was to make a tender offer for Conoco shares and then trade them back for the 53-percent share in Hudson's Bay. Conoco fought the tender, but Dome got what it wanted in June 1981 for $1.7 billion.

To finance the acquisition, Dome started the borrowing binge that brought it to the brink a year later, and Conoco, exposed as vulnerable by Dome's tender, fell victim to Du Pont's new-found acquisitiveness when the U.S. chemical company took over Conoco in the biggest acquisition in American corporate history. Meanwhile, Dome bought out Hudson's Bay's minority shareholders, who extorted a further $1.8 billion for the remaining 47 percent. Canadian banks refused any further credit, so Richards turned to a foreign syndicate led by Citibank. Foreign bankers had for years all but salivated over the prospect of Dome Pete business, and the twenty-five-bank syndicate quickly signed the loan in March 1982. This new, huge credit brought Dome's debt to $5.2 billion, nearly as big as Exxon's, in a company that realized sales of less than $2 billion a year.

Smilin' Jack and Richards had quite a reputation for financial juggling. A homely dictum in Western Canada had it that the two could move a ton of pigeons in a half-ton truck by keeping them all flying. The pigeons this time were the banks. Dome had pledged its 53 percent of Hudson's Bay shares to the four biggest Canadian banks—Canadian Imperial Bank of Commerce, Toronto-Dominion Bank, Royal Bank of Canada, and Bank of Montreal—to secure the original $1.7 billion credit. Now Dome proposed to pledge Hudson's Bay's assets to secure the foreign credit. Of course, the backing for the shares also consists of the physical assets of the company. The Canadian banks were upset at this violation of their loan covenants and exercised their right to change conditions, too, by demanding a repayment by September 1982 of a $1-billion loan originally due in ten years. Such a repayment schedule went far beyond Dome's liquid resources. If the Canadian banks held to their demand, Dome would be bankrupt. But the Citibank loan went ahead anyway. The foreign syndicate claims it found out about the change in maturity of the Canadian credit only months later, even though the two separate agreements with both the foreign banks and the Canadian banks were signed on March 10, 1981, in the same New York offices of the law firm Shearman & Sterling.

Dome's chief juggler, Richards, had hoped to meet the September 30 deadline for the Canadian loan by selling off U.S. and Indonesian properties, but the soft oil market had depreciated the value of oil assets. In early September, just as debt-shocked bankers were packing their bags for the World Bank–International Monetary Fund meeting in Toronto, the host country's flagship energy concern announced to the world that it could not pay its debt falling due at the end of the month.

Canadian Prime Minister Pierre Elliott Trudeau retorted in answer to an interviewer's question that the federal government would not bail out Dome. "Look at the banks that advanced money to Dome. The banks lent some $4 billion to Dome because they thought they were going to make a buck, and Dome was investing the money because it thought it would make a buck. So a lot of people around the world made a mistake, including our renowned and very responsible banks, and you are asking me, are we going to bail it out? The answer is no. We are not going to bail it out," concluded Trudeau firmly. The more nuanced view was that Ottawa could scarcely let such a prominent Canadian company go under. The rescue plan announced at the end of the month entailed substantial government support, but arguably fell short of a bailout.

The rescue terms dictated by the banks stunned the financial community for their severity. The government and the big four planned to inject a billion Canadian dollars of new capital into the company by means of ten-year convertible debentures, with the conversion price set at a paltry $2, a comedown from Dome's peak stock price of $25. The government and the banks had right of approval of directors and major business decisions. The rescue promised to give the rescuers majority ownership and effective control of the company. One angry shareholder brought a $5-billion class-action suit against the government and the banks for expropriation. Analysts speculated that original shareholders might get more if the company, which had total assets valued at nearly $10 billion, were liquidated. Russell Harrison, chairman of Canadian Imperial Bank of Commerce and one of the architects of the rescue plan, angrily disagreed. "The common shareholders should get down on their knees and thank God we came to an agreement," he sputtered. "If we hadn't done this, their shares would have been worthless now." Shareholders were also given the chance to subscribe to new shares.

As interest rates fell and Dome's cash flow improved—each one-point drop in interest rates saved the company an estimated $50 million annually—Richards tried to wriggle out of being rescued. All Dome really wanted was the debt-rescheduling part of the package, which essentially involved restoring the troublesome billion-dollar credit to its original ten-year maturity. The rescuers had

185

made it easy on themselves. The government was going to finance its share of the credit facility by a loan from those same four banks, always happy to get Canadian Government debt. The Government planned to pay off its credit with a half-penny gasoline tax that was already part of its National Energy Program. The banks wanted to finance their share by selling off some old Dome loans to that erstwhile eager syndicate headed by Citibank. But the foreign bankers felt they had ironclad security with Hudson's Bay's assets and were not interested in taking part in a rescue. "Lenders who are adequately secured have no reason to participate," Citibank telexed tersely to Bank of Montreal.

Smilin' Jack took a generous retirement. His pension was set at about $20,000 a month for eight years, enough to keep a smile on anyone's face. Richards felt that the company still had enough to offer private investors that it could forgo the "rescue" and meet its capital needs with a public offering.

4

The Main River carries its flotsam quietly through Frankfurt. As it curves gently past the historic city hall at the Römerberg, past the flea market, and flows under the Friedensbrücke, it enters a barren stretch of industrial wasteland. At the bridge, on the southern quay, stands a nondescript building. It is not very high and not very long. There is no decoration on the façade. The large sign on the top of the building identifies it as AEG-Telefunken. Despite its humble appearance, this modestly squat building is not a regional distribution center, but the world headquarters for a company that at one point employed nearly 160,000 workers around the globe.

The weather was typical for Frankfurt in August. Sticky and uncertain, the atmosphere alternated between hazy, lazy sunlight and threatening, oppressive gray. On Friday August 6, 1982, the public relations office of AEG rang around to the agencies and newspapers in Frankfurt to inform them of a press conference on Monday.

The company had been fighting a rearguard action all summer to keep afloat. The consortium of twenty-five West German banks with credits outstanding to the company had tried fitfully to reach an agreement on bailing out the cash-starved company.

They had leaped into the breach once before, in late 1979, when AEG had to restructure its balance sheet to cover hemorrhaging operating losses. In December of that year, shareholders summoned to an extraordinary meeting in Berlin had consented to a plan requiring them to write down their equity to one third of its nominal value. The bank consortium underwrote a new issue of shares at par value which then doubled the written-down capital. The maneuver eased AEG's financial bind for a while, but still left the company with a debt-equity ratio of nearly 10 to 1. The severe corporate surgery required in such a case was slow in coming. Interest rates rose and the cash drain became a torrent.

The journalists filed in Monday afternoon August 9 for the impromptu press conference. Something was in the air. West German companies usually hold one or maybe two press conferences during the year. They are formal affairs, with invitations and R.S.V.P. Had AEG found a white knight? Lord Weinstock's cash-heavy General Electric Company had reached a tentative agreement to inject DM 750 million into AEG. The offer had run into opposition from the German unions, who felt that the British company would force massive layoffs in Germany. AEG's domestic competitors also objected to a company with GEC's resources coming into their cozy market. Was AEG going to throw in the towel, declare bankruptcy? The federal government, stiffened in its resolve by the laissez-faire Free Democrats in the coalition, had refused so far to grant any aid to AEG. But could a Social Democratic chancellor countenance the bankruptcy of a company employing 100,000 persons in West Germany and keeping thousands of small enterprises alive with its orders?

The banks had refused to advance new credits to AEG without government guarantees. Bonn was not convinced the company could survive even with new money and delayed its approval. The beleaguered chief executive of AEG, Heinz Dürr, had jetted to the United States on Saturday August 7 in a last-ditch effort to interest United Technologies in taking a stake in the West German firm. GEC had quietly withdrawn its contested offer in the preceding week. The U.S. firm, for its part, declined to rush into an engagement of that magnitude. Dürr, a mild-mannered man who looks vaguely like a New England prep-school student, rushed back to Frankfurt. Together with Hans Friderichs, the chief executive of Dresdner Bank who was chairman of AEG's supervisory board, Dürr went up to Bonn on Sunday to explain the company's position to top cabinet members. It was a particularly difficult moment for Friderichs. The tall and affable ex-politician, who was a former Economics Minister, had been in the forefront of West Germany's liberals, the Free Democrats, in espousing laissez-faire economic policies. Now he was forced to ask the federal government for help.

When the AEG board met Monday morning, the company's fate was sealed. The board approved Friderichs and Dürr's recommendation to seek a court settlement of the company's debt. They applied for a West German version of Chapter 11, which allowed them to petition creditors for a substantial write-off of debt. AEG asked its banks and suppliers to forgive 60 percent of the company's DM 5 billion, about $2 billion, in debt.

Friderichs and Dürr descended to meet the press. Dürr read a prepared statement about the court filing. There it was, the largest corporate insolvency in the short history of the Federal Republic of Germany. If creditors failed to go along with the court settlement, the only alternative for AEG was bankruptcy and liquidation. Even if lenders forgave AEG part of its debt, the company that survived would be a vestige of the once-proud flagship of German industry.

The news of AEG's court petition flashed across the news wires in the same week that Mexican Finance Secretary Jesús Silva Herzog was watching the last cash drain out of his country.

AEG had grown fat and lazy. The world-famous producer of electrical goods relied on its reputation and market position to carry it along. Egregious management errors, like getting the company in over its head in nuclear energy, are easy to spot. Less obvious but more important in the long run was the failure to seize market opportunities, to develop new products, to control costs and productivity. The best indicator of how much deadwood the company was dragging around was management's projection in spring of 1983 that its 1984 sales of DM 14 billion, about $6 billion, would be realized by a work force of 82,000. It took 158,000 workers to produce the same turnover in 1979. Even allowing for

West Germany's moderate inflation and the higher Deutsche mark value of export goods, the comparison demonstrates the room for improved productivity.

The court settlement launched in such confusion in August came to a relatively swift conclusion. The court-appointed supervisor, a Frankfurt lawyer, tapped the former financial officer of the Thyssen steel group, Heinz Kuhn, to sort out AEG's finances. By the time the company laid a report before its creditors in February 1983, its cash situation bordered on rosy. The company had drawn only DM 890 million, or $370 million, of the more than $1 billion credit made available in wake of the August court filing. Half of the amount drawn was put into interest-earning deposits to guarantee contract commitments. AEG took advantage of the court settlement to bite the bullet hard and proper. It booked an operating loss of nearly a billion marks and wrote off another billion marks for the various layoffs and plant closings. The debt canceled by the court settlement coincidentally just covered these losses, so that AEG could report 1982 as a break-even.

The creditors finally convened in Frankfurt on March 9. The result was a foregone conclusion because the court supervisor had obtained written agreements from the majority of creditors. Not taking any chances in view of the 60,000 potential claimants, the court rented out the festival auditorium in Frankfurt's sprawling fairgrounds. Seating was set up for 5,800. But it was a case of calling the country's largest insolvency and nobody coming. Only 200 people, many of them journalists, showed up at the hall, lending an appropriately Kafkaesque atmosphere to the final scene of AEG's financial restructuring.

5

Bankruptcies around the globe reached record postwar levels in 1982 and proceeded to increase in 1983. The cumulative effect of insolvencies began to take their toll on bank earnings and morale. Several special cases of bankruptcy and near-bankruptcy contributed especially to the pervading desperation.

Massey-Ferguson had been a precursor of International Harvester. The Canadian firm was the largest manufacturer in the world of tractors and a leader in other farm equipment. Massey-Ferguson racked up a string of heavy losses beginning in 1978, so that the banks had to agree to a debt restructuring of $1 billion in 1981. But that only paved the way for more losses by the company, due in part to soft market conditions but in part also to management mistakes in the past. In 1983 the banks had to make further concessions on debt service for $900 million of Massey's total debt load of (U.S.) $1.2 billion.

Massey worried the banks because its debt was big, its capital base was small, and its market position increasingly poor. Massey's main banker was the Canadian Imperial Bank of Commerce. This was one of the big Canadian banks also dangerously exposed to Dome Petroleum. Because there were no lending limits for Canadian banks, CIBC had invested practically the equivalent of its entire capital base in these two corporations alone. This further disquieted foreign banks, who constantly feared that a collapse of a major bank anywhere would set off a chain reaction that first would pull down the other banks in that country and then the whole international banking system.

The worries from Hong Kong were even more arcane. *The Wall Street Journal*'s disaster scenario (see Chapter One) had the bankruptcy of a property company in Hong Kong triggering the global financial collapse. And in fact several real estate firms were in the process of collapsing. One of the biggest was Carrian, a high flyer that saw its net worth inflated during the property boom of 1979–81. The mood shifted in Hong Kong and the bottom fell out of the real estate market, making several Carrian properties worth only half what the company had paid for them. Carrian had been a good customer to lots of foreign banks trying to get a toehold in the local market. Most of them established branches in the British crown colony to participate in the "Asian dollar" market, but they saw local business as a source of added profit. When Carrian said it could not service $1 billion in debt on a timely basis, many of the world's leading banks were affected through their Hong Kong subsidiaries.

Again, Hong Kong and the world could easily survive the disappearance of another real estate wheeler-dealer, but the impact on the banks was more worrying. If the Hong Kong property companies had been the banks' only worry, that, too, would have been all right. But these were often the same international banks that had loans out to International Harvester, Dome Petroleum, AEG-Telefunken, and Massey-Ferguson, as well as Mexico, Brazil, and Argentina.

What emerged in case after case was that banks lent not necessarily to the most creditworthy customers. They lent the most to whoever needed the most. Often enough, though, those who needed to borrow a lot did so because they were not making any money.

One company even managed to expand while it was in bankruptcy. GHR Cos. was a large oil and natural gas company based in Good Hope, Louisiana. Entrepreneur Jack Stanley got ahead of himself in 1975 and had to put his company into Chapter 11 proceedings. But the company emerged from bankruptcy five years later with assets doubled at $530 million. Stanley talked a fourteen-bank consortium into lending GHR $750 million in the early 1980s. By the fall of 1982, when declining oil prices were creating trouble for a lot of people, GHR was in trouble too. It had trouble paying its bills, asked the bank to delay loan repayments, and sold off some gas leases to raise cash.

One of the leaders of the GHR consortium was trusty old Continental Illinois. In fact, it was the same John Lytle who later was fired for his role in the Penn Square Bank loans (see next chapter) who got the Chicago bank deeply involved in GHR. Another perennial in bad debt cases, Chase Manhattan, was also a GHR fan. But the biggest exposure to Jack Stanley's dream machine was held by the Banque de Paris et des Pays-Bas, a high-powered French merchant bank known as Paribas. Until it was nationalized with other French banks in 1982, Paribas had a reputation for banking with flair. As a merchant bank on the French model, a *banque d'affaires,* Paribas was not a simple conduit for funds. It did more than just take in deposits and make loans. It invested directly in industry and took an active role in managing the companies. Paribas somehow managed to take fully one third of the consortium's exposure, or $245 million.

Even Citibank, always pushing for more profits, kept its distance

191

from GHR. Among other things, Jack Stanley's idiosyncrasies put bankers off. These went beyond personal habits or managerial attitudes. For instance, Stanley did not believe in budgets. One former executive related that the accounting department told him to stop asking for a budget. "I was just supposed to spend money until I was told to stop," this executive said. The banks eventually told Stanley to stop spending money, but they had to see just where the interest on their $750 million was going to come from.

Bankers could spin the globe and stop it by sticking in a pin. Chances were there was a problem where the pin landed.

Wienerwald went bust. West Germany's contribution to the universe of fast food, Wienerwald started humbly enough in 1955 in Munich's Amalienstrasse. Friedrich Jahn franchised roast chickens and Bavarian *Gemütlichkeit* around the world. He made a lot of money and put that into a hotel chain, a tour operation, and other catering activities that did not do nearly so well. He also did the Swiss a big favor by moving his headquarters to Switzerland. When the holding company filed for restructuring in late 1982, it was the Swiss banks who were left holding the bag. The big West German bank, Deutsche Bank, displayed a startling lack of solidarity with its Swiss brethren and moved to secure its loans with claims against Wienerwald's assets in West Germany. These were mostly very profitable roast chicken places, so Deutsche Bank was in good shape. The Swiss banks had to figure out what to do with a holding company that no longer held anything worthwhile.

Spin again. Caterpillar reported its first quarterly loss in four decades for the third quarter of 1982. After Massey-Ferguson and International Harvester, bankers were understandably edgy about this farm and construction equipment manufacturer. In the Netherlands, the country's biggest shipbuilding company, RSV, foundered after years of government bailouts. After pumping more than 2 billion Dutch guilders into RSV since 1977, the Dutch Government rejected an appeal in February 1983 for 300 million guilders. The shipbuilder applied for a debt moratorium. Meanwhile, in Spain the biggest industrial company not owned by the state, Union Explosivos Rio Tinto, haggled with eighty foreign banks and fifty Spanish banks about rescheduling its billion-dollar debt.

It was all there—mismanagement, speculation, bad luck, bad

planning, and lots of risk. It seemed to come to a head in 1982 as the four-year-old recession caught up with those who had thought they could just wait it out, or those who thought there was a pot of gold at the end of the rainbow.

BREAKING THE BANK
CHAPTER NINE

———∽———

1

Banks make loans, loans go bad, banks go bust. This stubbornly simple sequence of events was the cadence that kept bank executives, central bankers, and government officials dancing through the fall and spring of 1982–83. Default and bankruptcy meant not only the collapse of an economy or the failure of a firm. They meant that a bank would have to write off an asset. If the asset was big enough, the bank might find out that it no longer had the resources to cover the loss. The bank itself would go bankrupt. Those not affected directly by the payments difficulties of a developing country or the travails of a farm-equipment manufacturer still had a lot to worry about. The fear was that if a Chase Manhattan or Citibank failed, the shock waves would cause the collapse of many smaller banks and companies. The greatest anxiety came from simply not knowing what would happen. Chase had never failed before. Who could say what the consequences would be?

May, June, and July of 1982 brought three successive bank shocks. They revealed how weak the foundation was supporting banks. These events enhanced the uncertainty and alarm about the credit system when Mexico initiated the crisis. An obscure trading firm in Wall Street bet on the wrong horse, and a big bank, Chase

Manhattan, lost millions of dollars. A man convicted for currency violations in Italy fled incognito to London, to end up hanging from Blackfriars Bridge. The bank he headed, Italy's largest privately owned, found a gap of $1.4 billion in its books and went into receivership. A small bank in Oklahoma went belly up and giants like Chase and Continental Illinois suffered huge losses.

Each case struck suddenly, surprisingly. It turned out later that there should have been no surprise. The signs of coming disaster were plentiful. Scalawags were at work, but the worrying recognition was that the system to protect banks from scalawags had holes big enough that such things could happen. Supervisors suffered from cowardice, sloth, and plain incompetence. Internal control systems within huge, sophisticated banks did not keep young and irresponsible junior officers from dangerously overextending a bank's credit. No one—not supervisors, not bank chief executives, and certainly not the public whose money was at stake—could see the big picture.

If bolts like these could come out of the blue, what other nasty surprises were in store? The Rock of Gibraltar supposedly supporting the banks turned out to be a sandbar that any passing wave could wash away. Banks were seen to be fragile institutions, vulnerable to the greed and incompetence of individuals as well as to the unpredictable shocks of an unstable financial environment. Small wonder that fears in the United States, Europe, and Japan immediately focused on the fate of the banks. Small wonder that the spontaneous public outcry was for bringing the banks under control.

2

David Heuwetter wanted to be a big player. His special ambition was to corner a single Treasury issue—to buy, for instance, a $1.5-billion issue at one fell swoop. He was not a con man, not a fraud, and probably did not break any laws. He *was* a big player, but he was playing at something that most of us would not regard as a game.

David Heuwetter, a onetime bond salesman in his early forties, played high stakes in government securities. This erstwhile humdrum market had mushroomed since Washington started running up big budget deficits. By the spring of 1982 there was $750 billion worth of government bonds and notes floating around in the investment world. Rapid rises and falls in interest rates forced big institutional investors to manage their portfolios "actively"—that is, to buy and sell bonds frequently to maximize their return. A small number of Wall Street houses specialized in trading government securities. They made a market in Treasury issues, so that anyone who wanted to buy or sell them could do so easily. Lots of people did. About $30 billion worth of government securities changed hands every day. The New York Stock Exchange, by comparison, traded "only" $2 billion a day.

By convention, investors regard U.S. Government securities as the best risk of all. They bear the lowest interest rates because there is no risk premium. If the U.S. Government does not repay its debt, the reasoning goes, the world must have ended. And so it never occurred to anyone that a market in federal government securities needed to be regulated. If the securities were virtually riskless, what risk could there be in buying and selling them? There was a fallacy in this reasoning. Whatever the standing of the securities themselves, a trading environment with short sales, repurchase agreements, reverses, and the deleterious effect of personal greed and ambition can spawn a lot of risk. A volatile, multibillion-dollar market with no rules invites the likes of David Heuwetter to make a lot of trouble.

Heuwetter was the force behind Drysdale Government Securities, a spinoff from a sleepy securities house founded in 1889. Heuwetter persuaded Drysdale Securities Corporation to franchise the new firm so that he could play freely in the government securities market. With a modest capital of $10 million, Heuwetter set out to be a big player. He traded blocs of $50 million without blinking an eye. He ran up positions of as much as $10 billion. With volumes like this, the ability to make a sixteenth or an eighth of a percent on a trade can mean millions of dollars of profit on a deal.

Heuwetter seemed to be doing well. He had a personal fleet of three Mercedeses and a limousine, a farm in upstate New York, and sported wads of cash. But Heuwetter's prosperity was a bubble, inflated by some peculiarities of the government securities market. One peculiarity was the wide use of repurchase agreements. Technically a sale of securities with a promise to repurchase, these agreements amount to a loan with securities as collateral. When the "loan" is paid back, the securities are returned. A second peculiarity is that securities were used in "repo" agreements without taking account of interest. Repurchase agreements are sometimes very short—overnight, or a few days. It hardly seemed worthwhile, especially in days when annual interest rates were 3 to 4 percent, to figure out the interest for that length of time, especially since it does not play a role in the repurchase agreement itself. The government securities market had established a tradition that the firm borrowing the securities would simply remit any interest payments made while the securities were in their possession. Simple enough. But the firms who borrowed securities did not necessarily have to keep them. They could sell them, just so long as they bought new securities of similar terms to replace the borrowed ones when it was time for them to be "repurchased." This was the enticing setup that enabled Heuwetter to play a type of shell game. When you sell a security outright, you do take account of the interest that has accrued. That is, a security close to the date of the interest payment is worth more than one not so close.

Heuwetter could borrow securities, entering into what was called a reverse repurchase agreement, paying a price that does not take account of interest. He could turn right around and *sell* these securities at a price that *does* take account of the interest—that is, a slightly higher price. That markup represents a sizable amount of money, which Heuwetter then had available to borrow more securities and continue the process. But the procedure leaves a trader exposed. He is "short" in the securities he borrowed and then sold. He has to replace those securities before it is time to return them to whomever he borrowed them from. If he fails to cover his short position on time, he has to bear the financing charges until he does. Worse, if an interest payment falls due while the trader is short, he still has the obligation to remit the interest payment to the original owners. It also left the lender of securities exposed for the amount of accrued interest. Because no borrower of securities had gone bust since the market reached its new dimensions, this risk was often overlooked.

Always keep in mind that the percentages involved are small, but they are percentages of big numbers and add up very quickly. One eighth of one percent seems minuscule, but amounts to $16 million on a position of $10 billion. Keep in mind, too, that Heuwetter had only $10 million of equity. Keeping a position of $10 billion, he could not afford a mistake of even one eighth of one percent. Traders are greedy, but not stupid. They came to regard Drysdale as overextended and stopped dealing with Heuwetter. But Heuwetter needed a steady supply of peas to keep his shell game going.

Enter the banks, particularly Chase Manhattan. Chase, it emerged later, had adopted a volume incentive scheme for its executives in the securities trading department. The more they traded, the more they made. So Chase traders were happy to do business with Drysdale, even after other Wall Street traders had backed off. Chase would go off and borrow securities from Merrill Lynch or Goldman Sachs and turn around and lend them to Drysdale. Merrill Lynch and Goldman Sachs had stopped trading with Drysdale. They did not know, or did not want to know, that the securities they lent to Chase went on to Drysdale. What Chase did with their securities, they reasoned, was Chase's business. It seems, though, that Chase's securities traders, keeping an eye on the bonuses that eventually matched their salaries, were not aware of the risk they were running by trading with Drysdale. The accrued interest in the securities lent to Drysdale amounted to an unsecured loan. It seems also that Chase's top executives were not aware that their government securities traders were not aware of the risks.

Everyone—Chase's traders, Chase's top executives, Merrill Lynch et al—became aware of the risk when Drysdale said it would not be able to remit $160 million in interest, due May 17, 1982, on $2.3 billion of securities it had borrowed from Chase. Chris Welles, in his prizewinning report on the Drysdale collapse, alleged that other traders, eager to get Heuwetter out of the market, had made sure he could not buy the securities he needed to cover his short position. So Heuwetter came up short, Chase came up short, and once the full extent of Drysdale's position was known, all of Wall Street came up short.

At first, Chase tried to explain to the securities houses that they had better see if they could get their money back from Drysdale somehow. The securities houses explained to Chase in no uncertain terms that they expected to get the money from the bank to which they had lent the securities, and it was up to Chase to see if it could get the money back. Merrill Lynch, according to Welles, threatened to dump hundreds of millions of Chase certificates of deposit it was holding onto the market, which would have made it very difficult for Chase to issue any more. The fact was that many Wall Street brokers themselves did not have a strong enough capital base to sustain heavy losses from Drysdale. Rumors coursed up and down Wall Street about how shaky some firms were. Laws regarding re-purchase agreements were hazy and had never been tested in court. So Chase had little choice but to pick up the tab. Chase reported a special after-tax loss of $117 million. Its loss in credibility on Wall Street was immeasurable. Willard Butcher, the unlikely successor to David Rockefeller at the head of Chase, had a penchant for sports analogies. "We were like a champion boxer who dropped his guard and got slugged," he said of the Drysdale loss. "It certainly wasn't a fatal accident, but it did deck him. And he clearly has a black eye." Manufacturers Hanover reported a much smaller loss, $9 million.

The New York Fed jumped in with billions of dollars of liquidity. The Fed's president, Anthony Solomon, went before Congress to explain what had happened. He promised to increase the Fed's monitoring of government securities trading.

The public was left with the realization that a small, apparently insignificant firm could deal a hard blow to the prestige and profits of a big and very significant bank. They realized that regulators could not be counted on to regulate markets that change and grow. They learned that banks are willing to get into deals where they not only fail to assess the risk, but do not even know there *is* a risk. An obscure and arcane sector of the financial market was exposed to the glare of publicity. It was not a pleasant sight.

An executive from Manufacturers Hanover, the big New York bank, found himself in Oklahoma City one night at Cowboys, a local bar. He saw something that stunned him. Bill Patterson, the pushy thirty-three-year-old senior executive vice president of a local bank, Penn Square, was drinking beer out of his boot. The beer feat was just one in Patterson's repertoire of tricks. It was enough for the New York banker, who muttered, "There's no way we will ever do business with this guy."

Other New Yorkers did do business with that guy, chief among them the ubiquitous Chase Manhattan. One of the other tricks Patterson had was the participation loan. It was his down-home way of bankrolling Oklahoma's voracious oilmen far beyond the capacity of the tiny shopping-center bank, which had equity capital of only $39 million. Penn Square Bank would arrange the loan, provide a small part of the funding, and then sell participations in the loan to big money-center banks like Chase. Patterson kept his customers happy, and the big-city banks got a piece of Oklahoma's oil action. Chase eventually bought about $200 million of Penn Square loans. Chicago's giant Continental Illinois bought in for $1 billion worth, inspiring some wags to call Penn Square a loan production office for the Chicago Bank. Seattle-First National Bank, the largest in the Pacific Northwest, bought $400 million of Patterson's loans.

Patterson's salesmanship earned him the accolade that "he could sell snowmobiles to the Okies." He certainly snowed the big banks, selling off more than $2 billion of his participation loans. It turned out that Patterson was better at selling than banking. Loans to wildcatters are notoriously risky, and a lot of Penn Square's loans went bad. By the summer of 1982, loan write-offs had risen to $47 million, more than enough to wipe out Penn Square's $39 million in capital. When the Comptroller of the Currency, the federal official responsible for supervising banks, found this out, he closed the bank on July 5. Subsequent investigation found that fully three thousand of Penn Square's energy loans suffered from inadequate documentation. The downturn in the oil market pushed even relatively healthy firms into cash flow difficulties.

Chase had to charge off $75 million in loan loss reserves for its Penn Square participations. The most dramatic impact came, logically, at Continental Illinois. The bank, seventh largest in the United States, reported a $61-million loss for the second quarter. It was a black day for Continenal Illinois. Some dark fate caused a crane on top of Continental's New York skyscraper to fall the day the loss was announced. A pedestrian was killed. Continental became the butt of business jokes. Lee Iacocca, the celebrated savior of Chrysler, entertained a Chicago audience with his irony. "If I had known how easy it was to get a loan from Continental Illinois, I would never have gone to the government," he quipped.

Continental was a go-go bank that chafed constantly under Illinois' peculiar banking laws, which forbade banks to maintain any branches at all. Deprived of the grass-roots deposits and customer base that provide the bread-and-butter business for commercial banks, Continental ranged far and wide for deposits and loans. In the wake of Penn Square, Continental had to leave the "run" of nine leading banks whose certificates of deposit trade in New York money markets on an equal basis. The Chicago bank had to pay a premium for funds, which further cut into its profitability. The vice president who signed up for Patterson's loans, John Lytle, had to resign. So did three of his superiors, including George Baker, the head of corporate lending, and one of the forces behind Continental's aggressive stance in the market. The Oklahoma loans continued to stalk Continental. Its first quarter earnings in 1983 were down by half, due to a $99-million net credit loss. Half of the loss came from Penn Square loans.

Penn Square set back Continental Illinois. It did worse to Seafirst, as the holding company of Seattle-First National Bank was known. William Jenkins, who had built up Seafirst in twenty years at the helm and shared Willard Butcher's fondness for boxing analogy, described the Penn Square collapse as a "body blow that slows you down a little." More than a little, as it turned out. When the full impact was evident, Jenkins had to go. "I offered to fall on my sword," Jenkins explained, switching metaphors. "The board offered me a sword."

Richard Cooley, the successful chief executive of the Wells Fargo Bank in California, was helping Seafirst find a new chief executive in the wake of the Penn Square fiasco. Finally Cooley took the job himself. When he saw how bad Seafirst's fourth-quarter earnings were going to turn out, he talked Bankers Trust into mustering a group of banks to provide a safety-net line of credit. Thirteen banks pledged $1.5 billion to keep depositors from panicking when Seafirst announced a net operating loss of $90.2 million for 1982, compared to its net profit of $78.5 billion in 1981. The support group included all the familiar faces—Citibank, Chase, Morgan, Manufacturers Hanover, Bank of America.

But Cooley's troubles were just beginning. A World War II pilot who lost an arm when he was downed in Europe, Cooley considered himself a risk-taker. But the yawning gaps in Seafirst's earnings were too big even for a veteran risk-taker. When Cooley saw that Seafirst's first quarter loss would total $133 million, he realized there was no solution but to put the bank on the block. After some quick and discreet inquiries, Bank of America made a bid, $250 million in cash and preferred shares plus $150 million in new capital for Seafirst to help cover the losses. Depositors from out of state and abroad began withdrawing funds and Seafirst had to tap its safety-net credit line. The twenty-sixth-largest bank in the United States, the largest in the state of Washington, had to stumble into the arms of a big brother to keep from collapsing. In the end, even the safety net fell apart, and the Federal Reserve Bank of San Francisco had to throw out a lifeline.

A small bank in a shopping center far away from the madding crowd crippled one giant bank and mortally wounded another. Nearly a hundred investigators from three federal agencies, including the FBI, descended on Oklahoma City to do an autopsy on the little bank that couldn't. Examiners from the Office of the Comptroller of the Currency had failed to spot the impending trouble in Penn Square when they visited in the fall of 1981. When they returned for the routine checkup in the spring, the bank was beyond saving. There was no evidence that Patterson sought to defraud anyone, or that he personally profited from his deals. His main failing seemed to be his exuberance, coupled with a lack of judgment. Patterson's college nickname was "Monkeybrain".

Penn Square had outstanding claims of $506 million. For the first time in the history of federal deposit insurance, depositors lost money in a bank failure. Seafirst and Continental Illinois, not to mention Chase Manhattan, certainly had other problems. The $400 million in loans that Seafirst bought from Penn Square was only part of the bank's $1.3-billion energy portfolio. Many of the other engagements went bad, too, in the soft oil and gas market. Once again, as in the Drysdale case, internal controls in America's biggest banks proved to be deficient. Credit assessment and review were too lax or too decentralized to prevent risky involvements with unreliable partners. The freewheeling buying and selling of loan participation without independent review had disturbing parallels to the syndicated loans of the Euromarket.

4

Italy's peculiar seedbed of corruption has spawned many a scandal, but few have been as messy as the collapse of Banco Ambrosiano. It was odd enough that Italy's largest private-sector bank should reelect as chairman a man convicted of currency evasion and sentenced to jail. It was odder still when that man, Roberto Calvi, fled Italy in disguise and went underground. Oddest of all, though, was the early morning discovery of Calvi's body hanging from Blackfriars Bridge in London, near the financial district.

It was grisly. The day before Calvi's body was found swinging from that London bridge with ten pounds of stones in his pockets, Calvi's secretary plummeted the four stories from the executive suite in Ambrosiano's Milan headquarters to her death. She left behind a note with a full-fledged curse on Calvi: "He should be twice-damned for the damage he did to the group and to all of us, who were at one time so proud of it."

The affair reached into the murkiest depths of Italy's opaque power relationships. Calvi bore the nickname "God's banker" for his close links to the Vatican. He was the protégé of the ill-fated Michele Sindona, whose fraudulent manipulation of banks in Italy and the United States made him a prize for courts on both sides of the Atlantic. After Sindona's fall, Calvi kept his hand in Vatican finances through close ties with Archbishop Paul C. Marcinkus, the enigmatic American prelate who functioned in the unlikely combination of chief papal bodyguard and chief Vatican banker. Marcinkus packed a Magnum and also wrote letters of comfort for certain Banco Ambrosiano loans abroad that later turned out to have vanished into thin air.

More sinister even than the links to the Vatican was Calvi's implication in the P-2 Masonic lodge scandal. This secret organization linked politicians, the military, and financiers in a conspiratorial power apparatus. Calvi's place in this spiderweb of money and politics may never be fully discovered. A London inquest first ruled Calvi's death a suicide, even though the circumstances were not typical for suicides. Eight months later, three high court judges overturned this verdict. It was widely felt in Italy that Calvi was murdered, but speculation about the perpetrator ranged from the Mafia, inevitably, to Opus Dei, the conservative, secretive lay Catholic organization that increased its power under Pope John Paul II's patronage.

So bizarre were the details of Calvi's career and demise that his saga distracted from the significance of Ambrosiano's collapse. What forced the Bank of Italy to liquidate Banco Ambrosiano and transfer its healthy business to a Nuovo Banco Ambrosiano were $1.4 billion in loans to "ghost companies." Whether the proceeds were used to buy Banco Ambrosiano shares and give Calvi control of the bank, or to finance arms purchases for anti-Communist dictators in Latin America, or to aid the Solidarity trade union in Poland, the fact that Calvi was able to make that much money vanish in complicated maneuvers among real and ghost companies confirms everybody's worst fears about the potential for wrongdoing in an unregulated banking world.

Calvi had booked the loans through subsidiaries in Peru and Nicaragua. He funded them with borrowings in the Euromarket. Whenever anyone wanted to know more about these ghost companies, which had names like Bellatrix and Manic, Calvi flashed his letters of comfort from the Vatican bank, Istituto per le Opere di Religione. The letters apparently amounted to a guarantee. Only, it emerged later, Calvi had written Marcinkus some letters of his own, explicitly releasing IOR from any obligation with regard to these loans. When the Bank of Italy came breathing down Calvi's neck in the spring of 1982 Calvi turned to Marcinkus for succor, but the cleric flatly refused. After Calvi's death, the Vatican's role in the affair became a political issue in Italy and led to diplomatic altercation between Rome and the Vatican. Beniamino Andreatta, an independent-minded Christian Democrat, gave a pungent speech in parliament, calling upon the pope himself to clear up the matter. A summons sent directly to Marcinkus in the Vatican was returned unopened with the direction to send it through diplomatic channels.

After Calvi was found dead, his deputies, who evidently remained in the dark about their boss's machinations, could only get the IOR to honor one direct loan to Banco Andio, the Peruvian subsidiary. The rest still totaled a billion dollars, more than Ambrosiano could afford to lose. Michel Leemans, a displaced Belgian who ran Ambrosiano's financial holding company, La Centrale, minced no words with the bank's board. "You'll have to call in Grandmother," he said, referring to the Bank of Italy. Grandmother acted quickly, appointing three commissioners to run the bank.

By mid-July, the central bank had to ask six other Italian banks to form a consortium to rescue Ambrosiano. The consortium was supposed to underwrite the bank's liabilities. But only its liabilities in Italy. Something wicked this way comes, sensed the Eurobankers. What about the $400 million that Ambrosiano's Luxembourg subsidiary owes on various syndicated loans? What about it, indeed, asked the Bank of Italy with its silence? The gloves were taken off. Midland Bank, one of the Big Four British clearing banks, jumped the gun and declared a $40-million loan to the Luxembourg unit formally and officially in default. That shot triggered the cross-default clauses. In the end, eighty banks rushed to various courts with claims against the Luxembourg unit.

Banco Ambrosiano was giving Luxembourg a bad name. Luxembourg was not Liechtenstein nor the Cayman Islands. The banks there were more or less real banks, not just nameplates on mailboxes. Pierre Jaans, the intelligent, mild-mannered banking commissioner in the grand duchy, had labored conscientiously to keep Luxembourg banking honest. The Bank of Italy's failure to provide for Ambrosiano's Luxembourg subsidiary pulled the carpet out from under the banks' integrity. The problem was that Banco Ambrosiano Holding in Luxembourg was not technically a bank, did not have a banking license, and did not come under Jaans's piercing surveillance. But its failure to honor its debts was nonetheless tarnishing Luxembourg's reputation as a banking center. Since the banks are the duchy's major taxpayers (Luxembourg is *not* a tax haven), this was a serious matter. Jaans reacted vigorously. He issued an ultimatum that all Italian banks with operations in Luxembourg immediately issue a formal guarantee for these operations or their licenses would be withdrawn. Even those other foreign bankers who were upset about the Bank of Italy's stance termed Jaans's action a "brutal procedure." The Bank of Italy, which had to approve the guarantees because foreign exchange was involved, was decidedly irritated. Reports began to circulate that the loans to BAH would eventually be made good. The Bank of Italy's action, it was said, was a tactic for forcing the Vatican to cover Ambrosiano's losses.

The Vatican meanwhile appointed its own three-man commission of financial advisers. Already tarnished by Sindona, the Vatican's standing in financial circles was anything but sterling after the Ambrosiano disclosures. Marcinkus stayed in his sanctuary within the Vatican walls.

On Friday August 6 (the week before the Mexican Weekend), Banco Ambrosiano closed its doors. On Monday August 9, like a phoenix out of the ashes, Nuovo Banco Ambrosiano opened its doors and life went on. So did the court battles. In addition to their legal actions, international banks sought further leverage against Italian officials with an "unofficial lending blockade" against Italian borrowers. Like any blockade, it had its weak points, but there was no question that as time wore on Italy felt the pain of having its flow of international funds reduced.

The Banco Ambrosiano fiasco exposed the shortcomings of the Basel Concordat. This agreement, simple enough in concept, had taken on mythological proportions in the Euromarket. The 1975 accord between major central banks attempted to make sure that somebody, somewhere, was keeping an eye on the banks. Central banks were responsible for supervising not only those banks headquartered in their jurisdiction, but also foreign branches, because these belonged juridically to the parent. Subsidiaries of foreign banks that were locally incorporated were the responsibility of the host central bank. In Luxembourg, for instance, most foreign banks incorporate juridically separate subsidiaries rather than maintaining branches. Under the Basel Concordat, Luxembourg's banking commissioner is responsible for supervising these subsidiaries. Because central banks cherish their freedom of action, the Basel agreement remained somewhat vague (it was not even published until some years later). No one specified anything, for instance, about bank holding companies. This was the crack that Banco Ambrosiano, not altogether accidentally, fell into.

5

By the time Penn Square broke, investors were worried enough that they began unloading bank shares. Drysdale and Penn Square were bad enough, but no one wanted to wait around to see what nasty surprise the next month would bring. In fact, the next month brought Mexico. In the initial uncertainty, spreads widened in the secondary marked for floating rate notes issued by U.S. banks in the Euromarket.

Life goes on, though. Once it was clear that the U.S. Government was not going to abandon American banks to the dark fate of sovereign default, investors gained heart. Standard & Poor's index of money-center banks bounced back with a gain of 49 percent in November against the low in July. Banks were doing other things than worrying about Third World loans. Citibank, for instance, was poised to cash in on its long-term investment in retail electronic banking. Barriers to interstate banking were crumbling, promising rich new markets to the money-center banks in a safe home environment. Stock market analysts turned bullish on banks. Many of the big banks reported a decline in fourth quarter profits, but the results for the entire year were reassuring. Citicorp boasted a 35-percent gain on the year, while J. P. Morgan, Manufacturers Hanover, and Chemical all reported respectable gains. Chase and Continental Illinois were not so fortunate. Chase's profit fell 25 percent on the year and Continental's was off 67 percent. At that, the banks still reported profits and still paid dividends.

By the first quarter of 1983, banks were back in the pink. Most of them, again with the exceptions of Chase and Continental, reported earnings gains for the period, some quite substantial. Banks usually rack up higher profits when interest rates are falling, because they are able to lower the rates they pay to depositors more quickly than the rates they charge to borrowers.

An unexpected windfall came from the reschedulings themselves. In the Mexican operation, for instance, the banks charged a rescheduling fee of 1 percent on the $20 billion involved. They also levied a 1 1/4-percent front-end fee on the $5 billion in new money. Fees alone added up to $262.5 million, more even than the first quarter net of Citicorp, the top earner among the banks. The loans were rescheduled at much higher interest margins, too, which promised even greater returns as long as these countries could pay their interest.

In the end, it seemed the only crisis was whether the banks would be able to increase their quarterly profits. While the banks and the Administration were moaning to legislators about the importance of increasing contributions to the International Monetary Fund, the supposedly endangered banks produced 30-percent-plus gains in profit. Most annoying of all was that a good portion of these gains came from increased fees from developing countries. And these countries were able to pay the increased fees only because the IMF and the central banks pumped emergency funds to them. The rescue money was not only bailing out the banks, it was actually making them rich.

Legislators quickly spotted the anomaly in all this. Senator John Heinz, a Pennsylvania Republican who chaired subcommittee hearings on foreign lending, and Senator William Proxmire, a Wisconsin Democrat with long experience as a gadfly to American banking, cosponsored a bill to regulate foreign lending. The bill authorized the Federal Reserve to set limits on how much banks could lend to individual countries. It also mandated the Fed to establish minimum loan loss reserves for endangered sovereign loans. Thirdly, the bill ordered regulation of loan fees so that charges exceeding actual administrative expenses would be stretched out over the life of the loan. The banks would not report that $262 million from Mexico in the quarter they happened to receive it, but in installments over the life of the loan itself.

The legislation sought to bring bank accounting into accord with the real situation. Accounting is more than bookkeeping. Its goal is to make financial reports reflect the actual financial state of the organization. It made no sense from an accountant's point of view to say on the one hand that banks were endangered because of their loans to developing countries, and on the other hand to let the banks carry these loans on the books at face value or to report windfall profits from forced reschedulings as ordinary income. Looking at it another way, the bankers justified the high rescheduling fees and interest margins to reflect the higher risk. But they failed to show that higher risk in their own accounts to the extent that they treated this extra revenue like any other.

Previous regulations designed to protect the banks did not always work. There was, for instance, the rule that banks could not lend more than 10 percent of their own capital to any single borrower. John Heimann, who as Comptroller of the Currency was the official responsible for supervising federally chartered banks, tried in 1978 to apply this rule to sovereign loans. He did not have a chance. The banks, which are ostensibly subject to the regulators, objected. So did the countries in question, notably Mexico. In the end, Heimann compromised by accepting the "sources and means" test. This allowed the banks to treat a particular government and its state agencies or state-owned companies as separate borrowers so long as it could be shown that the agencies or companies had their own means of support or their own sources of revenue. So the Mexican Electricity Commission, which had its own revenues, could be counted as a separate borrower from the United Mexican States for the purposes of the 10-percent rule. The speciousness of this distinction emerged at the time of Mexico's moratorium, which took in all public sector credit, regardless of which agency was involved. John Heimann, like most regulators, took a job in banking when he left government, becoming co-chairman of Warburg Paribas Becker, an investment bank.

The banking lobby is so strong that banks do not worry too much about possible congressional action. When legislative fervor was at its height in April 1983, Citibank vice chairman Thomas Theobald laconically remarked in a press conference abroad that the upshot of congressional concern was likely to be "more disclosure—a typically American response." Theobald did not think much would come from other suggestions. Even Heinz and Proxmire, zealous as they were, left the actual determination of the requirements on lending and loan loss reserves to those very regulators they castigated for having been too lax in the past.

In their testimony before congressional committees in spring 1983, a succession of bankers urged against loan restrictions on specific countries. The thrust of the bankers' argument, as usual, was that American banks would be at a competitive disadvantage in the world market because other countries do not have such strict regulation. It was the same argument the banks had advanced against unilateral regulation of the Euromarket a few years earlier, and on numerous other occasions as well.

What the bankers failed to establish was why they should not be at a competitive disadvantage. Perhaps they would regret losing this or that deal, or taking a back seat in this or that market. Too bad. What lawmakers and regulators fail to do when they accept this argument from the bankers is to maintain the priority of a secure financial system over the profits of individual banks. Of course banks have to be profitable for the financial system to work, but no one has ever demonstrated that the marginal profitability of unrestricted lending to sovereign borrowers is essential to maintaining bank profits at an adequate level.

The debate in the United States was paralleled in other countries, in a less public fashion. The Bank of England nodded and winked more furiously than before; the West German Bundesbank became a little less gentlemanly in enforcing its gentlemen's agreements on disclosure. Peter Cooke, the Bank of England official in charge of bank supervision and chairman of the international committee on supervision, hinted strongly that banks should keep their dividends down in order to reinforce their capital base.

This prompted *The Economist* to observe that the challenge to regulators was not to tell banks how much dividend to pay. "It is to discover a way to allow even big banks to fail, and their shareholders and managers with them, without damaging the depositors' or a country's financial stability." Well and good, but the banks have long since discovered that there's safety in numbers. A managed collapse worked in fact when Franklin National Bank in the United States and Herstatt in West Germany failed in 1974. But there was no question in 1982 and 1983 of just Chase or Continental Illinois collapsing. These banks had more problems than Citibank or Morgan Guaranty, but the dimensions of Latin-American exposure were such that a default by a big borrower on that continent jeopardized all the big banks. When Seafirst fell victim to its Penn Square loans, the Fed could keep it afloat long enough to merge into Bank of America. But if the Bank of America fell victim to a Brazilian moratorium, what could it be merged into?

The whole regulatory debate seemed like shadowboxing. The Cooke Committee, which brought together the G-10 countries, Switzerland, and Luxembourg under the aegis of the Bank for International Settlements, issued in June 1983 a new version of the so-called Basel Concordat. The original concordat, reached in 1975, sought to establish that no bank should escape supervision and that supervision should be adequate—objectives of such stunning banality that it was no surprise they failed in the case of Banco Ambrosiano.

The Cooke Committee, when it reached the original concordat, also urged supervisors to get consolidated accounts from their banks. Consolidation simply means that a bank reports all the operations from its myriad branches, subsidiaries, and affiliates in a single balance sheet. This is the only way that the bank's overall loan exposure can be measured against its resources. Consolidation provides an overview that gives regulators a chance to review a bank's true position. It is also very important even for the bank's executives, who may not themselves be aware of the bank's situation.

The United States requires consolidated accounts from its banks as well as from other public companies. Other countries as a rule do not (Italy only got around to requiring an independent audit in 1982). Despite the Cooke Committee's 1975 recommendation to consolidate bank accounts, the *Financial Times* survey of 1981 annual reports found that only twenty-four of the world's 100 biggest banks published consolidated balance sheets.

The revised concordat was equally vague and likely to be as

211

effective as the original. Its main purpose was to plug the gap exposed by Banco Ambrosiano's ability to evade supervision by operating as a holding company rather than a bank. Once again the supervisors emphasized that the concordat itself was concerned exclusively with supervision and not with the function of lender of last resort. It remained difficult for outsiders to accept the distinction because it seemed to divorce the responsibility for monitoring a bank's activities from the consequences of a failure in supervision—namely, picking up the tab.

The very existence of the Cooke Committee and the Basel Concordat served as alibis whenever the question of regulating international lending came up for discussion. It fell to U.S. legislators in the course of their hearing to call the Cooke Committee to account. Fernand St. Germain, the Democratic chairman of the House Banking Committee, excoriated the supervisors because they "watched while international lending expanded out of control at record-breaking rates." He continued: "I am personally concerned about the relative secrecy surrounding this committee's action and I feel that a far greater degree of accountability should be needed in the future."

The standard argument of the Cooke Committee and central bankers in general is that secrecy is necessary so that banks do not take support for granted. But bankers very clearly did take it for granted that central banks would not let them fail. Citibank, Chase, Bank of America, Deutsche Bank, Bank of Tokyo, Barclays, Banque Nationale de Paris, Banca Commerciale Italiana—how worried could they be?

THE
POLITICS OF DEBT
CHAPTER TEN

In August and September 1983, residents of Rio de Janeiro, São Paulo, and several towns in northeastern Brazil looted 225 supermarkets, taking sacks of rice, black beans and whatever else they could get their hands on. At one confrontation in the Vila Kennedy suburb of Rio, a thousand demonstrators threw stones at 150 soldiers using tear gas. "We are hungry," chanted the crowd.

Earlier in the southern hemisphere's winter, unionists in São Paulo had staged a series of violent strikes protesting the government's economic policy, a policy largely dictated by the requirements of the International Monetary Fund. Public discussion in Brazil turned quite openly to the subject of a debt moratorium or even repudiation. President Joao Figueirido and Delfim Netto rejected these ideas, but Delfim did not hesitate to use this public sentiment in extorting new money from reluctant Western banks and governments.

By October 1983 *The Wall Street Journal* was astounded to report that "national political issues" were "intruding" in international debt. Bankers, it emerged, were getting worried that riots, looting, and demonstrations might sabotage the rescue packages. No one had realized, the *Journal* reported, that the masses of people who are thrown out of work, have their wages cut, and find their staple foods priced out of sight might rise up and actually meddle with the delicate financial balances so cleverly constructed by the IMF and the banks.

The IMF formula for "stabilization" throws up numerous anomalies. One key prescription is to reduce government spending as a way of dampening overall demand in a country. Next to arms spending, the one big item in most developing-country budgets is food subsidies. Arms budgets remain sacrosanct, so IMF-ordered cuts in public spending usually come in the food subsidies. This obviously entails very sharp rises in food prices, particularly of the staples that are directly subsidized.

When Egypt followed this classic course in 1977 it unleashed the worst riots the country had seen since its revolution in 1952. The official count for the dead was seventy-nine. The Sadat government banned strikes and demonstrations and imposed a curfew.

Hapless Peru had a worse experience with its IMF program in 1979. The central bank president of the period, Manuel Moreyra, told the New York *Times* that the IMF program "means death for around 500,000 children and brings an incontrovertible reality with it: The Peruvians are being subjected to a hunger cure." Many poor people subsisted, literally, on chicken feed. The feed, Nicovita, is made from fish and contains some toxic substances. Finance Minister Silva Ruete, who negotiated the IMF program, admitted the widespread consumption of Nicovita, but added, "What is even more serious is the fact that there are people who don't even get chicken feed regularly to eat."

Richard Gerster, a young Swiss development specialist, lists several undesirable side effects to IMF "stabilization" programs. The IMF, for instance, seeks to keep borders open for the free flow of trade, even when a country is suffering from a trade deficit. When a country needs to reduce its imports, it often finds the simplest thing is to restrict certain types of imports by denying them entry to the country. This gives the government some voice in choosing just what foreign products it will spend its precious foreign currency on. The IMF on the other hand, committed to free trade, wants to achieve the same effect by devaluing the country's currency, making imports much more expensive across the board, and by reducing government spending. But this does not mean that the country will automatically import only those goods necessary for economic growth.

The Philippines benefited from a surge in U.S. aid and IMF credits after it removed import controls in 1962. But the effect of lifting the restrictions was a dramatic increase in imports of consumer goods like cars, television sets, and electrical appliances. Imports rose 68 percent in the period 1963–67, while exports grew only 7 percent, obviously aggravating the Philippine trade deficit. The money came from those foreign credits, so that the country's indebtedness also rose. In the vicious circle that was to become the classic syndrome in the 1982–83 credit crisis, payments on the debt itself then became a major drain on foreign currency resources, and the major use of money obtained in new credits.

IMF advisers "welcomed" Haiti's decision in 1978 to remove restrictions on the import of luxury cars. They urged the government to lift controls on all automobile imports. The IMF economists ignored the question of whether the economic interests of Haiti, the poorest country in the Western Hemisphere, were best served by the free import of new Mercedeses for "Baby Doc" Duvalier's friends. Free trade was what counted.

Gerster uses these examples to document his theses on the bad effects of IMF programs. The agency's formula, applied to developing countries, makes it harder to fulfill basic human needs. IMF programs generally make food staples and services like mass transit much more expensive. They curb nominal wage increases, which means that the populace bears the brunt of breaking inflation by suffering a cut in real purchasing power. The stabilization programs usually entail a recession, which increases unemployment. Supplies of basic goods become sharply limited.

On the domestic front, IMF programs tend to heighten social tensions, block social reforms, and encourage political repression. Internationally the IMF prescriptions favor big business, which means a concentration of domestic industry and a prejudice toward multinational corporations. They increase foreign dependency by increasing foreign debt and making it all but impossible to selectively "decouple" a developing economy from the world economy in general.

2

Numerous developing countries have aimed their rhetoric at the IMF. Often enough this was political posturing using the IMF in one of its favorite roles, that of whipping boy. The government's technocrats would meet with IMF representatives in an atmosphere of enlightened camaraderie, whatever excoriations the politicians delivered for their constituencies.

One notorious case, though, went beyond rhetoric—that of Michael Manley's Jamaica. When the tiny Caribbean country was de facto bankrupt in 1980 and in the normal order of things completely at the mercy of the Washington technocrats, Manley's populist party, the People's National Party, decided on a complete and immediate break with the IMF. The country had failed its review tests on one IMF-mandated program, and the break came while negotiations were underway for a new one. Manley, a charismatic and articulate leader whose father was founder of the PNP and Jamaican premier in the 1950s, explains the party's decision this way: "They saw an absolute and disabling contradiction between the philosophy of the IMF and the model of economic development on which its programs were predicated, on the one hand, and the goal of a socially controlled, egalitarian society seeking to maximize its independence of economic actions, on the other."

Manley succinctly describes the Third World's main objections to the IMF prescription for financial distress. The twin measures of devaluation and reduced government spending are to redress the trade balance by making imports more expensive and exports more competitive, and by reducing domestic demand. But most developing countries lack two prerequisites that enable this formula to succeed. One is a diversified economy that can respond to these incentives and shift resources to accommodate the indicated shift in production. The other is a system of social benefits like unemployment payments that protects individuals as the economy shifts. Because Jamaica and other developing countries lack these two prerequisites, they suffer disproportionately from the bad effects of the IMF program while hardly ever reaping the benefits.

Manley made the IMF a central election issue that year. He lost the election and retreated to England to write his cogent and crisp apologia. His opponent in the election, Edward Seaga, painted the choice as being between Manley's "one-party Marxist state with a planned economy" and a "multiparty democratic system based on a market economy," which does not do justice to the PNP's stated program of "democratic socialism."

Street violence became the hallmark of that hotly contested election. Manley suggests in his book that some of the violence at least was the result of "destabilization" like that practiced in Allende's Chile. He stops short of openly accusing the CIA of suborning this destabilization, but strongly hints at it. Manley links all this to the IMF. "The break with the IMF was regarded by the opposing forces at home and abroad as the final confirmation of their view that we must be removed. The argument was couched in terms of foreign exchange statistics and needs. But there was a deeper concern. The IMF was seen as a guarantee of dependence upon an economic strategy in which the free enterprise system would be increasingly entrenched. Foreign banking support would balk if free enterprise was not promoted visibly in successive programs. The logic of events would drive us along that path. A break meant freedom to explore the non-capitalist path, the democratic socialism of the third way."

For Manley, as for many Third World leaders before and after him, the IMF was a representative of "capitalist" interests—i.e., the industrialized countries of the West. Ostensibly a multilateral organization of 146 sovereign countries, the IMF was set up to promote a world monetary and economic order that served the interests of those countries. Of course, that order might correspond to a natural law of economics. It might be the ideal order that would guarantee well-being to every country in the community of nations. Rightly or wrongly, though, many in the Third World perceived it as inimical to their interests, as the attempt of a powerful group of countries to subordinate a less powerful group of countries, to impose on them the structures and ideologies that benefit the more powerful group.

Michael Manley found other things to do after he lost his election. Earlier Third World leaders who crossed the IMF also lost power, not always according to the amicable by-laws of a functioning democracy. In her 1974 broadside on the International Monetary Fund, Cheryl Payer documents several cases where there is a suggestive correlation between opposition to the IMF and military coups. Of course, opposition to the IMF usually is just one part of a "revolutionary" ideology that brings tremendous external pressure down on a Third World regime. Payer's point is that the IMF, as representative of the industrialized countries, is one of the main instruments in applying this pressure. "Since its founding at the end of the Second World War, the IMF has been the chosen instrument for imposing imperialist financial discipline upon poor countries under a façade of multilateralism and technical competence."

In August 1965 President Sukarno announced Indonesia's withdrawal from the IMF and World Bank, proclaiming a "Year of Self-Reliance." Fed up with the strings attached to their money, he said, "The hell with your aid." In March 1966 General Suharto seized power and reopened Indonesia's borders to foreign investment. The country rejoined the IMF in early 1967, but an IMF mission was already at work in mid-1966 on an economic program. Western nations put up new credits and the Paris Club dispatched Hermann J. Abs, Germany's leading postwar banker, to put Indonesia's foreign debt on a payable basis. Abs wisely rescheduled the government-to-government debt over thirty years, to 1999, "the most lenient debt settlement which has been voluntarily granted to a Third World government by its creditors."

There were many issues at stake in Sukarno's fall besides the IMF and economic policy. But it was very clear whose side the IMF took and what the repercussions were.

In 1964, President João Goulart of Brazil fell off his political tightrope. Abandoned by Western aid agencies, including the World Bank and IMF, Brazil adopted increasingly leftist policies. Goulart imposed tighter restrictions on the amount of profits that foreign companies could send home. Then he announced land reform measures and nationalized the oil refineries. The military seized power on April 1. On April 2 the United States recognized the new government and mobilized the full panoply of aid at its disposal, including the IMF and World Bank. "The haste with which the United States moved to congratulate, recognize, and

218

send aid to the new military leaders of Brazil was embarrassing even to their sympathizers," writes Payer.

In the Cold War mentality of the 1960s, the United States and its foreign policy mattered much more than it did two decades later. The U.S. role and intentions were much more overt in Indonesia and Brazil and the seven other cases Payer documents (Philippines, Indochina, Yugoslavia, India, Chile, Ghana, and North Korea). The IMF functioned as an alter ego of the United States because its purpose was to maintain the economic order that the U.S. and its allies wanted. When this clashed with the policies and goals of less important countries, even those rich in resources and people like Indonesia and Brazil, the stronger group won.

Payer and other critics of the IMF contend that the organization's sole purpose is to keep capital flows free for the benefit of the industrialized countries. IMF stabilization programs, ostensibly designed to redress the imbalance in foreign payments, serve first and foremost to make it easy for multinational corporations to invest in a country and then earn a stable return on that investment by taking home the profits. That hardly sounds sinister, but the argument continues that this priority does not necessarily serve the economic and social development of the country. At any rate, it imposes an external policy that often runs counter to the country's perceived political goals.

3

The IMF was founded to prevent devaluations because too many countries prior to World War II used devaluation as a trade weapon. The irony now is that the IMF spends most of its time compelling Third World countries to devalue their currencies. The agency's response to one glaring competitive devaluation by an industrialized country—Sweden's 16-percent devaluation in 1982 —was to gently reprimand the country and make a study. There was no sanction and no reversal of policy by the Swedish Government. The IMF has no power to make a Sweden, let alone a United States or Japan or Great Britain, heed its behests, and none of these industrialized countries acknowledges the authority of the IMF to demand this or that.

In fact, the authority of the IMF is an illusion. It is simply a convenient front man for the real powers. Throughout the credit crisis, the IMF's apparent strength was largely a mask to disguise the real actors. When the IMF withheld its loans to Brazil in the summer of 1983 because the country failed to meet the agreed-upon targets for inflation and trade, Brazil had to modify its already stringent policies even further. But only because the Western governments, the creditor banks, and everybody else said they had to obey the IMF. The IMF is only a club. It is the governments and the banks who wield it. The IMF has no authority; it is simply an alibi for powerful countries to impose suitable policies onto less powerful countries.

The subordinate role of the IMF became very clear during the Mexican Weekend. The Mexicans consulted De Larosière, but the crisis was resolved at the Treasury, across the street from the White House. The funds came predominantly from the United States. The backup came from the Bank for International Settlements, which groups the central banks, the lenders of last resort.

The IMF is in fact what it claims to be, a technical ancillary. But these are not technocrats serving some vague, altruistic goal. They are serving the interests and ideology of the industrial countries who founded the IMF, and the World Bank, for that matter. The IMF experts are very partisan technocrats. They have a function in the established order of things. Expecting them to take the side of Third World countries or to take seriously indigenous goals for development is like expecting Exxon's corporate lawyers to sympathize with OPEC's position in 1973, when the producers' cartel unilaterally raised prices.

Once the rescue package for Mexico was agreed upon in August 1982, the lawyers for the Department of Energy, the Department of Defense, and the Mexican oil company, Pemex, had the important task of drawing up the actual contracts. Likewise, the IMF had the important task of working out contractual details with the Mexican Government for getting the country's payments back in balance. Both measures were political, agreed on at a political level.

The lawyers and the IMF were the instrument of execution, not the policymakers themselves.

IMF staffers cultivate an anonymity suitable to their technocratic status. Only with the credit crisis did public interest focus on these people and certain personalities begin to emerge. Department directors and their deputies, who often turn out to be mission heads, come from diverse countries—Burma, India, Zambia, Mali, Egypt, Colombia, Chile, as well as the G-5 countries and many others.

Ted Beza does not appear sinister or cruel. He has an engaging smile, but smiles only briefly because he has a lot to do. He is a former professor but has lost any trace of academic detachment. He is an economist, but not woolly-minded or abstract. More than anything else, he seems like a negotiator who knows how to dole out syrup and vinegar in appropriate measure. He bears a passing resemblance to Lee Iacocca, and his job made saving Chrysler look like a piece of cake. Ted Beza led the Mexican mission for the IMF. He negotiated with Mexican officials to set targets for imports and exports, government spending, and inflation.

"You have to see how things hang together," is how Beza sums up his pragmatic approach to economics. Beza believes in the IMF. He believes in Mexico. He speaks Spanish like a native, obviously enjoys his contacts with the Mexicans, and spends twelve hours a day working. The IMF program might entail hardships, he says, "but the problem would be if they didn't have a program."

That is a standard IMF line. If Beza is almost avuncular, Johannes Witteveen, onetime managing director of the IMF, is downright grandfatherly in semiretirement as an adviser to Amsterdam-Rotterdam Bank in Holland. Sitting in his office overlooking Herengracht in Amsterdam, Witteveen notes reflectively that the IMF does not make the rules of the international economy. "It is not the IMF that withdraws the money," he says of countries who run into trouble because banks lose confidence in their creditworthiness. The agency is simply a "disciplinary mechanism."

The quiet men at the IMF know better than to believe the propaganda spread about them. Hailed as heroes of the debt crisis, they shyly refuse to step up and accept the medals, with good reason. They work hard, like good foot soldiers slogging along. But it is the generals who reap the glory or the blame. Much of the praise lavished on the IMF comes from those bankers, politicians, and central bankers who would like to distract the public attention from their own responsibilities and mixed performances in the crisis.

The main criticism of the IMF, during the credit crisis and before, concerned the rigidity of its formula for "stabilization." That very rigidity betrays the limits of the IMF mandate. The agency's experts have no choice. Imagine Ted Beza coming back to Washington from Mexico with a novel "stabilization" program for Mexico that called for a ten-year moratorium on *all* payments of interest and principal on the foreign debt, including that owed to the World Bank, with a twenty-year repayment schedule following that. Suppose Beza suggested that all manufactured imports from Mexico be given concessionary tariffs by the United States and other industrial countries. All this to avoid the harsh impact of 40-percent unemployment and skyrocketing food prices on the poor people of Mexico, let alone the depressive effect on industry of drastic cuts in imports. Even if Beza would propose it, imagine Jacques de Larosière accepting such a preposterous program. He would be out of a job quicker than his countryman, Pierre-Paul Schweitzer, who lost the IMF post in 1973 after crossing the U.S. administration.

Asking the IMF to change its policies or its programs is asking the leopard to change its spots. Payer refuses to discuss a reform of the IMF as a possible solution to Third World financial problems. "Since the international monetary system is controlled by the rich nations, it is utopian to expect the guardian of the system to be the champion of the have-nots as well." Change at the IMF, she continues, is hopeless, "for it would have to tear up its constitution and become a different animal altogether before it could conceivably play a positive role in the development of the Third World."

A top Fund official affirms this view, without the prejudicial implications, even in the wake of the 1982–83 credit crisis. Bahram Nowzad, who was longtime chief of the IMF department responsible for debt questions, noted that the debt crisis prompted some people to call for even greater involvement of the agency in debt questions. But Nowzad cautioned that there were limits to what the Fund could do. "At the broadest level, the Fund is limited by its Articles, which prescribe not only its purposes but also, to some degree, the manner in which it is to reach these purposes (an example being the provision regarding the promotion of an open international economic system—the Fund's objectives cannot be met by resort to restrictions)." Which leaves us all with the question of what to do about the IMF if it turns out that restrictions, on imports or foreign exchange or investment, serve the best interests of a particular economy.

4

In the United States, the Third World debt crisis cut across party lines. Republicans and Democrats were divided among themselves for different reasons. Some wanted to aid the developing countries, punish the banks, and save the financial system. Others wanted to forget the developing countries, punish the banks, and let the marketplace work its magic. Debate on the debt crisis and the budget deficit joined such unlikely advocates as the conservative supply-sider Jack Kemp, a congressman from New York, and the liberal crusader Ralph Nader. These two opposed the increased U.S. contribution to the International Monetary Fund because it was a bailout for the banks. Reagan, Regan, and all the bankers in the world insisted that the new IMF funds were the linchpin for global salvation.

Lobby groups were formed to whip up public opinion on an issue the public could not begin to fathom. Investment adviser Howard Ruff mounted a whimsically titled "Save the Eagle" campaign against the IMF contribution. Their argument, repeated in various ways by other opponents of the IMF contributions in the United States and elsewhere, was that the government could not afford to shell out billions of dollars to aid faraway countries or bail out banks when budget trimming was already depressing the domestic economy. It was a curious mirror image of the IMF opponents in developing countries, who also wondered why they should suffer further austerity just to shell out money to faraway countries or bail out banks. Of course, they had contracted a debt.

In the United States and other developed countries, the credit crisis exposed political malfeasance with regard to the banks. Politicians and governments were not willing to recognize the consequences of international payments transfers resulting from higher oil prices. That one very concrete, immediate event was of course just the most obvious manifestation of a shift in world economic power. A politician with a moderate measure of common sense and an uncommon measure of political courage would have advocated appropriate changes in world economic and monetary institutions.

Instead, Western politicians quietly stopped worrying about the "recycling" problem. As much by their silence as anything else, they encouraged the banks to increase their financial mediation to handle the problem. Governments abdicated their responsibilities for the world financial system to the banks. They allowed the banks to expand their power over the conduct of international finance. After generations of banking frauds, failures, and collapses had taught governments how to control banks in a domestic environment, the Western governments of the 1970s gave free rein to private banks in a vastly expanding international environment.

The biggest irony was that just as U.S. banks were getting caught short in the international sphere, they were finally breaking out of the domestic restrictions imposed on them in the wake of the great crash of 1929. Limits on interstate banking and combinations of commercial banking and investment banking activities crumbled even before Congress could remove them. The banks simply rode roughshod over the law. Even as legislators inveighed in Congress against the irresponsibility of the banks, the financial magazine *Institutional Investor* heralded the arrival of a new era in nationwide banking in a panegyric to Walter Wriston's accomplishment. Just as the world was trembling with the message that money and credit require strong political control, banks were planning an unprecedented and practically uncontrolled expansion in the biggest capitalist market in the world.

5

Debt is political. It diminishes sovereignty. A debtor no longer owns what is his; he is no longer master of his own house. The creditor has power over the debtor, and politics is the allocation of power.

224

The problem with sovereign lending by banks is that the parties are mismatched. A bank represents private, anonymous interests—its shareholders. A country ostensibly represents a sovereign nation of people with certain political rights. The common good traditionally has priority over the individual or private good. The state can appropriate land to build a highway or nationalize a basic industry to ensure its survival. The anomaly of the credit crisis is that a sovereign state is supposed to bend its will and its understanding of the common good to the demands of private interests, foreign ones at that.

Bankers are acutely aware of this, which is why they hide behind the shield of the International Monetary Fund. A multilateral, governmental institution, the IMF can back up the bankers' demand with overwhelming political weight. A state will not kowtow to a group of banks, but can submit to an organization representing 145 other nations. But this is where the political problem really begins. The IMF is not a democratic institution based on one man, one vote. Rather, it is an oligopoly based on one dollar, one vote. The five biggest nations effectively control the agency and determine its policies. The other 141 cannot even play the role of loyal opposition, because there is no chance that they will ever gain control.

Conservative writer Paul Craig Roberts pointed out that banks might rue the involvement of political heavyweights like the International Monetary Fund, the U.S. Treasury, and the Bank for International Settlements. Bankers like to view their sovereign loans as simple business contracts. But when these and other governmental entities "intervened in the relationship between debtors and private creditors, the psychology of the situation changed. The involvement of such prestigious third parties allowed debtors to cease viewing their debts as private contractual obligations and to begin seeing them as something subject to politics and international diplomacy." Roberts has turned things upside down, though. Precisely because loans to sovereign countries cannot remain "private contractual obligations," the United States and other governments had to get involved.

No one expects the Third World countries nowadays to get a generous settlement like Indonesia's thirty years. That debt was "official"—that is, government-to-government—debt. It is gener-

225

ally conceded that governments may have overriding political interests for treating development loans as something other than a
purely financial contract. Until recently it seemed clear that rich
Western governments also could afford to indulge in such overriding political interests.

The debt owed by Mexico, Brazil, and Argentina is overwhelmingly bank debt. It is *not* generally conceded that banks have any
political interests, overriding or otherwise. Their loans, most would
agree, *are* purely financial contracts and should be respected as
such. Governments may have the luxury to take political dividends
of a generous aid policy into account, but banks are in business to
make money.

But the loan is still a matter of political interest for the borrowing
country. No less than Indonesia in the 1960s, Brazil in the 1980s
has compelling reasons, in view of its overall development goals, to
want more extensive debt relief than bankers have been willing to
give. The anomaly, once again, arises from the disparity of con-
tracting partners: a private, profit-motivated bank, and a government responsible for the welfare of a sovereign nation. The rescue
packages of the 1982–83 credit crisis focused on the banks. Their
whole purpose was to keep debtor nations liquid enough to keep
interest payments current and to reorder principal repayments in a
proper contractual manner.

Banks are private, profit-oriented institutions. But they are headquartered in one country or another. Ultimately their political
backing comes from their home country. During the Falkland Islands dispute between Britain and Argentina, it was British banks
which did not receive payments from Argentina. During the U.S.
hostage crisis with Iran, it was American banks which froze Iranian
assets. Political crisis exposes the ultimately political character of
banks.

The banks took on a further political dimension in the credit
crisis of 1982–83. The size of the debts and the importance of the
banks involved meant that the crisis threatened the whole financial
structure of the Western world. Although the governments of the
industrialized countries had abdicated much of their responsibilities
toward the financial system in the decade following the first oil

shock, they could hardly overlook the clear and present danger posed by the crisis.

The presumption of the political authorities involved—the finance ministries and central banks in the industrialized countries—favored this focus on the banks. That was neither necessary nor logical, though. After a year of short-term financial rescue packages, it was becoming clear that these were not providing, and could not provide, a solution to the payments problems of the developing countries. As political pressures mounted in the debtor nations in 1983, the automatic backing of Western governments for their banks' position became harder to defend. As with Indonesia, overriding political interests were coming into play. Political risks and benefits had to be balanced with the financial risks and benefits.

The more intractable the debt crisis became, the more evidently political it appeared. Bankers and businessmen have always tried to preserve the illusion that business is just business, and has nothing to do with politics. They tried it again with international lending. They tried it again with multinational corporations. But business determines the flow of wealth within a country and around the world. Money is power and politics is the practice of power. Debt is not political only when it drives slum dwellers to loot supermarkets. It is political at heart, from the moment it is conceived in the mind of ministry planners or approved in the bank's boardroom. Debt is not political just when it cannot be paid. It is political also when it is signed in secret and quietly retired.

It is too late to protest and riot when the IMF mission arrives. The protests and riots should have taken place when those slick bankers in their pin-striped suits first checked in to the local Sheraton or Meridien. The IMF team is simply following through on the original loan agreements. It insists on a banker-approved program which puts the country in a position to resume normal international payments, whatever the domestic cost.

There is much talk about the IMF's "Good Housekeeping Seal of Approval." That is putting the cart before the horse. The IMF "seal" has validity only because the bankers and the governments approve the IMF policy. The bankers do not put up more money because the IMF adopts a program in a particular country. The IMF adopts a program because that is the only way to get bankers to put up the money. The bankers are the motive force.

True enough, in Peru in 1978 the bankers tried to enforce a stabilization program without the help of the IMF and failed (see Chapter Five). The missing ingredient in the Peru experience was the political backing that the IMF enjoys by virtue of its status as a supranational organization. Successful interference in the policies of a sovereign nation requires a tremendous political force.

Politics is everywhere. Whenever public policy is at stake, politics has a role and debt is clearly a matter of public policy. Perhaps too much attention has always been paid to government *spending,* or to the trade-off between spending and taxes. Debt then appeared as an easy out to legislators and politicians because finance always was arcane. Debt pushes off the cost of consumption now onto an anonymous future generation of taxpayers.

But there are limits to obscurity. Politicians turned too often to this easy out, and it was no longer so easy. Credit is not infinite.

The debt crisis pits North against South, but it also creates tensions between East and West, between Europe and America. It aggravates class tensions in developing as well as developed countries. But debt is neutral. It is neither left nor right. It befuddles them both, because it is ineluctable, unavoidable.

Debt seems to write its own rules. By definition, it must be paid back. Otherwise it's not debt, but something else—a grant, a concession, a gift. The problem in resolving the debt crisis is the failure to transcend this legalistic definition. The megadebt of the 1970s and 1980s took on a social significance. It was no longer a question of just money, but of people's lives and well-being. Just as society could no longer tolerate uncontrolled industrialism and bossism and other versions of primitive capitalism, it could no longer put up with debt imperialism.

As the crisis ran its course, the feeling grew even among officials in the industrialized countries that the issue was long-term and political, rather than short-term and financial. A managing director of the Morgan Stanley investment banking firm, Barton Biggs, summed it up concisely: "Somehow the conventional wisdom of 200 million sullen South Americans sweating away in the hot sun for the next decade to earn the interest on their debt so Citicorp can raise its dividend twice a year does not square with my image of political reality."

6

The injustice of the world monetary system represented by the IMF arises not so much from the powerful industrial countries' imposing their rules on the developing countries. It would be bad enough if it were a simple case of forcing weak players to follow the same rules as strong players, but the situation is worse than that. The rules formulated by the powerful countries and enforced by the IMF bind the poor countries, but do not bind the rich countries themselves, who regularly and routinely ignore the rules they dictate to others.

There was Sweden's brutally competitive devaluation in 1982 to improve its own trade balance at the expense of its Scandinavian trading partners. It was precisely the type of tactic prevalent before World War II that the IMF was designed to check. But the IMF was so busy running around telling indebted countries to devalue their currencies, it had time to scold Sweden only mildly.

While the IMF was forcing country after country to reduce its government spending deficit to a fraction of its former size, the United States blithely proceeded to double its deficit. In fact, IMF managing director Jacques de Larosière did chide the United States about its deficit, but his was just one voice in a veritable chorus of criticism from within and without the country. Fact is, the United States did not feel obliged to bend its policies to any of this criticism, let alone respond specifically to the admonitions of the IMF.

The IMF, child of the Bretton Woods agreements, continues its work even though the Bretton Woods system has fallen apart. In place of that system, based on the dollar and anchored in gold, is a de facto dollar system based on nothing other than the whim of U.S. fiscal policy and the decisions of speculators. With the collapse of the Bretton Woods system, the IMF lost its original legitimacy. Its actions now represent the exercise of naked political power. The unilateral decision of the United States in 1971 to throw off the

229

discipline of the link to gold eliminated whatever benignity remained in the dollar's despotism.

The Europeans managed to shield themselves partially from the unmitigated impact of the dollar with the creation of the European Monetary System. That system, established only through the combined political willpower of two exceptional politicians, West German chancellor Helmut Schmidt and French president Valéry Giscard d'Estaing, has proven surprisingly resilient. Time and again it has demonstrated its ability to respond to the *political* needs of European economies and trade. The EMS has nothing to do with the International Monetary Fund. For the Fund, the EMS is a nonentity and exists in spite of the system defended by the Fund. A moderate reform of the world monetary system put forward repeatedly by Europeans, particularly the French, to create three currency blocs based on the dollar, the European Currency Unit, and the Japanese yen has been ignored by the United States and by the IMF.

But not even the Europeans can escape the dollar. The oil-producing countries are forced to sell their oil for dollars, they are forced to keep their financial assets in dollars, the banks are forced to take dollar deposits, the developing countries are forced to borrow dollars and repay dollars, and pay dollar interest rates on their debt. Dollars, dollars everywhere, but the United States no longer has the economic and financial clout to match the preeminence of its currency. The United States is not stingy. It really does not have the money for floating the International Monetary Fund, for funding the International Development Agency, for bailing out Brazil. It does not have the political will or the institutions for redressing its own runaway finances.

In 1983 the dollar was not strong. Its apparent strength rested on a number of technical and mutually supportive factors all boiling down to the fact that everybody had to use dollars for everything. The debt bubble that threatened to burst in the credit crisis of 1982–83 was a dollar bubble. The problem was not financial; it was not a question of shuffling around credits and debts, but of coming to grips with a dollar-dominated monetary system that had outgrown the *political* capability of the United States to cope. The calls from the Third World and from Europe for a new monetary system recognized the fact that new political relationships based on shifts in economic strength had to be institutionalized in the way the world managed its money.

THE
FUTURE OF DEBT
CHAPTER ELEVEN

———∞———

1

There's no solution to the debt crisis, only a resolution. The problem is not debts, but money. The only "solution" for debts is to get rid of them, either by paying them back or writing them off. The various solutions proposed for ending the crisis presumed that the debtors were capable of honoring their commitments, but that they needed more time to do so than original loan terms allowed. They were countries short of cash, but with the means of generating enough income over time to pay back the debt, was the way this argument ran. If that really were true, though, the bankers would not want the debtors to pay back the debt. As long as a debtor is able to pay on debt, he should have some.

When Mexico, Brazil, and Argentina and all the other countries ran into trouble paying on their debt, the bankers adopted a very ambivalent attitude. On the one hand, they did not want to lend any more money because it suddenly seemed risky to lend to those countries. On the other hand, they maintained that it really was just a liquidity problem, and in the long run those countries would get back on the track of prompt debt repayment. You can't have it both ways. Either it's risky or it's not. If Walter Wriston and the others really believed it was just a liquidity problem, they should have been happy to put up any amount of new money to tide over such wonderful long-term clients. Good debtors should have debt.

Much of the problem solving by bankers, monetary officials, and governments was so much shadowboxing. They were trying to find a way to keep loan payments current, either by shelling out new money or postponing the date of payment. But their hope was forlorn. The banks cannot prevent losses on their loans, because the losses *have already occurred*. Most of the shilly-shally in rescheduling loans was simply a shell game to preserve legal fictions. The question was not how to keep the banks from losing money—the money was gone. The problem was to find a genteel way of recognizing that loss in the bank's accounts. The overhang of debt that's on the banks' books can be taken care of in two ways. The banks can write it off and take a corresponding loss. Because of the sums involved, they could not do that right away because they would have been bankrupt. So they played their shell game and postponed the day of reckoning until they had a few years to build up loan loss reserves. Once these are big enough to cover the write-offs, the banks will make the loss official. This was the attitude of most European banks. The reality is the same: The losses have already occurred, whether this is acknowledged now or later.

No less an authority than Fritz Leutwiler, the president of the Swiss central bank and the Bank for International Settlements, prophesied during the Washington meeting of the IMF in September 1983 that big banks had huge losses ahead of them. Even without a banking collapse, the outspoken Swiss warned the banks, "the world debt problem will leave deep marks on their balance sheets."

Former Secretary of State Henry Kissinger put it to a group of international bankers meeting in Cannes, France, in June 1983, well after the various "rescues" were underway. "Can you believe," Kissinger asked rhetorically of the group, "that of the top ten debtor nations not one of them will rally public opinion by declaring a debt moratorium or limiting payments to a percentage of exports?" The pained silence in the auditorium spoke for itself. "Will you then," continued Kissinger, driving his point home, "cut that country completely off?"

The other way to take care of these losses is to inflate the debt away. This wipes out the loss by wiping out the value of money. It

233

is effective in purifying the banks' books, but obviously has other costs. It not only purifies away the banks' bad loans, but the well-intentioned savings of the rest of us.

There is no calculable, realistic way for countries to keep up their debt service and to grow economically if money retains its value. Ninety billion dollars is just too big a yoke even for a country as rich as Brazil. The only way to make it manageable is to reduce it to $30 billion or $20 billion, which is what a good double-digit inflation would do in a very short time. Whatever lip service American bankers paid to preserving low inflation, this seemed to be their gamble regarding Third World debts. They were not making reserves on the order of their European counterparts, but continued to declare higher profits and dividends as though everything were hunky-dory.

If no amount of rescue programs for Third World debtors could bring back the money the banks have lost, what good were such programs? For one thing, they postponed recognition of the banks' illiquidity until one or the other of the above alternative solutions became possible. For another thing, the rescue programs preserved the fiction that there was still a monetary order in the world, and that the countries who thought they maintained that order were still in charge. But that hope was equally forlorn. The monetary order had already collapsed. The United States and its allies were no longer in charge.

2

The U.S. administration and most American bankers rejected the need for grandiose solutions. They maintained that the problem was a temporary liquidity crisis and did not require a fundamental solution. The crisis originally arose from an extended recession. The obvious way to overcome the difficulty, then, would be an extended period of growth. Simple. Perhaps the only hitch was the experience of the previous decade which demonstrated decisively that all the king's horses and all the king's men seemed powerless to move the economy one way or the other, regardless of what policy was decided upon. So this school of thought boiled down to keeping your fingers crossed that growth would resume and continue, then the debt problem would disappear. Simple, but chancy.

Pedro-Pablo Kuczynski, a clever Peruvian who became president of First Boston International, an investment banking firm, said, "The way out is to grow out." Wilfried Guth, the immensely influential head of Deutsche Bank and a nephew of Ludwig Erhard, father of West Germany's economic miracle, saw the rescue packages themselves as flanking operations. "What we need even more urgently is an economic recovery in the major industrial countries. Indeed, we could look upon the debt problem with far greater equanimity if such a broad recovery were to materialize." Indeed, but it was the same Wilfried Guth who had been preaching the gospel of low growth in the industrialized West. He had maintained for years that the days of rapid growth in Europe were gone forever. His born-again economic optimism seemed prompted more by the need to maintain public confidence than genuine conviction. Even as he spoke, Guth prudently put aside a good portion of Deutsche Bank's profits as reserves against eventual losses on sovereign loans.

Geoffrey Howe, the soft-spoken Chancellor of the Exchequer in Britain who later became Foreign Secretary, put forth a four-point "program" for economic recovery: more stable exchange rates; a correct balance of national policies, especially regarding budget deficits; an increase in resources for the International Monetary Fund; and an avoidance of protectionism. This "program" just listed the measures favored by the Establishment consensus. Most basic of all was Paul Volcker, the harried chairman of the U.S. Federal Reserve Board. He spelled out those flanking measures that Guth and everyone else took for granted. He urged increased lending authority for the IMF and encouraged the banks to restructure old loans and provide new credit if necessary. He even promised a relaxation of bank supervision to accommodate this cooperation by the banks: "In such cases where new loans facilitate the adjustment process and enable a country to strengthen its economy and service its international debt in an orderly manner, new credits shouldn't be subject to supervisory criticism."

One prominent retired banker was not willing to let the banks off so easily. George Champion, former chairman of Chase Manhattan

235

Bank, repeated his long-held belief that commercial banks had no business making sovereign loans to begin with. He suggested that banks immediately stop making loans to developing and Eastern bloc countries. Supervisors, he continued, should insist that banks use at least 50 percent of their pretax profits to write off bad loans to those countries until they are down to no more than 50 percent of face value. In the meantime, the banks should not be allowed to increase their dividends or acquire any institution that did not strengthen their capital. Needless to say, these suggestions, tougher than what any legislator would have dared propose, were not enthusiastically taken up by Champion's former colleagues.

One think-tank economist ran a computer program on nineteen national economies and concluded that the only thing necessary for solving the debt crisis was for industrialized countries to grow an average of 3 percent a year in the three years 1984 through 1986. The report drew criticism from several quarters for its optimism. After all, sustained economic growth even at that modest level had eluded industrialized countries for more than a decade.

Perhaps the most charming suggestion for solving at least one country's debt problems was that from a San Diego resident in a letter to *The Wall Street Journal.* James G. Dunn proposed that "in exchange for the immediate and unconditional forgiveness of all debts to U.S. banks, the Mexican Government will pass title to the Baja California Peninsula." The U.S. Government would just sell all this land and turn the proceeds over to the banks in lieu of those forgiven loans.

Other plans were more sophisticated. But the "solutions" that began to proliferate like mushrooms in 1983 shared one fundamental error. They failed to address the problem. The plans from investment bankers, professors, and other pundits filled Op-Ed pages around the world. They followed a typical formula: Take a supranational organization [multiple choice: (a) International Monetary Fund, (b) World Bank, (c) a new world central bank, (d) all of the above]; strip the banks of their Third World loans at a discount [(a) of 10 percent, (b) of 20 percent, (c) negotiated according to country]; stretch out the loans over a longer period [of (a) 15, (b) 20, (c) 30 years] at a subsidized rate of interest. That would take care of existing debt. For the future, the designated agency should issue bonds, with industrial country guarantees, that the banks would buy. The agency then would lend the money from selling the bonds to the developing countries. Presumably, given the past performance of loans by the IMF and World Bank, the agency's new loans would not be prey to the same imprudence that marked banks' direct loans to the Third World. A variation would be to have this superagency assess the creditworthiness of each borrowing country, set limits to borrowing, and allocate available loans accordingly. This would be like a super credit-rating service with IMF enforcement.

Spinning out global solutions to the debt crisis became a pastime for everyone. Financial wizard Felix Rohatyn, the mastermind for New York's "Big MAC" rescue, drew a lot of attention with his variation of the formula solution. His was one of the first. With the best will in the world, it is hard to see it except as a plan that would afford a major and continuing role for an investment banking firm like Rohatyn's Lazard Frères. Who is going to tabulate all those loans, compute the discounts, and underwrite the bonds, after all?

Peter Kenen, an economics professor at Princeton, proposed a similar plan. His neighboring New Jerseyite, Senator Bill Bradley, the former basketball star who took the debt issue and ran with it, also espoused this solution. But then so did Antoine Lafont, Joseph Grunwald, and other people never heard of before and maybe never heard of again. Jacques de Larosière, the managing director of the International Monetary Fund, got quite irritated with these Monday-morning quarterbacks, wondering why "some professor in Princeton" should know the best way.

Norman Bailey, an acerbic if slightly pompous adviser on President Reagan's National Security Council, devised a latter-day version of gunboat diplomacy, in a departure from the formula solution. He suggested impounding a certain percentage of a debtor country's export revenues to retire the debt. Instead of fixing maturities and a repayment schedule, this plan took account of the chief variable in the fortunes of developing countries—how much they can export from year to year. Unfortunately, the plan very much resembled the nineteenth-century solution of sending in the Marines to occupy customs houses and collect a certain portion of tariffs to pay off debts. Bailey was something of an odd man out in the Administration and particularly annoyed the Treasury.

Some problem solvers decided to attack the root of the problem, money. Ronald McKinnon, a Stanford University economist, argued that money should be managed on a world basis, because multinational corporations, institutional investors, and central banks all shift funds around the globe, from one currency to the next, and a strictly domestic monetary policy does not take this into account. But the concept that even the three or four main central banks—the Federal Reserve and those in Japan, England, and Germany—should coordinate money supply growth and interest rates to reflect these movements sounds like an if-wishes-were-nickels proposal.

The heavyweight economic commentators at the British financial newspaper the *Financial Times,* Samuel Brittan and Anthony Harris, suggested various kinds of monetary indexation to smooth out the sharp fluctuations in debt servicing due to the swings in currency rates. Brittan proposed an interest rate subsidy to compensate for the erratic movements of the dollar. Harris wanted any plan that should be adopted to shift the debt into investors' portfolios so that bank debt would no longer be frozen, and to reduce the dollar's share of debt in favor of other strong currencies. Their colleague at Bracken House, Nicholas Colchester, preferred to revive an old idea: the use of the IMF's artificial currency, the Special Drawing Right (SDR), for commercial and trade transactions. This would achieve a de facto indexation by averaging the rates of the world's five strongest currencies.

Rohatyn, Kenen, Bailey, Bradley, Brittan and all the other plan proposers conveniently forgot one insuperable obstacle toward adopting their plans. Nobody wanted them. Reagan, Regan, Wriston, and De Larosière could scorn these pipe dreams because there was absolutely no political pressure to adopt such plans. Until a full-scale financial collapse actually happened, there was no motivation to adopt such far-reaching solutions. Rather the opposite. Like the bankers themselves, the voters in Western countries who bothered to follow the roller-coaster debt crisis mostly felt that the thing to do was to cut your losses and get out of sovereign lending altogether.

Westerners felt themselves suddenly poor. Government deficits, social security deficits, and high unemployment do not inspire confidence. There was no loose cash for the beggar. Rohatyn and company continued to cast the debtors in the role of beggar. But the tycoon had lost his fortune and the beggar no longer wore rags. The countries who began borrowing money in the early 1970s were not the same ones who owed money in the early 1980s. These big debtors in the 1980s were ready to sell steel, cars, and petrochemicals to the countries that invented these products. The *industrialized* countries had been the beggars. They had for two decades begged the developing countries to take their excess liquidity and to pay for their excess productivity by buying their exports.

One thing that became clear as the debt crisis moved into its second year was that the "solution" found in the first panic could not last long. The package of a short-term loan from the Bank for International Settlements, an IMF program and standby credit, and new loans from the banks enabled most of the countries in trouble to limp through 1983. But Brazil's intractable situation alone demonstrated that this type of medicine provided only temporary relief.

Brazil failed to meet the inflation targets set in its IMF program, so the agency withheld its credit installment. The IMF demanded that Brazil modify its wage indexation law so that wage increases matched only 80 percent in the rise of prices, instead of 100 percent. But the newly liberated Brazilian congress had the temerity to repeatedly vote down this IMF requirement. Meanwhile Brazil lined up an $11-billion rescue package for 1984, including $6.5 billion in new money from the banks. Also, it wanted a "bridging loan" of $3 billion still in 1983 to bring its payments arrears up to date. The 1983 rescue, far from putting Brazil back on its feet, just paved the way for a bigger package in 1984. Only the most courageous bankers dared to look forward to 1985 and beyond.

3

The U.S. Congress seized upon a solution that directly attacked one of the causes of the problem—it established restrictions on banks' foreign lending. The banking lobby and the regulators themselves eventually softened the blow so that precise limits were avoided. The success of the law depended upon its enforcement by regulators, although lawmakers, among others, had expressed dissatisfaction with the performance of regulators.

Banks did not really worry a lot about this law. They were no longer so keen on international lending anyway, and objected mostly because they object to any legal interference in their freedom of operation. Far more important for the American banks was the de facto collapse of the restrictions on domestic banking in power since the Great Depression. On balance, the banks stood ready to realize great new advances, the debacle of the 1982–83 credit crisis notwithstanding. The law on foreign lending seemed like a mild chastisement compared to the new vistas of profitmaking afforded by Congress's inability to keep up with the evolution of financial services in the United States. Banks bought brokers, banks bought banks in other states, insurance companies bought securities firms, and Sears, Roebuck became one of the biggest financial services conglomerates in the world. Legislators blinked. Regulators balked. Walter Wriston prepared to retire a happy man.

If the 1982–83 credit crisis demonstrated anything, it is that credit is too important to be left to the banks. Credit requires political control. Public opinion no longer countenances the laissez-faire attitude toward the economy that prevailed in the eighteenth century when Adam Smith wrote his classic analysis *The Wealth of Nations.* In those days workers were workers, bosses were bosses, and the government ran the army and the navy. Money was made and spent according to the law of the jungle, and the fittest prospered. It was primitive capitalism's finest hour, but it was unacceptable as a social system and underwent a series of violent changes.

In those days the government had no economic policy and the central bank was privately owned. Nowadays the government intervenes in every aspect of economic life. Economic policy shares top priority with military policy in the United States and is preeminent in most other industrialized countries. The central bank belongs to the state.

Presumably the next stage of evolution will entail a nationalization of credit. Many European countries have already nationalized the banks themselves: In France, Italy, Austria, and Greece, the state owns all major banks. Even in a country like West Germany, largely seen to have a classic liberal economy, about half of the banking apparatus is government owned. Although West Germany's private banks are very big and strong, the central bank has nearly absolute control over credit by virtue of its carefully wielded moral power. Likewise, the Bank of England holds considerable sway over the private banks in the United Kingdom.

Someday, preferably soon, it will seem as anachronistic that banks determine credit ceilings and interest rates as the thought of a privately owned central bank seems today. One "solution" to the debt crisis would be for politicians to take control of these mechanisms which have such an effect on the lives of the populace they are supposed to govern. It is ridiculous for a government that cannot control money or credit to pretend that it has a decisive role in managing a domestic economy. Nor is it possible that the world move to any coordinated economic policy as long as interest rates, exchange rates, credit creation, and capital allocation remain the exclusive province of profit-oriented private institutions. The public good is at stake, and banks are not built to serve the public good. That is what governments are for.

The United States is unlikely to nationalize banks in the way France did in 1982. It is not the American way. But Congress and the executive branch of government must regain control of the banks, nonetheless. The parameters of banks' operations must be so constructed that public interests are protected. That means reversing the trend of the past decade, where banks have held the initiative and Congress has not even been able to comprehend, let alone control, what banks are doing.

The bigger the bank, the easier a target it is for full-scale nationalization. When the political wind blows in the direction of greater control of banks, it is tempting to accomplish that in one fell swoop by acquiring a dominant banking institution. The Big Three banks of West Germany—Deutsche Bank, Dresdner Bank, and Commerzbank—and the four big British clearing banks—Barclays, National Westminster, Midland, and Lloyds—have this eventuality constantly in the back of their minds. If Citibank, Bank of America, and Chase Manhattan realize their more grandiose dreams of aggrandizement—expanding across the nation and dealing in every form of financial service from savings accounts to life insurance—then the nation that never even wanted a central bank may decide that it is more unAmerican to have a bank that big and powerful than it would be to expropriate its shareholders. (More likely, the Justice Department will come along and break these banks into little pieces again.)

A corollary to controlling banks' authority in setting interest rates and creating credit is closer political supervision of central banks. The impact of monetary restraint, tight credit, and high interest rates on the jobs, lives, and well-being of the public has demonstrated that these questions cannot be left to a group of cigar-smoking men meeting in a closed room. The nature of money markets demands a certain discretion in central bank activity, but the predilection of central bankers to wrap themselves in a cloak of gnosticism has no place in the 1980s. Of course, most central banks, whatever their protestations to the contrary, are subject to political pressure already. But this process should be brought out in the open to increase public accountability.

4

The old order is past saving. Only a catastrophe can compel a consensus on a new monetary order. Short of that, the new order will arrive bit by bit, with jerks and dips that will necessitate sharp adjustments.

There will be a second debt shock, just as there was a second oil shock. The debt shock is not an economic event any more than the oil shock was. It is political. It is a tremor caused by a massive shift in power. The real issue was not resolved after the first oil shock because it was hardly even recognized. The Arabs and other oil producers wanted a voice in how the world was run. Amplified by the double oil shock, their voice was very prominent for a time, sometimes harsh and strident. Now it has blended more into a harmony, but the world is different.

The same applies to the credit crisis. The first shock wave did not convey the message. The second one might finally get the point across and the world will be different. Even after the first debt shock, it was no longer quite the same.

The second debt shock will be worse than the first. It will be bigger, although perhaps less shocking because of the experience of the first one. The second debt shock, which may have taken place by the time this book is published or could wait till the end of the decade, will deal with debt overhang in the only way it can be dealt with: It will wipe it out. No amount of fifteen- or twenty-year bonds will save those debts. Either a new high inflation will reduce the value of the debts to a fraction of their original, or there will be a confrontation that will end with 40 or 50 or 60 percent of the debts being written off.

The second debt shock will change the world monetary system. The world has grown too big to sway upon the whims of U.S. domestic policy. Not only developing countries, but Europe and Japan are growing restive under the dictatorship of the dollar.

One of the red herrings in the discussions about solutions was trying to figure out now just how to finance economic development of Third World countries in the future. Where there is a will, there's a way. Where there's an opportunity, there will be the will. Already after the first debt shock, many developing countries began to modify their restrictions on direct investment. Foreign ownership of economic resources does present problems, but these should not be exaggerated. History has shown that foreign-owned resources generally come to be domestically owned. The polite, economical way of putting it is that domestic savings reach the point of replacing foreign capital. This often takes place in an amicable manner; other times, through war or expropriation. Risk is part of investment.

Some modest solutions proposed during the credit crisis of 1982–83 tried to find ways to convert some of the debt into equity. One suggestion was to have debtor governments sell stock in their state-owned enterprises. The theory was that there might be genuine interest in Pemex or Eletrobraz shares.

André Coussement, a stocky Luxembourger with twinkling eyes, devoted his time before his premature death in a car accident to selling bonds. He broached some years ago the notion that developing countries should be able to sell bonds to private investors.

Not exactly issues for widows and orphans, but for more venturesome investors willing to take the risk for a matching return. This need not mean a return to the wild and woolly days of the Kingdom of Poyais. But, after all, those poor investors in the bonds of mythical Poyais did not do any worse than the savvy banks who lent money to the preposterous but unfortunately real Zaire of Mobutu.

The World Bank Group and regional development banks, not to mention bilateral aid, will still have a role to play in financing countries where opportunity is absent or obscure. World Bank president A. W. Clausen and the pundits who wanted the Bank to become a sort of super loan syndication leader and performance bond for Third World loans may have pinned too many hopes on the organization, though. After so many years of mythmaking and myth shattering, the myth of World Bank infallibility should not have had so many believers by the early 1980s. Like the IMF toward the end of 1983, the World Bank was headed for a financial squeeze of its own. The soft loan subsidiary of the World Bank, the International Development Agency, was already caught in an inextricable financing bind.

5

Prime Minister Robert Muldoon of New Zealand was the first politician in the industrialized countries to call loudly for a new Bretton Woods conference. U.S. Treasury Secretary Donald Regan floated the notion to a select group of journalists in the fall of 1982. President François Mitterrand of France, anxious to cut a figure on the world stage, solemnly urged a new Bretton Woods just weeks before the Williamsburg Summit in May 1983. What they meant was an international conference to reform the world monetary system, like the one held in Bretton Woods, New Hampshire, in 1944. One commentator actually suggested convening the new conference in the same place. The management of Mount Washington Hotel, which housed delegates at the original conference, sent a letter to Treasury Secretary Regan offering the hotel's facilities for a new meeting.

But the Williamsburg summiteers diplomatically shelved the

Bretton Woods idea with a vague commitment to study the matter. Neither Muldoon nor Mitterrand commanded enough authority to make their suggestions stick. Regan retracted his suggestion practically the next day. The world had grown cynical about international conferences. The Williamsburg summit itself, complete with costumed fife and drum bands, seemed more a circus than a serious event.

The original Bretton Woods conference took place while men were dying on the battlefields. Roosevelt, Churchill, Stalin, and Hitler were ruling the world. The biggest financial collapse in history had taken place the decade before the most destructive war. In this cauldron two men, John Maynard Keynes and Harry Dexter White, backed by the authority of Great Britain and the United States, forged a monetary system and imposed it on the world. The world was not in a position to complain.

As harried and dangerous as the world was in 1982–83, it could hardly match the Armageddon of the 1930s and 1940s. The idea of having a new Bretton Woods conference in the 1980s sounded good. The system of the original conference was falling apart: let's get everyone together and make a new system. But it was not a realistic idea. Who would come—all 146 nations of the IMF? Or also the Eastern bloc countries who mostly do not belong to the IMF? Who would prepare such a conference? (Bretton Woods originally required three years of preparation.) Finally, where on earth was anyone going to find a good idea for a world monetary system? Keynes was dead. Most concrete ideas for stabilizing money seemed to involve some sort of return to a gold standard, which seemed like simple nostalgia.

The problem with anything like a new Bretton Woods conference is national sovereignty. It is sovereignty that emerges time and again as the central issue in the debt crisis. Any monetary agreement requires some sacrifice of sovereignty. The minting of coins has represented the highest authority throughout history. It was the jealously guarded privilege of rulers from emperors to the heads of countless German principalities. If you control the money, you are master of the wealth of the land.

As World War II drew to a close, the United States was practically a world sovereign. In the end, it was the United States which de-

245

cided the rules governing the monetary system. It is no coincidence, of course, that the two institutions founded at Bretton Woods are headquartered in Washington, just as the United Nations is located in New York. Neither the IMF nor the World Bank could be founded today. It is equally inconceivable that a new organization could be formed, or even that the authority and scope of the other two could be significantly expanded without a much greater catastrophe than the 1982–83 credit crisis had created.

We are prisoners of our past. Along with the calls for a new Bretton Woods came those for a new Marshall Plan. The idea was to mount an aid program for Latin-American and other Third World countries like that established for Europe after World War II. It is generally accepted that the United States was doing itself the biggest favor of all by giving Europe the money to get back on its feet. The Europeans' ability to finance purchases for postwar reconstruction lent added zest to the U.S. boom.

The suggestions for a new Marshall Plan were too late, though. *It had already taken place.* The transfer of capital came under the guise of bank loans to Third World countries. It was only when the fiction of contractual debt became difficult to maintain—that is, during the 1982–83 credit crisis—that the resource transfer of the 1970s emerged as an aid program. The only thing that remained was to apportion the costs. The banks, which were among the biggest beneficiaries as the program's agents, would certainly bear a good portion of the cost. But to the extent that this aid program benefited the American economy as a whole, the public authorities were going to have to take over some of the costs. Dividing the bill is always the most unpleasant part of a dinner out together, so both the banks and the authorities decided to have another cup of coffee rather than pay the check when presented.

One way to smooth the transition to a new economic order would be to abandon the rhetoric of free trade. The rhetoric is largely empty and the ideology behind it no longer acceptable. Free trade implies that the country with the competitive advantage—that is, the most efficient producer of something—will sell that something to everybody else because its price is the lowest, and will buy the other things it needs from the most efficient producers of those things. Price regulates supply and demand as goods flow freely across borders. But Jan Tumlir, the economist for the General Agreement on Tariffs and Trade in Geneva, demolishes the notion that price determines trade flows. By implication, he denies the existence of free trade:

"The services provided by public administrations, now a substantial part of total output everywhere, are clearly not priced by the spontaneous interplay of the cost and the demand side. Agriculture, an industry perhaps closest to the demanding conditions of atomistic competition, produces without competition, under prices set entirely by the political process. Textiles and clothing, an industry with vigorous internal competition, is effectively sheltered against competition from developing countries; the average level of prices is raised in this way and relative prices of particular textile and clothing products distorted. Steel, without significant competition on the national level, is extensively regulated in international trade. Shipbuilding in industrial countries continues to exist only by virtue of subsidies, a national self-indulgence; petrochemicals are largely cartelized; the world's most efficient producer of automobiles is severely constrained in foreign trade; an extensive and increasingly acrimonious international political negotiation is going on about where and under what conditions the latest technological innovations will be produced. Energy is under purely political pricing, most services both politically regulated and protected against imports, medical costs pushed upwards by the profession's power to control its own numbers . . . what remains?"

An economist, Tumlir plainly doesn't like all this political interference in the economy. He bears eloquent witness, though, to the overwhelmingly political motivation of economic actions. After all, that "self-indulgent" shipbuilding industry is usually seen by jaundiced politicians and admirals as having some middling strategic importance.

Trade is not free, and most discussion of it in those terms is hypocritical and cynical. Trade, like debt, is political. The two are inextricably tied together, because debt is just the financial side of trade. Trade is the only reason countries have anything to do with one another, in fact.

247

As the debt crisis rolled into its second year, the optimists seemed to be wrong. Even the consensus formed in the wake of the Mexican debt shock seemed to be falling apart. On a single day in October, Johannes Witteveen, former head of the International Monetary Fund, gloomily warned that the IMF and World Bank had to play a bigger role in debt reschedulings. In sunny Honolulu, meanwhile, Milton Friedman, the Nobel Prize-winning economist who championed monetarism, drew the loudest applause from delegates representing four thousand banks at the American Bankers Association meeting when he suggested dismantling the IMF because it was trying to turn itself into the world's central bank. The Philippines, rocked by demonstrations in the wake of the assassination of Benigno Aquino, convened commercial bankers in New York to broach the subject of rescheduling the country's $18 billion in foreign debt. The Philippines became the first major Asian debtor to join the ranks of reschedulers in the 1982–83 credit crisis. Brazil, ready for its second dose of rescue, rented the Mermaid Theatre in London so that City bankers could listen to their pitch for $6.5 billion. The meeting resembled an $8-million-a-plate charity dinner.

The United States, as it had throughout the crisis, continued to demonstrate an ambivalent attitude. The Administration's sense of urgency waxed and waned depending on the immediate threat to the banks. Domestic economic issues, particularly the recovery, dominated political thinking. The message of the debt crisis seemed to get lost once the immediate danger of default receded. The resistance of Congress to a straightforward measure like increasing the resources of the International Monetary Fund reflected the mood of a public which saw through the Administration's attempt to shore up the banks, but which did not see the bigger issue.

The credit crisis is an issue for all of us. Whatever its inclinations, the United States cannot withdraw from the world stage and live in blissful autarky. The American people have to learn to live in a diffuse economic and political environment. The United States is still dominant politically and economically in the West, but is no longer sovereign. It has to learn to share sovereignty gracefully.

A generation of Americans jaded by Vietnam and Watergate has grown cynical about international affairs. But the United States still has a constructive leadership role to play. Neither political leaders nor the public will be ready for that role until they recognize the scope of the problem.

The 1980s, for better or for worse, does not seem to be a decade for grand designs. The transition to a more stable political and economic order was not going to be accomplished in one fell swoop. But as the course of the credit crisis demonstrated, it was going to be accomplished one way or the other. The role of the United States as well as Japan, Great Britain, West Germany, France and the other industrialized countries is to take a lead in that transition process, to extend and reform the existing, crumbling system before a series of shocks brings it down.

The rest of the world is readier now for serious dialogue than ever before. Sobered perhaps by the serious consequences of the debt crisis, Third World groupings noticeably moderated their rhetoric. Gone were the strident, unrealistic demands of the 1960s and 1970s. Meetings of the nonaligned nations in New Delhi and the Group of Seventy-seven in Buenos Aires quietly abandoned sweeping calls for a new international economic order right here and now for a more moderate, step-by-step approach to reform in the interests of all parties, developed and developing countries alike.

The British Commonwealth, as fair a mix of industrialized and developing countries as one is likely to find, commissioned a report on the need for a new Bretton Woods. That report, published in the fall of 1983, made several concrete recommendations for immediate, near-term, and long-term action, including preparations for an international conference on trade and finance.

Earlier in the year, the Brandt Commission issued its second report. The urgency of the credit crisis had prompted the group, which disbanded in 1980 after presenting its first report on North-South relations, to reconvene and recommend even more concrete measures. The panel's chairman was Willy Brandt, a former chancellor of West Germany and winner of the Nobel Peace Prize, who is by any measure one of the most prominent Western statesmen of the postwar period. The commission's members came from all continents in both Northern and Southern hemispheres.

Both of these heavyweight groups recommended full use of existing international institutions while looking ahead to a reform that would give more countries a say in managing the world's economy. A key suggestion from both studies was the allocation of the IMF's Special Drawing Rights, its artificial currency, to all members and greater use of these SDRs in settling international accounts. The big developed countries which control the IMF had resisted issuing new SDRs, arguing that such a move would be inflationary because it would involve printing money, in effect. This argument came, though, from the same people who were quite content to ignore the potential inflationary effect of credit creations by private banks. Handing out SDRs, in the end, is the same as giving credit, only in this case the allocation is subject to the concerted political will of the countries involved and not the judgment of profit-oriented banks.

Greater use of the SDR as a reserve currency or a trade currency might be part of a monetary reform. Or the European notion of three currency blocs based on the dollar, the European Currency Unit, and the yen might be workable. Either system would liberate the world from the absolute dictatorship of the dollar.

The Commonwealth and Brandt Commission studies hardly afford a blueprint for salvation, but they were serious efforts by representative experts to cope with a crisis. They merited at least serious consideration, and not the chronic myopia demonstrated by *The Wall Street Journal* in dismissing the Brandt Commission editorially as a group of political has-beens.

Whether now or later, willingly or unwillingly, the government and people of the United States will have to pay attention to these questions. Debt shocks like that of 1982–83 will demand it. Achieving political consensus on such broad issues is difficult and frustrating. It requires a type of political leadership that Americans have been missing since the 1960s. No number of Mitterrands, Schmidts, or Muldoons can make up for that absence. But making the effort is preferable to letting events run their course. The debt crisis will not go away. The world monetary system will not reconstruct itself.

The situation is dangerous. A full-scale collapse would increase economic hardship even beyond the bad experiences so far. But the greatest danger is the added strain on a complex and volatile network of international relations. A fragile financial system increases the already great risk of political and military confrontation. It magnifies the repercussions of revolutions, boycotts, coups, and assassinations. In the strained atmosphere of the second Brazilian rescue, what if Iran had closed the Strait of Hormuz, blocking oil tankers in the Persian Gulf, as it threatened? What if the Burmese bomb had killed Chun Doo Hwan, as it nearly did, and set off a long succession struggle in South Korea? What if there had been a Moslem fundamentalist revolution in Saudi Arabia that turned that country into a second Iran?

The debt shock was the first tremor. There will be others. In their own interest, it is time for industrialized and developing countries alike to abandon rhetoric and deal with the real political crisis that underlies that shock.

NOTES

The notes have been kept to a minimum, and provide references primarily for quotations. References to sources are abbreviated; full details can be found in the bibliography. Quotations in the text that do not have a reference generally came from discussions with the author.

PROLOGUE

The description is based on conversations with several participants in the Mexican Weekend, including most notably José Angel Gurría Treviño. Two lengthy newspaper accounts, in the Washington *Post,* January 30, 1983, and *The Wall Street Journal,* March 14, 1983, provided other details.

CHAPTER ONE

P. 6 *The Sunday Times* headline appeared September 5, 1982.

—*The Economist* cover was October 22, 1982.

—The *Time* story appeared January 10, 1983.

P. 7 The OECD report was published in December 1982 under the title *External Debt of Developing Countries.*

P. 7 Details of bank rescheduling came from Mendelsohn, *Commercial Banks,* p. 3.

P. 8 U.S. cumulative deficit cited in Tumlir (see Bibliography), p. 28.

—Kaufman's figures in his October 19, 1982, speech in Tokyo, "A Difficult Transition."

P. 9 Hartford anecdote reported in Hershman, "Bankruptcy Scare," *Dun's Review,* September 1982, p. 33.

—The Chicago jobless scene was reported in *Le Monde,* January 17, 1983.

P. 10 *The Economist* report ran March 26, 1983.

P. 10 Bell's comment was in a speech he gave at the International Monetary Conference in Philadelphia, November 1982.

—De Vries quoted in *Time,* "The Debt Bomb," p. 9.

P. 12 The Coca-Cola problem was reported in *The Wall Street Journal,* September 9, 1983.

P. 13 Volcker's statement before Senate subcommittee on February 8, 1983, in Government Printing Office, "The International Debt Crisis," p. 288. Emphasis in the original.

P. 14 Rothschild's analysis in her article, "Banks: The Coming Crisis," *The New York Review of Books,* May 27, 1976, p. 16.

—The Citibank economists were Cleveland and Brittain, "Are the LDCs in Over Their Heads?" *Foreign Affairs,* July 1977, pp. 732–33.

P. 24 *The Wall Street Journal* scenario appeared November 10, 1982.

P. 26 The counter-trade examples came from *The Wall Street Journal,* August 11, 1983.

—Soros's remark in his monograph "The Crisis," p. 8.

P. 26 Hayek's remark in an interview in *La Vie française,* January 27, 1983, p. 20 (in French).

P. 28 Commodity prices from Inter-American Development Bank, *Economic and Social Progress,* 1982, p. 396.

CHAPTER TWO

P. 36 Analysis of trade flows in Hallwood and Sinclair, *Oil, Debt and Development,* pp. 60–64.

P. 36 Healey's observations in his article "Oil, Money and Recession," *Foreign Affairs,* Winter 1979–80, p. 226.

P. 39 Tanzanian anecdote in *Time,* "The Debt Bomb," January 10, 1983, p. 8.

P. 51 Morgan's statistics appear in the bank's monthly publication, *World Financial Markets.*

CHAPTER THREE

P. 53 Baring's problem detailed in Sampson, *The Money Lenders,* pp. 35–37.

P. 54 Quotations from Feis's book, *Europe, the World's Banker:* on Brazil, p. 244; on Turkey, pp. 18–19; financial distress, p. 20.

P. 54 Kindleberger quotes from his article "Debt Situation," p. 375 and p. 378.

P. 57 Exasperated banker quoted in Meynel, "Erwin Blumenthal," *Euromoney,* February 1979, p. 14.

P. 58 Friedman's deal described in Belliveau, "Heading off Zaire's default," *Institutional Investor,* March 1977, p. 24.

P. 59 Wriston's quote in Meynel, p. 11.

—Costanzo quote in Belliveau, p. 28.

P. 60 Blumenthal's assessment reported in *Le Monde diplomatique*, November 1982 (in French).

P. 60 *Financial Times* comment from September 7, 1982.

P. 62 Ghana's settlement described in Krassowski (see Bibliography), p. 147.

P. 64 Phrase "financial war zone" from Asheshov, "Peru's Flirtation with Disaster," *Institutional Investor*, October 1977, p. 37.

P. 64 Details from Cohen, *Banks and the Balance of Payments*, p. 213 and following.

P. 66 Turkey's "seventy cents" in Bleakley, "The Rush to Rescue Turkey," *Institutional Investor*, November 1978, p. 50.

—Demirel's accusation of Ecevit in MacLeod, "Turkey Refuses to Be Rescued," *Euromoney*, June 1979, p. 49.

P. 66 Banker's peanuts comment in Bleakley, p. 51.

P. 69 Kafaoglu's complaint reported in *Middle East Economic Digest*, April 8, 1983, p. 44.

CHAPTER FOUR

Some of the material in this chapter appeared also in my story "What Next for East European Debt?" *Institutional Investor*, January 1983, co-authored with Jane Baird.

P. 70 *Wall Street Journal* comment from August 8, 1981.

P. 71 WEFA comment in Centrally Planned Economies Survey, September 1981, p. 124.

—Comecon loan data based on OECD figures analyzed in Schröder (see Bibliography), p. 38.

P. 72 Portes quote in "East Europe," p. 768.

P. 73 Nyers quote in *International Herald Tribune*, December 15, 1982.

P. 74 Laulan comment in "L'Occident," *Problèmes Économiques*, July 28, 1982, p. 6 (in French).

P. 75 WEFA, June 16, 1981.

—Project loan shadow comment in Hindle, "A Nightmare of Debt," *The Economist*, March 26, 1982, p. 16.

P. 77 Schwartz quote in Hindle, p. 21, as is the ultimatum to Krzak.

P. 78 Hurd's comment in *Financial Times*, March 2, 1982.

P. 79 Pitchfork anecdote in "Was sollen Mistgabeln in Warschau?" *Der Spiegel*, No. 41 1982, p. 209.

P. 80 Stealing on the job reported in *Frankfurter Allgemeine Zeitung*, December 16, 1982 (in German).

P. 81 Giraffe joke in Van Meer, "Banks, Tanks and Freedom," *Commentary*, December 1982, p. 22.

—Theobald quote in *The Wall Street Journal,* December 21, 1981, among other places.

—Dresdner executive was Jurgen Sarrazin in speech October 18, 1982, "Problems," p. 2.

P. 82 Rohatyn comment in the New York *Times,* June 11, 1982. His congressional testimony was before the Senate Committee on Banking, Housing and Urban Affairs, February 23, 1982.

P. 83 East-West trade figures in Leland, "U.S. relations" testimony to House Appropriations Subcommittee, July 21, 1982.

P. 84 Wharton's approval of Romania reported in *Financial Times,* September 17, 1982.

P. 87 Fekete's odyssey to Vienna reported in Dornberg, "The Communists' Best Banker," *Institutional Investor,* April, 1979, p. 55.

P. 90 Andropov accolade in *The Wall Street Journal,* February 14, 1983.

P. 93 Shultz telex reported in *The Wall Street Journal,* December 8, 1982.

P. 94 Puzzled comments on East Germany from *The Wall Street Journal,* December 7, 1982.

CHAPTER FIVE

P. 96 Poyais bond detailed in Rippy, *British Investments,* p. 19.

—Conversion schemes describe in Jenks (see Bibliography), p. 113.

P. 97 French expert's comment in Sosa-Rodriguez, *Les problèmes structurels,* p. 49.

—Defaulted bonds documented in Sosa-Rodriguez (see Bibliography), p. 105.

P. 97 Morrow quote from Bodayla, "Bankers versus Diplomats," *Journal of Inter-American Studies and World Affairs,* November 1982, p. 464. The anecdote comes from this article. The quoted comment on Lamont and Morrow is on p. 478.

P. 99 *The Economist* figures in December 11, 1982.

P. 100 Inter-American Development Bank figures in *Economic and Social Progress in Latin America: The External Sector,* 1982, p. 81.

P. 101 Finance minister turnover in *The Wall Street Journal,* February 17, 1983.

P. 102 Asheshov's rhetorical question in "The Mexican Petrotrauma," *Institutional Investor,* November 1981, p. 69.

P. 103 Tello's remark on tyranny reported in *Financial Times,* September 11, 1982.

—Legorreta's fainting spell reported in *Euromoney,* October 1982, p. 48.

P. 104 Dog joke told by Lawrence Rout in *The Wall Street Journal*, January 18, 1983.

P. 107 Banker's remark about upsetting the cart in *Financial Times*, September 10, 1982.

—"Yes" alternatives quoted in Asheshov, "How Mexico Unraveled," *Institutional Investor*, November 1982, p. 90.

—Mexico's step reported in *The Wall Street Journal*, September 7, 1982.

P. 108 Monterrey businessmen's problems described in *The Wall Street Journal*, October 7, 1982.

P. 109 Gavin's telex reported in the *International Herald Tribune*, October 11, 1982.

P. 112 Banker's telexed comment in *Financial Times*, December 16, 1982.

P. 114 Wehbe's witticism related in *Frankfurter Allgemeine Zeitung*, November 15, 1982 (in German).

—McNamar's "elevator shuttle" recounted in Wilson, "Treasury's Mr. Inside," *Institutional Investor*, May 1983, p. 82.

P. 115 "Trojan horse" reported in *Neue Zürcher Zeitung*, September 13, 1982.

P. 117 Banking in Brazil reported in *Transnational Banks: Operations, Strategies and Their Effects in Developing Countries*, 1981, p. 4.

P. 119 Brazilian diplomat's remark quoted in *Financial Times*, March 1, 1983.

P. 121 Sugar analyst quoted in *The Wall Street Journal*, December 14, 1983.

P. 124 *Exame* headline reported in the *International Herald Tribune*, December 20, 1982.

P. 124 The "Sambatorium" was coined by *The Economist*, January 8, 1983, which reported its designation as an "operational procedure."

CHAPTER SIX

P. 130 The term "bankers' international" coined by Petit, "Le maître chanteur," *Économie et politique*, April 1978, p. 41.

P. 132 Leutwiler quoted in "The Bankers' Banker," *Fortune*, January 10, 1983, p. 83.

P. 132 Muldoon's comment in speech at European Management Forum, Davos, Switzerland, January 1983.

P. 134 French headline in Le Fournier, "Nouveaux Maîtres," *Expansion*, March 6, 1980, p. 85.

P. 135 Galbraith's comment in his book *Money*, p. 40.

P. 141 De Larosière's press conference reported in *IMF Survey*, F ary 21, 1983, p. 55.

P. 142 The Brandt Commission recommendations are in *Common C* pp. 13–14.

P. 145 Witteveen's speech, "Growing Financial Interdependence," given on October 7, 1982, in New York.

P. 145 BIS report quoted in *Financial Times,* January 27, 1983.

P. 147 French writer's comment was in Le Fournier, p. 89.

P. 147 Pöhl's praise in speech before Statistisch-Volkswirtschafliche G sellschaft in Basel, November 8, 1982.

P. 148 Leutwiler's comment reported in *The Wall Street Journal,* Febr ary 1, 1983.

P. 149 Clausen's remarks came in the 1983 Jodidi Lecture at Harvarc on February 24, 1983.

P. 151 *The Wall Street Journal* editorial appeared on February 22, 1983.

P. 152 Simonsens' suggestion reported in the *International Herald Trib une,* February 2, 1983.

P. 152 Richardson's valedictory was on February 8, 1983.

CHAPTER SEVEN

P. 157 Beame's rhetoric quoted in Ferretti (see Bibliography), p. 325.

P. 157 Ford's speech quoted in Ferretti, p. 357.

P. 158 New York's potential impact on banks was described in Jensen, *The Financiers,* p. 150.

P. 159 Rohatyn's remark quoted in Jensen, p. 156.

—Connors' analogy in Ferretti, p. 153.

P. 163 Hoffmeyer's remark quoted in *Financial Times,* January 21, 1983.

P. 164 The Guadeloupe pension was reported by Werner Adam in the *Frankfurter Allgemeine Zeitung,* January 25, 1983.

P. 168 Galbraith's cable quoted in *The Wall Street Journal,* October 22, 1982.

P. 171 Stockman's remark was in Greider, "The Education of David Stockman," *Atlantic Monthly,* December 1981, p. 38.

P. 171 Regan's remark quoted in the *International Herald Tribune,* February 9, 1983.

P. 172 Feldstein's remark in *The Wall Street Journal,* November 10, 1982.

P. 173 Regan's CEO comment in interview with Steinberg, "How the Debt Bomb Might Be Defused," *Fortune,* May 2, 1983.

—His trading experience related in *Newsweek,* May 9, 1983.

P. 174 De Larosière's pleas was in a speech at the University of Neuchâtel, Switzerland, March 3, 1983.

P. 174 Galbraith's comment in "The Budget and the Bust," *The New Republic*, March 17, 1982, p. 9.

CHAPTER EIGHT

P. 177 Banker's remark on workout quoted in *The Wall Street Journal*, January 28, 1983.

P. 178 The figure on shipping exposure was reported in *Financial Times*, February 10, 1983.

—The coincidentally equal sum in energy exposure was in the *International Herald Tribune*, February 14, 1983.

P. 179 *The Economist*'s criticism was in Hindle, "The Other Crisis," March 26, 1983, p. 20.

P. 180 Johnson's claim reported in *The Wall Street Journal*, November 19, 1982.

P. 181 The pensioner's check reported in *The Wall Street Journal*, December 20, 1982.

—Menk's confession in *Financial Times*, November 3, 1982.

P. 183 McCardell's phone call in Gurwin and Wittebort, "The Game of Nerves," *Institutional Investor*, September 1982, p. 128.

P. 185 Trudeau's remarks reported in *Financial Times*, September 8, 1982.

P. 185 Harrison's remark quoted in *Financial Times*, October 7, 1982.

P. 186 Citibank's telex reported in Tully, "How Dome Petroleum Got Crunched," *Fortune*, January 10, 1983, p. 90.

P. 191 GHR executive's comment on the budget in *The Wall Street Journal*, September 21, 1982.

CHAPTER NINE

P. 196 Details of government securities trading in Welles, "Drysdale," *Institutional Investor*, September 1982. This story was a main source for the section.

P. 199 Butcher quote in Welles, p. 467.

P. 200 Patterson's beer feat reported in *Financial Times*, August 24, 1982.

P. 200 Accolade for Patterson recounted in Rowan, "The Swinger Who Broke Penn Square Bank," *Fortune*, August 23, 1982, p. 11.

P. 201 Continental Illinois' crane reported in *Financial Times*, February 16, 1983.

—Iacocca's quip in *The Wall Street Journal*, January 5, 1983.

P. 201 Jenkins "body blow" quoted in *Financial Times,* April 26, 1983. His "sword" metaphor was in *The Wall Street Journal* of May 5, 1983.

P. 202 Patterson's nickname reported in Rowan, p. 23.

P. 203 Calvi's secretary's curse quoted in Gurwin, "Death of a Banker," *Institutional Investor,* October 1982, p. 123.

P. 205 Leemans' advice reported in Alison Macleod, "The Heirs of Calvi Fight for Honest Banking," *Euromoney,* September 1982, p. 243.

P. 210 Theobald's remark quoted in the *International Herald Tribune,* April 13, 1983.

P. 210 *The Economist's* recommendation was in the issue of March 5, 1983.

P. 212 Congressman St. Germain made his points in a letter to *Financial Times,* April 21, 1983.

CHAPTER TEN

P. 213 Vila Kennedy demonstration described in the *International Herald Tribune,* October 13, 1983.

—*The Wall Street Journal* surprise was shown in a front page story, October 10, 1983.

P. 214 Moreyra's comment was in the New York *Times,* August 24, 1979, quoted in Gerster, *Fallstricke der Verschuldung,* p. 71 (in German).

—The Nicovita anecdote is from the Los Angeles *Times,* December 9, 1979, quoted in Gerster, p. 72.

P. 216 Manley's comments on party policy from his book *Struggle in the Periphery,* p. 184.

P. 217 Seaga's comment in Baird, "Michael Manley Against the World," *Institutional Investor,* October 1980, p. 51.

P. 217 Manley again from *Struggle,* p. 191.

P. 218 Payer's remarks in her book *The Debt Trap,* p. x.

—The comment about Indonesia's debt is from Payer, p. 83.

P. 219 The embarrassing recognition of Brazil from Payer, p. 155.

P. 222 Payer's remark from her book, p. 221.

P. 222 Nowzad's remark in paper published by American Express Bank, October 1983, p. 19.

P. 225 Roberts's comment in *The Wall Street Journal,* October 17, 1983.

P. 228 Biggs was quoted in *Fortune,* July 25, 1983, p. 6.

CHAPTER ELEVEN

P. 233 Leutwiler's warning reported in the *International Herald Tribune,* September 27, 1983.

P. 235 Kuczynski was quoted by columnist Tom Wicker in the *International Herald Tribune*, May 20, 1983.

—Guth's remark came at an Atlantic Institute symposium in Paris, July 4, 1983.

—Howe's program detailed in *Financial Times*, February 1, 1983.

P. 235 Volcker's comment was in a speech before the New England Council in Boston on November 16, 1982.

—Champion's suggestions were in an editorial page piece in *The Wall Street Journal*, January 11, 1983.

—William Cline of the Institute for International Economics did the computer model, reported in *The Wall Street Journal*, May 26, 1983.

P. 236 Dunn's letter appeared December 7, 1982.

P. 237 Bailey's plan was in Bailey, Luft, Robinson (see Bibliography).

—McKinnon's suggestion was reported by columnist Robert Samuelson in the *International Herald Tribune*, August 12, 1983.

P. 243 Coussement's suggestion appeared in "Why the bond market should open up for developing countries," *Euromoney*, August 1980.

P. 245 The role of sovereignty in the debt crisis is argued most cogently by Hervé de Carmoy, a senior executive at Midland Bank.

P. 247 Tumlir's brilliant analysis of the debt crisis appears in *National Westminster Quarterly*, Summer 1983. The quotation is from p. 36.

P. 248 Witteveen's warning reported in *Financial Times*, October 13, 1983. Friedman's remark, the Philippines situation, and Brazil's dinner party all reported in *Financial Times*, October 14, 1983.

P. 249 The Commonwealth report was published in September 1983 under the title "Toward a New Bretton Woods."

—The Brandt Commission's second report appeared under the title *Common Crisis*.

BIBLIOGRAPHY

Bibliography and Note on Sources

My main "source" on the history and operations of the Euromarket and the international monetary system was eight years' experience covering this beat as a journalist, in New York, Frankfurt, and Paris.

The credit crisis was a breaking story. There is a vast academic literature on development economics and government finance, but this story was reported in the daily newspapers. The world's two leading business newspapers, the *Financial Times* of England and *The Wall Street Journal* of the United States, covered the debt crisis thoroughly with news reports and analysis. The *International Herald Tribune* carried the salient reports of the New York *Times* and the Washington *Post*, and its editorial page was especially attentive to the credit crisis. Three European newspapers—*Frankfurter Allgemeine Zeitung, Neue Zürcher Zeitung,* and *Le Monde*—were also very helpful. The newsweeklies, particularly *The Economist* of England and *Der Spiegel* of West Germany, often delved even further into the story.

This is a story of people, too. Over the years, in the course of my reporting, I have met and talked to a good many of the monetary experts, government officials, economists, and bankers portrayed in the book. In addition, I conducted more than a score of interviews specifically for this book. The credit crisis also was *the* subject of conversation in many other interviews, press conferences, and symposiums. Monetary officials and bankers rarely speak extemporaneously, so there were reams of printed speeches from the numerous conferences and seminars on the debt crisis. The personal impressions of the players in this crisis provided not only information, but also a feeling for the future course of events.

I would like expressly to single out the value of *Institutional Inventor,* the magazine I have been writing for since 1977. This magazine and its English counterpart, *Euromoney,* have chronicled the boom and bust of international lending month after month with in-depth "insider" stories. Although written for an audience of bankers and investors, these two magazines cumulatively provide an invaluable primary source material for both critics and

261

supporters of the financial establishment. They successfully portray for public scrutiny a world that previously remained closed and obscure.

The following is a partial listing of works consulted for this book.

I. Documents and Periodicals

Agefi International Financing Review (London). Weekly.

Amex Bank Review (London). Monthly.

Bank for International Settlements, *Annual Report* (Basel); and quarterly analysis of international banking.

Bank of England, *Quarterly Bulletin* (London).

General Agreement on Tariffs and Trade, *International Trade* (Geneva). Annual.

Inter-American Development Bank, *Annual Report* (Washington).

————, *Economic and Social Progress in Latin America: External Sector* (Washington). Annual.

International Insider (London). Weekly.

International Monetary Fund, *Annual Report* (Washington).

————, *IMF Survey* (Washington). Biweekly.

————, *International Financial Statistics* (Washington). Monthly.

————, *World Economic Outlook* (Washington). Annual.

Morgan Guaranty Trust Co., *World Financial Markets* (New York). Monthly.

Organization for Economic Cooperation and Development, *Financial Market Trends* (Paris). Quarterly.

————, *World Economic Outlook* (Paris). Annual.

United Nations Conference for Trade and Development, *Trade and Development Report* (Geneva). Annual.

United States Federal Reserve Board, *Federal Reserve Bulletin* (Washington). Monthly.

World Bank, *Annual Report* (Washington).

————, *World Debt Tables* (Washington). Annual.

II. Books and Articles

Abbott, George C., *International Indebtedness and the Developing Countries,* London: Croom Helm; White Plains, NY: M. E. Sharpe, 1979.

Aliber, Robert Z., *The International Money Game,* 2d edition, New York: Basic Books, 1973, 1976.

Aronson, Jonathan David, *Debt and the Less Developed Countries,* Boulder, CO: Westview Press, 1979.

———, *Money and Power: Banks and the World Monetary System,* Beverly Hills and London: Sage Publications, 1977.

Asheshov, Nicholas, "How Mexico Unraveled," *Institutional Investor,* November 1982, pp. 87–97.

———, "Let's Hope the Mexicans Know What They're Doing," *Institutional Investor,* December 1980, pp. 61–79.

———, "The Mexican Petrotrauma," *Institutional Investor,* November 1981, pp. 63–87.

———, "Rescheduling, Costa Rica Style," *Institutional Investor,* September 1982, p. 43ff.

Asheshov, Nicholas, and Reich, Cary, "Has Delfim Worked His Last Miracle?" *Institutional Investor,* August 1980, pp. 43–65.

Bailey, Norman A., Luft, R. Donald, and Robinson, Roger W., "Exchange Participation Notes: An Approach to the International Financial Crisis," in De Saint-Phalle, Thibaut, ed., *The International Financial Crisis: An Opportunity for Constructive Action,* Washington: Center for Strategic and International Studies, Georgetown University, 1983.

Baird, Jane, "The Mexican Nightmare," *Institutional Investor,* November 1982, pp. 81–87.

———, "Michael Manley Against the World," *Institutional Investor,* October 1981, pp. 47–51.

Balogh, Thomas, and Graham, Andrew, "The Transfer Problem Revisited: Analogies Between the Reparations Payments of the 1920s and the Problems of the OPEC Surpluses," *Oxford Bulletin of Economics and Statistics,* August 1979, pp. 183–91.

Beim, David O., "Rescuing the LDCs," *Foreign Affairs,* July, 1977, pp. 717–31.

Bell, Geoffrey, Speech at International Monetary Conference, Philadelphia, November 1982.

Belliveau, Nancy, "Heading off Zaire's Default," *Institutional Investor,* March 1977, pp. 23–30.

Bleakley, Fred R., "The Rush to Rescue Turkey," *Institutional Investor,* November 1978, pp. 47–67.

Bodayla, Stephen D., "Bankers versus Diplomats: The Debate Over Mexican Insolvency," *Journal of Interamerican Studies and World Affairs,* November 1982, pp. 461–82.

Brandt Commission, *North-South: A Programme for Survival,* London: Pan Books, 1980.

———, *Common Crisis,* London: Pan Books, 1983.

Brunner, Karl, et al., "International Debt, Insolvency and Illiquidity," *The Journal of Economic Affairs,* April 1983.

Business Week, "Dome Petroleum: Going for Broke in a Risky Search for Arctic Oil," March 29, 1982, pp. 117–26.

————, "Worry at the World's Banks," September 6, 1982, pp. 33–37.

Camps, Miriam, with Gwin, Catherine, *Collective Management: The Reform of Global Economic Organizations,* New York: McGraw-Hill for the Council on Foreign Relations, 1981.

Clausen, A. W., "Third World Debt and Global Recovery," Jodidi Lecture, Harvard University, February 24, 1983.

Cleveland, Harold van B., and Brittain, W. H. Bruce, "Are the LDCs in Over Their Heads?" *Foreign Affairs,* July 1977, pp. 732–50.

Cline, William R., "Mexico's Crisis: The World's Peril," *Foreign Policy,* Winter 1982–83, pp. 107–19.

Cohen, Benjamin J., *Banks and the Balance of Payments: Private Lending in the International Adjustment Process,* Montclair, NJ: Allan Held, Osmun, 1981.

Cohen, Stephen D., "Forgiving Poverty: The Political Economy of the International Debt Relief Negotiations," *International Affairs,* Winter 1981–82, pp. 59–77.

Colvin, Geoffrey, "International Harvester's Last Chance," *Fortune,* April 19, 1982.

Cooke, Peter, "The Role of the Banking Supervisor," speech at the Institute of Chartered Accountants Banking Conference, November 4, 1982.

Coussement, André, "Why the Bond Market Should Open up for Developing Countries," *Euromoney,* August 1980, pp. 117–27.

Cumming-Bruce, Nicholas, "Jan Woloszyn's Struggle for Poland," *Euromoney,* October 1980, pp. 100–8.

Davis, Christopher, *Financing Third World Debt,* London: Royal Institute of International Affairs, 1979.

Dell, Sidney, *On Being Grandmotherly: The Evolution of IMF Conditionality,* Princeton Essays in International Finance, No. 144, October 1981.

Davis, L. J., *Bad Money,* New York: St. Martin's Press, 1982.

De Vries, Rimmer, "International Debt," statement to U.S. Senate Subcommittee on International Economic Policy, January 19, 1983.

De Vries, Tom, "Jamaica, or the Non-Reform of the International Monetary System," *Foreign Affairs,* April 1976, pp. 577–606.

Dhonte, Pierre, *Clockwork Debt: Trade and the External Debt of Developing Countries,* Lexington, MA: Lexington Books, 1979.

Dizard, John, "The End of Let's Pretend," *Fortune,* November 29, 1982.

————, "Paul Volcker: Is He Really Tough Enough to Defend the Dollar?" *Institutional Investor,* October 1979, pp. 39–46.

Dornberg, John, "The Communists' Best Banker," *Institutional Investor,* April 1979, 54–65.

Eaton, Jonathan, and Gersovitz, Mark, *Poor-Country Borrowing in Private Financial Markets and the Repudiation Issue,* Princeton Studies in International Finance, No. 47, June 1981.

The Economist, "The Crash of 198?" October 22, 1982.

Einzig, Paul, *The Euro-Bond Market,* London: Macmillan, 1965, 1969.

Einzig, Paul, and Quinn, Brian Scott, *The Eurodollar System,* London: Macmillan, 1964 (6th ed.), 1977.

Emden, Paul H., *Money Powers of Europe in the 19th and 20th Centuries,* London: Sampson, Low, 1938.

Emminger, Otmar, "Petrodollar Recycling: völlig neue Dimension," *Wirtschaftswoche,* April 11, 1980, pp. 72–82.

Erb, Richard D. (interview), "The IMF and World Economic Stability," *Challenge,* September–October 1981, pp. 22–27.

Erdman, Paul E., *The Crash of '79,* London: Secker & Warburg, 1976.

———, "Living on the Default Line," *Playboy,* January 1983.

Feis, Herbert, *Europe, the World's Banker, 1870–1914,* New Haven: Yale University Press for the Council on Foreign Relations, 1930.

Ferretti, Fred, *The Year the Big Apple Went Bust,* New York: G. P. Putnam, 1976.

Fishlow, Albert, "Debt Remains a Problem," *Foreign Policy,* Spring, 1978, pp. 133–43.

Friedman, Irving S., *The Emerging Role of Private Banks in the Developing World,* New York: Citicorp, 1977.

———, *Inflation: A Worldwide Disaster,* Boston: Houghton Mifflin, 1973, 1980.

Galbraith, John Kenneth, "The Budget and the Bust," *The New Republic,* March 17, 1982, pp. 9–13.

———, *Money: Whence It Came, Where It Went,* London: Penguin, 1975.

Gall, Norman, "How Much More Can the System Take?" *Forbes,* June 23, 1980, pp. 91–98.

———, "The World Gasps for Liquidity," *Forbes,* October 11, 1982, pp. 150–54.

Gerster, Richard, *Fallstricke der Verschuldung: Der internationale Währungsfond und die Entwicklungsländer,* Basel: Z-Verlag, 1982.

Greider, William, "The Education of David Stockman," *Atlantic Monthly,* December 1981, pp. 27–54.

Gurwin, Larry, *The Calvi Affair: Death of a Banker,* London: Macmillan, 1983.

Gurwin, Larry, and Wittebort, Suzanne, "The Game of Nerves: The

Treacherous Art of Rescheduling," *Institutional Investor,* September 1982, pp. 125–43.

Guth, Wilfried, "Weltwirtschaft und Finanzmärkte in der Stabilisierungs-krise," Kölner Vorträge in Kommunikationsforum, Cologne, November 25, 1982.

Hallwood, Paul, and Sinclair, Stuart, *Oil, Debt and Development: OPEC and the Third World,* London: George Allen and Unwin, 1981.

Hardy, Chandra, *Rescheduling Developing Country Debt, 1956–1980: Lessons and Recommendations,* Overseas Development Council, Working Paper No. 1, March 1981: revised February 1982.

Harrod, Roy F., *The Life of John Maynard Keynes,* London: Penguin, 1951, 1972.

Hayek, Friedrich von (interview), "Le krach est inevitable," *La Vie fran-çaise,* January 23, 1983, p. 20.

Healey, Denis, "Oil, Money and Recession," *Foreign Affairs,* Winter 1979–80, pp. 217–31.

Helleiner, G. K., et al., *Towards a New Bretton Woods: Challenges for the World Financial and Trading System,* Report by a Commonwealth Study Group, London: Commonwealth Secretariat, 1983.

Hershman, Arlene, "Bankruptcy Scare," *Dun's Business Month,* September 1982, pp. 33–37.

Hindle, Tim, ed., "A Nightmare of Debt: A Survey of International Banking," *The Economist,* March 26, 1982.

———, "The Other Crisis: A Survey of International Banking," March 26, 1983.

Hogan, W. P., and Pearce, I. F., *The Incredible Eurodollar, or Why the World's Money System Is Collapsing,* London: Unwin Paperbacks, 1982–83 (revised edition).

Hope, Nicholas C., *Developments in and Prospects for the External Debt of the Developing Countries: 1970–80 and Beyond,* Staff Working Paper No. 488, Washington: World Bank, 1981.

Illingworth, Montieth M., "So Long to Smilin' Jack: The Sad Saga of Dome Petroleum," *Barron's,* May 2, 1983.

Jenks, Leland Hamilton, *The Migration of British Capital to 1875,* New York: Alfred Knopf, 1927.

Jensen, Michael C., *The Financiers: The World of the Great Wall Street Investment Banking Houses,* New York: Weybright and Talley, 1976.

Kaufman, Henry, "A Difficult Transition," speech given in Tokyo on October 19, 1982.

———, "Forces Affecting Near-Term Financial Behavior," speech given in New Orleans on November 15, 1982.

Killick, Tony, "Euromarket Recycling of OPEC Surpluses: Fact or Myth?" *The Banker,* January 1981, pp. 15–23.

Kindleberger, Charles P., "Debt Situation of the Developing Countries in Historical Perspective (1800–1945)," *Aussenwirtschaft,* Vol. IV, 1981, pp. 372–80.

———, *Manias, Panics and Crashes,* New York: Basic Books, 1978.

Krassowski, Andrzej, *Development and the Debt Trap: Economic Planning and External Borrowing in Ghana,* London: Croom Helms in association with the Overseas Development Institute, 1974.

Kuczynski, Pedro-Pablo, "Latin American Debt," *Foreign Affairs,* Winter 1982–83, pp. 344–64.

——— (interview), "Why the Music Stopped," *Challenge,* January–February 1983, pp. 20–29.

Landes, David S., *Bankers and Pashas: International Finance and Economic Imperialism in Egypt,* London: Heinemann, 1958.

Laulan, Yves, "L'Occident, peut-il utiliser l'arme économique et financière? L'exemple polonais," *Problèmes Économiques,* July 28, 1982, pp. 3–6.

Le Fournier, Philippe, "Les nouveaux maîtres des monnaies," *L'Expansion,* March 6, 1980, pp. 85–90.

Leland, Marc E., "U.S. Economic and Financial Relations with the Soviet Union and Eastern Europe," hearings before the U.S. House of Representatives subcommittee on foreign operations, July 21, 1982.

Leutwiler, Fritz (interview), "The Bankers' Banker Worries Out Loud," *Fortune,* January 10, 1983, pp. 82–83.

Lissakers, Karin, *International Debt, the Banks and U.S. Foreign Policy,* Staff Report for U.S. Senate Subcommittee on Foreign Economic Policy, 1977.

Lüke, Rolf E., *13. Juli 1931: Das Geheimnis der deutschen Bankenkrise,* Frankfurt/Main: Fritz Knapp Verlag, 1981.

McNamar, R. T., "Press Briefing Concerning the Mexican Financial Situation" (transcript), Washington: U.S. Treasury press office, August 20, 1982.

MacLeod, Alison, "Turkey Refuses to Be Rescued," *Euromoney,* June 1979, pp. 42–65.

Manley, Michael, *Jamaica: Struggle in the Periphery,* London: Third World Media Ltd. in cooperation with Writers and Readers Publishing Cooperative Society Ltd., 1982.

Martin, Sarah, "The Secrets of the Polish Memorandum," *Euromoney,* August 1981, pp. 9–15.

Mayer, Martin, *The Bankers,* New York: Ballantine Books, 1974, 1976.

Mendelsohn, M. S., *Commercial Banks and the Restructuring of Cross-Border Debt*, New York: Group of Thirty, 1983.

———, *Money on the Move: The Modern International Capital Market*, New York: McGraw-Hill, 1980.

Minsky, Hyman P., "Can 'It' Happen Again? A Reprise," *Challenge*, July–August 1982, pp. 5–13.

Muldoon, R. D., Address to the European Management Forum, Davos, Switzerland, January 27, 1983.

Mundell, Robert (interview), "Rally 'Round the Gold Standard," *Barron's*, March 14, 1983.

Nowzad, Bahram, *The Extent of IMF Involvement in Economic Policy-Making*, Amex Bank Review Special Papers No. 7, London, 1983.

Ogden, William S., "The Nature of the LDC Debt Problem," speech at the Manhattan Institute of Policy Research, October 25, 1982.

Organization for Economic Cooperation and Development, *External Debt of Developing Countries*, Paris, 1982.

Osborne, Neil, "Is International Banking Really Such a Good Idea?" *Institutional Investor*, June 1981, pp. 59–75.

Payer, Cheryl, *The Debt Trap: The International Monetary Fund and the Third World*, New York and London: Monthly Review Press, 1974.

———, "Third World Debt Problems: The New Wave of Defaults," *Monthly Review*, September 1976, pp. 1–22.

Petit, Juliette, "Un maître chanteur international de FMI," *Économie et Politique*, April 1978, pp. 340–51.

Portes, Richard, "East Europe's Debt to the West: Interdependence Is a Two-Way Street," *Foreign Affairs*, July 1977, pp. 751–83.

———, *The Polish Crisis: Western Economic Policy Options*, Chatham House Papers, London: Royal Institute of International Affairs, 1981.

Richardson, Gordon, Speech at Overseas Bankers Club, February 8, 1983.

Rippy, J. Fred, *British Investments in Latin America, 1822–1949: A Case Study in the Operations of Private Enterprise in Retarded Regions*, Minneapolis: University of Minnesota Press, 1959.

Rohatyn, Felix, "A Plan for Stretching out Global Debt," *Business Week*, February 28, 1983, pp. 8–9.

———, "The State of the Banks," *The New York Review of Books*, November 4, 1982, p. 3ff.

———, "We Cannot Create a MAC for Poland: Let It Go Bankrupt," New York *Times*, June 11, 1982.

Rose, Sanford, "Why They Call It Fat City," *Fortune*, March 1975.

Rothschild, Emma, "Banks: The Coming Crisis," *The New York Review of Books,* May 27, 1976, p. 16ff.

————, "Banks: The Politics of Debt," *The New York Review of Books,* June 24, 1976, p. 25ff.

Rowan, Roy, "The Swinger Who Broke Penn Square Bank," *Fortune,* August 23, 1982.

Sampson, Anthony, *The Money Lenders: Bankers in a Dangerous World,* London: Hodder and Stoughton, 1981.

Sanchez-Arnau, J. C., et al., *Dette et développement,* Paris: Éditions Publisud, 1982.

Sarrazin, Jürgen, "Problems in Banking Relationships with Eastern Europe," speech at Financial Times European Banking Forum, London, October 18–19, 1982.

Schröder, Klaus, "Aspekte zukünftiger Finanzbeziehungen zwischen Ost und West," speech from April 8, 1981.

Shapiro, Harvey D., "What Is John Heimann Up to?" *Institutional Investor,* June 1978, pp. 69–75.

Smith, Adam (pseud.), *Paper Money,* London: MacDonald, 1982.

Solomon, Robert, *The International Monetary System, 1945–81,* New York: Harper & Row, 1982.

Soros, George, "The International Debt Problem: Diagnosis and Prognosis," Morgan Stanley Investment Research, New York, July 1983.

Sosa-Rodriguez, Raul, *Les Problèmes structurels des rélations économiques internationales de l'Amérique latine,* Geneva: Librairie Oroz, 1963.

Spiegel-Report, "Was sollen Mistgabeln in Warschau?" Nr. 41/1982, pp. 209–21.

Steinberg, Bruce, "How the Debt Bomb Might Be Defused," *Fortune,* May 2, 1983, p. 128ff.

Time Magazine, "The Debt Bomb: The Worldwide Peril of Go-Go Lending," January 10, 1983.

Triffin, Robert, *Gold and the Dollar Crisis: The Future of Convertibility,* New Haven: Yale University Press, 1960.

Tully, Shawn, "How Dome Petroleum Got Crunched," *Fortune,* January 10, 1983, p. 84ff.

Tumlir, Jan, "The World Economy Today: Crisis or a New Beginning?" *National Westminster Bank Quarterly Review,* August 1983, pp. 26–44.

United Nations, *Transnational Banks: Operations, Strategies and Their Effects in Developing Countries,* Geneva, 1981.

U.S. Senate, *International Debt: Hearings Before the Subcommittee on International Finance and Monetary Policy,* February 14, 15, and 17, 1983, Washington: U.S. Government Printing Office, 1983.

Van Meer, John (pseud.), "Banks, Tanks and Freedom," *Commentary,* December 1982, pp. 17–24.

Volcker, Paul A., Testimony Before U.S. House of Representatives Committee on Banking, Finance and Urban Affairs, Washington, February 2, 1983.

———, "Sustainable Recovery: Setting the Stage," speech before the New England Council, Boston, November 16, 1982.

Welles, Chris, "Drysdale: The Untold Story," *Institutional Investor,* September 1982, pp. 454–68.

———, "The Making of a Treasury Secretary," *Institutional Investor,* March 1981, pp. 68–83.

Wilson, Stanley, "America's LDC Troubleshooter," *Institutional Investor,* May 1983, pp. 80–85.

Witteveen, H. Johannes, "Growing Financial Interdependence and Monetary Cooperation," speech in New York, October 7, 1982.

Wriston, Walter B., "Banking Against Disaster," New York *Times,* September 14, 1982.

INDEX

278

Z